I0605647

THE SUBVERSIVE ART OF A CLASSICAL EDUCATION

RECLAIMING THE MIND IN AN AGE OF SPEED, SCREENS, AND SKILL-DRILLS

MICHAEL S. ROSE

Regnery books may be purchased in bulk at special discounts for sales promotion, corporate gifts, fund-raising, or educational purposes. Special editions can also be created to specifications. For details, contact the Special Sales Department, Regnery, 307 Fifth Avenue, 4th Floor, New York, NY 10016 or info@skyhorsepublishing.com.

Regnery® is an imprint of Skyhorse Publishing, Inc.®, a Delaware corporation.

Visit our website at www.regnery.com.

Please follow our publisher Tony Lyons on Instagram @tonylyonsisuncertain.

10 9 8 7 6 5 4 3 2 1

Library of Congress Cataloging-in-Publication Data is available on file.

Cover design by David Ter-Avanesyan

Print ISBN: 978-1-5107-8612-7
Ebook ISBN: 978-1-5107-8613-4

Printed in the United States of America

To those who dare resist the glowing screen
And choose instead the patient work of hands,
Who find in ancient texts what moderns mean
By progress, yet refuse its swift demands.

To teachers who still trust the human voice
Above the algorithm's sterile song,
Who give their students depth instead of choice,
And know that wisdom ripens slow and long.

To children taught to think before they click,
To write with pen on paper, line by line,
Who learn that truth emerges not from quick
But careful cultivation, like fine wine.

This book's for those who know the rebel's art:
That revolution starts within the heart.

Contents

Preface

Why I Lead a Classical School

A quiet rebellion stirs in the shadowed corners of modern education, where a band of pedagogical heretics dares to champion the unfashionable. While the great machinery of progress thunders forward, promising ever more illuminated screens and ever less illuminated minds, these rebels stubbornly kindle the ancient lamps of learning. I count myself among their number, and this paradoxical revolution is my daily work. I lead a classical school.

To lead a classical school in this our bewildering century is to find oneself performing an act of magnificent absurdity, like a medieval scribe hunched over parchment while printing presses clatter in the neighboring room. There is something gloriously unreasonable about insisting upon Latin declensions when artificial intelligences compose essays at the press of a button, something delightfully obstinate about teaching Euclidean geometry when digital simulations promise to make thought itself obsolete.

The modern world, with its splendid scientific skepticism, would ask of us a perfectly reasonable question: Why persist in this antiquated endeavor? Why chain ourselves to dusty tomes when the whole of human knowledge glitters within a rectangle of glass and silicon? It is a sensible inquiry that demands an answer that transcends mere sense.

I lead a classical school because there are truths that must be known, not as files to be downloaded but as living realities to be encountered by living souls. The supreme jest of our age is that we have mistaken information for wisdom and facts for truth. We have built marvelous machines to tell us everything except what matters. We have created educational systems that teach the young how to operate devices while forgetting to teach them how to be human. The great catastrophe of our time is not that children fail to learn, but that they have never been taught what is worth knowing. The tragedy that unfolds daily in fluorescent-lit classrooms across the land is not the absence of technology but the presence of amnesia—a colossal forgetting of our inheritance. The inheritance of human genius and beauty—from Athens and Jerusalem, through Rome and the Renaissance, to Shakespeare's London and Lincoln's prairie—is what now stands in peril. It has not been violently seized; that would require too much effort and too much awareness of what was being lost. Rather, it has been carelessly misplaced, forgotten among the dazzling distractions of modernity.

The great catastrophe of our time is not that children fail to learn, but that they have never been taught what is worth knowing.

I lead a classical school because a generation unmoored from its intellectual patrimony is a generation adrift. A boy with the collective knowledge of humanity accessible through his smartphone may still be desperately ignorant if he has never confronted Hamlet's dilemma or pondered the paradoxes of Augustine's heart. He knows everything and understands nothing; he possesses the world and inherits dust.

I lead a classical school to teach what has been lost. We teach traditional grammar, for example, not because we are enamored with diagrams but because we recognize that language, when mastered rather than merely used, becomes the architecture of thought itself. We teach logic not as an academic curiosity but as the skeleton key that unlocks every other discipline. We teach rhetoric not as ornamentation but as the bridge between thought and action. We insist upon handwriting because there is wisdom in slowness, because the physical act of forming letters connects mind to body in ways mysterious and profound. We require memorization of poetry because the soul needs beauty stored within it, beauty that can be summoned without electricity, beauty that remains when all else fails.

I lead a classical school because there must exist sanctuaries of thought in a thoughtless age, islands of permanence in the rushing river of the ephemeral. The modern world moves with tremendous velocity but lacks direction; it speaks incessantly but has nothing to say. In such a time, the simple act of reading Dante or contemplating Euclid's elegant proofs becomes not a retreat from reality but an assertion of it. This is not, as our critics would have it, a fearful clinging to the past but a courageous reclamation of what is timeless. The past, properly understood, is not a museum to be occasionally visited but a workshop to be daily engaged.

I lead a classical school because education is not job training but soul-craft. The tragedy of modern schooling is not that it fails to prepare students for employment but that it succeeds only in this narrow task. We have mistaken utility for purpose, confusing the means of existence with its meaning. A human being is not merely an economic unit, a future employee, a consumer-in-training, but an inheritor of civilization, a potential guardian of wisdom, a soul capable of greatness.

In our classical academy, we espouse the Seven C's—curiosity, competency, creativity, culture, compassion, content-rich learning, and character—not as skills to be listed on a résumé but as attributes of a fully awakened humanity. We study history not as a catalog of disconnected events but as the great drama of human achievement and folly, a drama in which our students must take their own place, knowing what came before so they might wisely determine what should come next.

I lead a classical school because our republic depends upon it. The founders of this nation, steeped in classical learning and the Western tradition, created a system of government that requires virtuous, educated citizens to maintain it. A people ignorant of their own inheritance can neither preserve it nor improve upon it; they become strangers in their own land, citizens of nowhere, at the mercy of whatever ideology speaks loudest in the present moment.

This is the magnificent rebellion to which I have pledged my professional life: to remember what others forget, to preserve what others discard, to kindle what others allow to be extinguished. It is a rebellion fought not with swords but with sonnets, not with guns but with geometry, not with shouting but with Socratic questioning.

In the chapters that follow, you will discover why this rebellion matters—not just for the few students fortunate enough to receive a classical education, but for our culture, our democracy, and our shared future. The subversive arts of classical education are not dusty relics but radical acts of resistance against the machine of forgetting, against the cult of push-button immediacy, against the slow erosion of everything that makes us fully human. To be truly radical is not to tear up roots but to remember them, to nourish them, and to grow from their deep wisdom into something both ancient and new.

Introduction

The Great Forgetting

The most astounding feature of our age is not what we have invented but what we have lost. This paradox stands in plain view, like Poe's purloined letter, too obvious to be noticed. We have erected gleaming academies of unprecedented size, established departments of education sprawling with experts, and produced mountains of research on pedagogical methods, all while steadily forgetting what education is for. This curious amnesia is not an accident but an achievement, requiring the sustained effort of generations.

It deserves a name: The Great Forgetting.

There is an odd sort of modern fellow who, having heard that men once believed the earth to be flat (which, incidentally, educated men rarely did), concludes that all inherited wisdom must be similarly mistaken. This fellow does not merely doubt tradition; he prides himself on doubting it. He considers skepticism of the past to be identical to intelligence and dismissal of ancestors to be synonymous with progress. He has been educated into ignorance and schooled in forgetting.

The madness of our educational decay lies in this: we have mistaken movement for advancement. Like a man furiously rocking in a rocking chair, modern pedagogy generates tremendous activity while remaining in the same place—or rather, a place increasingly distant from wisdom. We have crafted elaborate systems to measure what students know without asking whether what they know is worth knowing. We have developed sophisticated methods for transmitting information while systematically destroying the conditions necessary for wisdom.

Consider the peculiar inversion that has occurred: we have made the means of education its end. Technology, once a tool to serve learning, has become its master. Assessment, once a method to gauge understanding, has become the purpose of instruction. Relevance, once a natural by-product of genuine education, has become its sole criterion. We no longer teach subjects; we teach strategies for subjects we never teach. Like a chef who spends all his time sharpening knives but never cooks, modern education has become splendidly equipped for a task it no longer performs.

What has been forgotten in this great educational amnesia? First and most profoundly, we have forgotten that education concerns the formation of souls, not merely the training of minds. The ancients understood, whether pagan like Aristotle or Christian like Augustine, that learning is inseparable from character, that knowledge without virtue is not merely incomplete but potentially monstrous. The modern educator, having dispensed with such "metaphysical" concerns, speaks blandly of "social-emotional learning" while avoiding any mention of the good, the true, or the beautiful. It is as if we have determined to build houses without foundations because foundations are bothersome things that take too long to construct and cannot be easily measured.

Next, we have forgotten that education is the transmission of civilization itself. What G. K. Chesterton called "the democracy of the dead," the great conversation across time in which the finest minds of every age participate, has been replaced by the tyranny of the trendy. Students encounter fragments of texts divorced from context, selected not for their enduring importance but for their contemporary "relevance," which is the quality least likely to endure. Having denied our students their rightful inheritance, we express surprise when they behave like disinherited castaways.

We have forgotten, too, that difficulty is not an obstacle to learning but its essential precondition. The modern educational establishment, seized by a misguided compassion, has systematically removed obstacles from the path of students, failing to recognize that the obstacle is the path. Learning to parse a complex sentence in Latin, to follow the elegant proof of a geometric theorem, or to discern the subtle arguments in Plato's *Republic*—these tasks demand effort because they develop intellectual capacities that cannot be developed without strain. Yet we have built educational systems dedicated to the proposition that learning should never cause discomfort, never require struggle, never demand discipline. This is like attempting to build muscle without resistance or endurance without exertion, a physical impossibility mirrored in our intellectual training.

Perhaps most perniciously, we have forgotten that words matter. Language, once understood as the vessel of thought, has been degraded into an instrument of manipulation. In our schools, grammar—the art of arranging words according to their proper relationships—has been abandoned in favor of "self-expression," as if one could express a self that has never been formed. Rhetoric, once the noble art of persuasion through truth beautifully articulated, has devolved into a collection of techniques for emotional effect without ethical foundation. Logic, the discipline of valid inference and coherent reasoning, has been replaced by its counterfeit: the appeal to feelings, to consensus, to anything but the merits of the argument itself.

This linguistic decay reflects a deeper intellectual corruption. We have forgotten how to think because we have forgotten the conditions necessary for thought. Concentration, that sustained attention to a single subject, has been shattered by devices that interrupt and fragments that distract. Contemplation, the patient consideration of an idea from multiple perspectives, has been surrendered to the cult of immediacy. Memory, the storehouse of wisdom acquired, has been outsourced to silicon, as if having information at one's fingertips were the same as having understanding in one's mind.

The consequences of this Great Forgetting are not merely educational but civilizational. A society that no longer transmits its defining narratives is a society suffering from a kind of cultural Alzheimer's disease—still physically present but increasingly unable to recognize itself. Citizens who cannot follow an extended argument or distinguish between assertion and evidence are citizens in name only. They may cast votes, but they cannot exercise the reasoned judgment that self-governance requires.

Moreover, a people severed from their intellectual tradition become vulnerable to whatever ideology speaks loudest in the present moment. Having no internal compass calibrated by the accumulated wisdom of civilization, they drift with every cultural current. The vacuum created by forgetting does not remain empty; it is filled with the crude simplicities of demagogues or the seductive banalities of technocrats.

Yet in this dire assessment lies a curious hope. For the great educational truths we have forgotten have not ceased to be true in our forgetting of them. They wait, like buried treasure, to be rediscovered. And herein lies the radical promise of classical education: not as a retreat into antiquity but as a recovery of what is most essentially human.

The classically educated student learns that freedom is not the absence of constraint but the capacity to choose rightly, that equality does not negate excellence but demands its cultivation in all, that democracy requires citizens formed in virtue, not merely informed of their rights. These truths have not grown antiquated; they have grown urgent.

What I propose in the pages that follow is not nostalgia but revolution, a turning again to the permanent things that make us human, a reclaiming of the intellectual heritage that belongs by right to every student. The subversive arts of classical education—grammar, logic, rhetoric, mathematics, history, literature, and all the rest—are subversive because they undermine the shallow presumptions of modernity. They challenge the notion that the new is always better than the old, that progress is inevitable, that tradition is inherently suspect, that efficiency is synonymous with effectiveness, that utility is the measure of worth.

We stand at a crossroads, facing a choice between continued amnesia and recovered memory, between the Great Forgetting and what might be called the Great Remembering. The chapters that follow make the case for remembering, not as an academic exercise but as a radical act of reclamation, an intellectual resistance against forces that would diminish both education and humanity itself.

For education, properly understood, is not the mere acquisition of skills or credentials. An authentic education shapes the soul so that students come to understand truth and develop a deep sense of beauty while learning to act with integrity. It fosters the growth of fully human persons by cultivating reflective minds and caring hearts that engage the world wisely. In short, education is the art of guiding each student toward the fullness of who they are meant to be. That we have forgotten this purpose is a tragedy. That we can remember it again is our hope.

Part I

Subversive Acts of Language

Chapter 1

The Subversive Art of Traditional Grammar

How studying language structure develops minds resistant to manipulation

In our enlightened age, an oddly prevailing conviction has taken hold: that rules of grammar, like arbitrary fashions in hats or hemlines, are mere social constructions, changeable at will and significant only to those pedants who have nothing better to occupy their diminishing minds. This belief, held with the remarkable confidence that accompanies all modern heresies, suggests that language is whatever we wish it to be, that a sentence, like a lump of clay, may be molded into any shape that pleases the potter, with no regard for its internal architecture or natural tendencies.

The grammar revolutionaries—for so they fancy themselves—have declared independence from the tyranny of the semicolon, the oppression of the properly placed modifier, and the authoritarian regime of the complete sentence. "Who," they ask with righteous indignation, "decided that a sentence needs a subject and a predicate? Who appointed the past participle to its lofty office? What right has any dusty rulebook to dictate how I express myself?" And having posed these questions with the air of having delivered unanswerable challenges to the established order, they proceed to communicate in fragments, in run-ons, in a sort of linguistic anarchy that they mistake for freedom.

What these revolutionaries fail to understand is that grammar is not a constraint upon expression but its very possibility. The irony that shadows their rebellion is that in casting off the supposed chains of grammatical structure, they have not liberated thought but confined it to a smaller, meaner province, where clarity is impossible and precision unknown.

Consider the humble comma, that modest punctuation mark that has provoked such fury in the breasts of modernists. "A mere convention," they insist, "a typographical ornament that we shall use or not as whim dictates." Yet in this dismissal they overlook the miraculous function of the comma, which, like a musical rest, creates the rhythm of thought itself. A misplaced comma does not merely offend some arbitrary rule; it transforms meaning. "Let's eat, Grandpa" and "Let's eat Grandpa" are not alternate expressions of the same sentiment. They are invitations to radically different activities; one a cordial summons to the dinner table, the other a proposal of cannibalism among cousins.

Or consider the much-maligned semicolon, that elegant hybrid that joins what might be separate but should not be divorced. The semicolon creates a relationship between clauses that is neither the loose association of the comma nor the complete separation of the period; it establishes a subtle hierarchy of thought that reflects the way ideas actually operate in the human mind. To abandon the semicolon is not merely to simplify punctuation; it is to eliminate a tool for expressing complex relationships, to flatten the topography of thought into a featureless plain. To misuse the semicolon, well, that is abominable.

But the war against grammar extends beyond punctuation to the structure of language itself. The modern educational establishment, with its peculiar genius for destroying the very things it claims to promote, has largely abandoned the teaching of structured grammar. Yes, you read that correctly. Many schools do not even pretend to teach grammar. And even in schools where they are at least going through the motions of teaching grammar, students no longer learn to diagram sentences, that magnificent exercise in which language is mapped like a newly discovered continent (see chapter 2), its features named and its relationships charted. The diagram reveals that a sentence is not a random collection of words but an organism with parts in specific relationship to one another. The subject and predicate form the spine from which dependent clauses hang like ribs, with modifiers attached in their proper places and conjunctions creating joints that allow the whole structure to move with grace and purpose.

This visual representation of language teaches more than rules; it reveals the inherent logic of expression. A student who has mastered the diagram understands that when we speak or write, we are not merely making sounds or forming letters; we are creating patterns that reflect the patterns of thought itself. Grammar, in this light, is not imposed upon language but discovered within it, much as the laws of physics are not invented but recognized and articulated.

The abandonment of grammar instruction represents more than an educational oversight; it constitutes a kind of cognitive disarmament, rendering students defenseless against the manipulation of language that characterizes our age. In a world where words are increasingly deployed not to clarify but to obscure, the ability to recognize and construct clear sentences becomes not merely an academic skill but a survival tool.

Consider the fog of verbal imprecision that envelops bureaucratic pronouncements. "Mistakes were made," announces the politician, employing the passive voice to avoid specifying who made them. "We are experiencing higher than normal call volumes," drones the automated message, using a present progressive tense that suggests a temporary condition rather than a permanent staff shortage. "Your application is being processed," intones the form letter, offering the appearance of action while committing to no particular outcome or timeline.

These linguistic evasions succeed precisely because their audience lacks the grammatical tools to dissect them. The citizen untrained in the parsing of sentences becomes the unwitting victim of his calculated ambiguities. He can neither identify the missing agent in the passive construction nor distinguish between the genuine accident and the deliberate obscurity. He needs the precision that only proper grammar makes possible.

Here lies the radical potential of traditional grammar instruction: it equips students not merely to speak and write correctly but to think clearly and to detect falsehood. A mind trained in the rigorous analysis of sentences develops an instinctive resistance to rhetorical sleight of hand. Such a mind recognizes immediately when an adjective has been substituted for evidence or when a string of impressive-sounding abstractions has been offered in place of concrete claims that could be verified or refuted.

Moreover, the study of grammar across languages reveals that while specifics may vary, the underlying principles remain remarkably consistent. Latin, with its intricate system of cases and declensions, may seem at first glance entirely foreign to English, yet both languages operate according to logical structures that reflect the fundamental characteristics of human thought. The student of Latin grammar discovers not merely the mechanics of an ancient tongue but the universal architecture of language itself.

This universality gives the lie to linguistic relativism, the notion that because languages differ in their particulars, they must be entirely arbitrary systems with no connection to objective reality. The fact that every Western language distinguishes between subjects and predicates, between statements and questions, between past, present, and future, suggests something profound about the relationship between language and the world it describes. Grammar, in this light, is not merely a set of conventions but a window into the structure of reality.

The traditional approach to grammar—systematic, structured, and rigorous—represents a form of intellectual training that transcends mere correctness. It instills the habits of careful analysis and logical organization that are the foundations of clear thinking in any field. The student who has learned to diagram sentences has also developed skills that easily transfer to expressing complex ideas with clarity and force.

Contemporary culture suffers from linguistic inflation, where words multiply but meaning diminishes. The discipline of grammar offers a counterweight, a return to the solid ground of meaning. It insists that words matter and that their arrangement is not arbitrary.

The study of grammar becomes, in this context, not a dry exercise in rule-following but a discipline that shapes the mind to recognize and value order, clarity, and precision.

For there is, in the end, something profoundly ethical about grammatical precision. To speak and write clearly is to respect both the truth and one's audience; to manipulate language for the purpose of deception is to commit an act of violence against both. The student trained in traditional grammar develops not only a technical skill but also a disposition toward honesty, a recognition that words have meanings that cannot be twisted without consequence, that language exists not merely to express personal preference but to communicate truth.

This understanding places grammar instruction at the heart of classical education, which aims not merely to impart information but to form character. The study of grammar becomes, in this context, not a dry exercise in rule-following but a discipline that shapes the mind to recognize and value order, clarity, and precision. It cultivates what might be called "grammatical virtue," the habit of using language not for manipulation or self-aggrandizement but for the clear expression of truth.

True freedom in language, as in life, comes not from the absence of constraints but from the mastery of necessary forms.

In this light, the teaching of traditional grammar emerges as a profoundly subversive act in a culture that increasingly treats language as a tool for dominance rather than communication. To insist that clarity is possible and precision valuable is to challenge the postmodern orthodoxy that reduces all expression to power plays and all disagreements to conflicts between equally valid "perspectives."

The student who has mastered traditional grammar potentially possesses a kind of intellectual immunity against the verbal epidemics of our age: the euphemisms that disguise harsh realities, the jargon that creates the illusion of expertise, the emotional appeals that bypass reason, and the calculated ambiguities that preserve deniability. Such a student can detect when language is being used not to illuminate but to obscure.

This capacity for linguistic discernment represents a form of freedom more substantial than the illusory liberty promised by grammatical anarchists. True freedom in language, as in life, comes not from the absence of constraints but from the mastery of necessary forms. The jazz musician improvises with such apparent ease because he has internalized the underlying structures of music; the poet crafts surprising metaphors because she understands the conventions she is transcending. Similarly, the writer who has mastered grammar gains not constraint but liberation, the ability to express nuanced thoughts that would be inexpressible without the disciplined use of linguistic structures.

The revival of traditional grammar instruction thus represents an advance toward intellectual clarity and moral seriousness. It is an acknowledgment that language matters, that precision is possible, and that the relationship between words and reality, while complex, is not arbitrary.

Let us then reclaim this ancient discipline, not as a collection of arbitrary rules but as the living architecture of thought itself. Let us teach our students to diagram sentences not to torture them with technicalities but to reveal the hidden structures that make communication possible. Let us insist upon precision out of respect for the precious gift of language, which, more than any other human capacity, allows us to bridge the chasm between mind and mind, to share not merely information but understanding.

A culture that abandons grammatical precision inevitably loses the capacity for logical thought and meaningful discourse.

In the end, the battle for grammar is not merely a skirmish over rules but a campaign for civilization itself. A culture that abandons grammatical precision inevitably loses the capacity for logical thought and meaningful discourse. The stakes, properly understood, could hardly be higher.

The semicolon, the diagram, and the properly placed modifier are not the fussy concerns of pedants but the essential tools of clear thinking. In their proper use lies not conformity but the precision that enables creativity's highest expression. Grammar, taught with understanding and embraced with intelligence, becomes thought's finest ally.

Recommended Further Reading

1. *The Elements of Style* by William Strunk Jr. and E. B. White. A classic, concise guide to clear writing that emphasizes precision and economy of language.

2. *Eats, Shoots & Leaves: The Zero Tolerance Approach to Punctuation* by Lynne Truss. A spirited defense of proper punctuation that demonstrates how small marks dramatically affect meaning.
3. *The Trivium: The Liberal Arts of Logic, Grammar, and Rhetoric* by Sr. Miriam Joseph. An essential text on how grammar forms one part of the classical approach to developing clear thinking.
4. *The New Well-Tempered Sentence: A Punctuation Handbook for the Innocent, the Eager, and the Doomed* by Karen Elizabeth Gordon. A witty exploration of how punctuation creates meaning and clarity.
5. "Politics and the English Language" by George Orwell. A seminal essay on how linguistic imprecision facilitates political manipulation.
6. *An Experiment in Criticism* by C. S. Lewis. While primarily about literature, offers valuable insights about how language affects perception.
7. *Dreyer's English: An Utterly Correct Guide to Clarity and Style* by Benjamin Dreyer.
8. Explores how well-constructed sentences contribute to clear thinking and meaningful communication.

Chapter 2

The Subversive Art of Sentence Diagramming

Why mapping the architecture of language builds intellectual independence

Sentence diagramming, that delightfully systematic mapping of language's underlying structure, has become one of education's most unfairly maligned practices. This curious discipline stands as a perfect paradox in our pedagogical discourse: dismissed as a relic by those who consider themselves progressive, abandoned as too difficult by those who fancy themselves practical, and regarded with a mixture of terror and nostalgia by those who experienced it in their youth. Far from being merely a relic of Victorian classrooms, sentence diagramming develops something increasingly vital: minds capable of independent analysis, resistant to manipulation, and skilled at recognizing the architecture of thought beneath the surface of words.

What makes this paradox so remarkable is not merely the antiquated appearance of the practice—though there is something delightfully subversive about suggesting that a teaching approach involving pencils, rulers, and slanted lines might offer something valuable in an age of digital algorithms and artificial intelligence—but the fact that it directly contradicts the most cherished assumptions of modern language instruction. Sentence diagramming proceeds by analysis and structure rather than by sentiment. It embodies the radical notion that language is not merely a vehicle for self-expression but a system governed by logical principles. It recognizes that sentences are not random collections of words but architectural marvels with parts in specific relationships to one another.

To diagram a sentence is to examine the intricate architecture of thought itself, exposing the hidden scaffolding where subject leans into predicate and clauses weave their filigree of nuance and intent. It is an exercise both maddeningly meticulous and beautifully transcendent, where the mundane grammar of daily speech unfurls into a vast latticework of logic and interdependence. Here, prepositions cling like ivy to their objects, modifiers dangle precariously, and conjunctions bridge the chasms between ideas, all laid bare, stark and luminous, under the unforgiving precision of diagrammatic lines. For the student, this academic exercise provides a slow awakening to the mechanics of meaning. It is a revelatory act of peeling back layers until only the raw essence of human communication remains: structured, deliberate, and infinitely expressive.

Consider, first, the act of drawing the diagram, or as Mrs. Schmidt, my seventh grade English teacher, always said, "Begin by drawing the skeleton." Here, the student becomes an architect, laying down lines and branches, separating subject from predicate, positioning modifiers like precarious ornaments, and tethering conjunctions to the spine of meaning. In this quiet act of construction, an analytical mind is born. The sentence, once an opaque block of words, becomes a lattice of relationships: nouns nesting snugly in their subjects, verbs marching forward with transitive clarity, prepositions bearing their objects like keys to hidden doors. Language ceases to be a formless fog and reveals itself as a machine of almost mechanical precision, one that with practice a student can disassemble and rebuild at will.

Take, for instance, the humble declarative sentence: "The cat sat on the mat." To the uninitiated, this is merely a string of mundane words. But to the diagrammer, it is an ecosystem. The subject—cat—claims the first perch on the horizontal line, the action—sat—its partner in predicate. Below, on the mat descends like the roots of a tree: the preposition on stretching its limb to clasp the object mat. Even here, in its simplicity, the diagram reveals an essential truth: the sentence is a world in miniature, a model of order. The student begins to see not just language but thought itself as structured, as something that can be analyzed, understood, and improved.

This revelation stands in opposition to the prevailing winds of modern language instruction, which often treat grammar as either an oppressive system of arbitrary rules to be minimized or an optional formality subordinate to personal expression. The contemporary emphasis on writing as primarily a vehicle for individual voice, on correctness as less important than creativity, on structure as less vital than sincerity, has produced generations of students who can express themselves with passionate incoherence but cannot construct a complex sentence with conscious control. They have been taught to prioritize what they say over how they say it, as if content and form were separable elements rather than interdependent dimensions of meaning itself.

The sentence diagrammer discovers a more profound truth: that form and content are not adversaries but allies, that structure does not constrain expression but enables it, that the architecture of a sentence is not external to its meaning but constitutive of it. The student who masters the diagram begins to understand that the difference between "The dog bit the man" and "The man bit the dog" is not merely a rearrangement of words but a transformation of reality, that the shift from active to passive voice represents not simply a stylistic choice but a substantive change in emphasis and agency, that the placement of a modifier can alter not just the rhythm of a sentence but its very meaning.

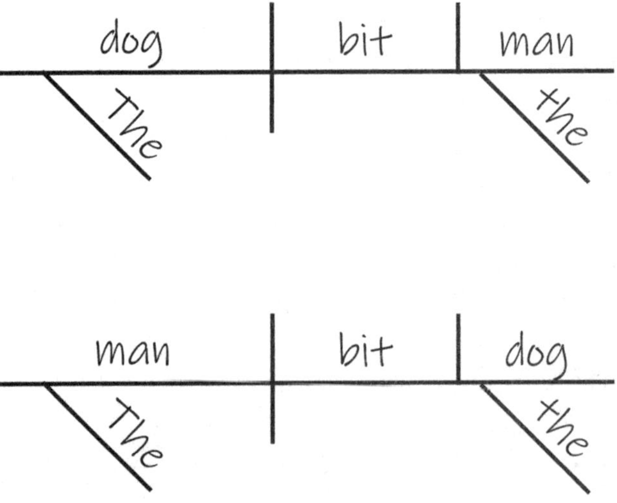

This understanding emerges through the visual clarity that diagramming provides. Consider a more complex example from Dickens: "It was the best of times, it was the worst of times, it was the age of wisdom, it was the age of foolishness." A student tasked with diagramming such a sentence faces a delightful challenge. The repetition of "it was" demands its own horizontal scaffolding, while each predicate nominative—"the best of times," "the worst of times"—branches off like tributaries from a mighty river. The modifiers—"of times," "of wisdom"—descend dutifully below their respective nouns, offering a cascade of meaning. Through this exercise, the student learns to untangle parallelism, to recognize patterns and contrasts, to see how structure reinforces meaning in ways that mere identification of parts of speech cannot reveal.

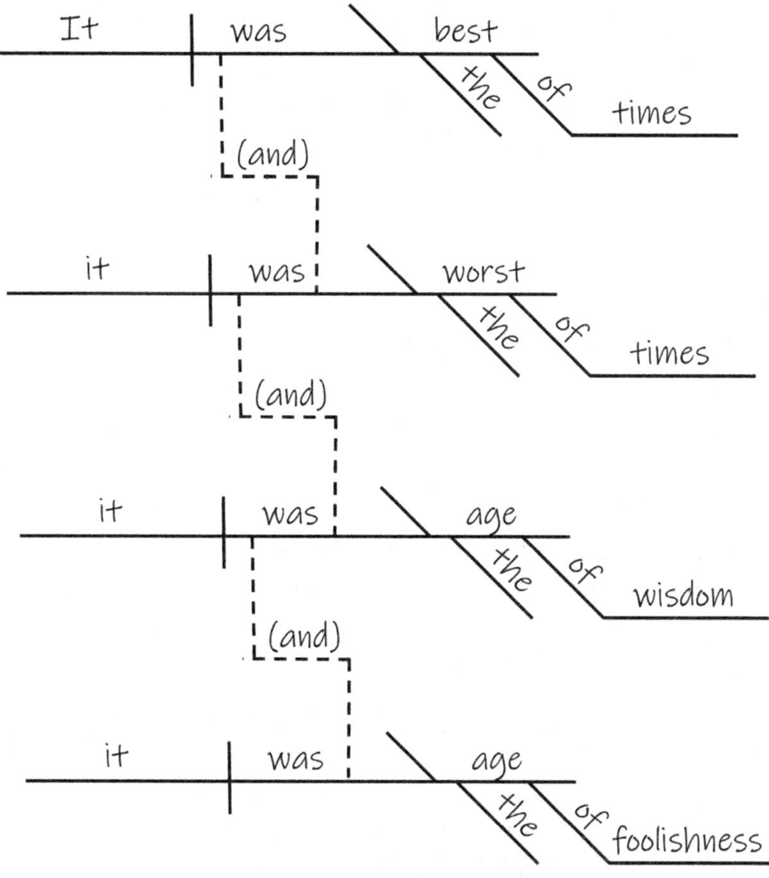

When approaching the intricate labyrinths constructed by masters like Hawthorne, we encounter sentences that test the very limits of diagrammatic art. Take this passage from "The Scarlet Letter": "The grass-plot before the jail, in Prison Lane, on a certain summer morning, not less than two centuries ago, was occupied by a pretty large number of the inhabitants of Boston, all with their eyes intently fastened on the iron-clamped oaken door."

Here the diagram begins with a deceptive simplicity: "The grass-plot . . . was occupied by a pretty large number." But then observe how the modifiers cascade in all directions! "Before the jail" hangs below "grass-plot," "in Prison Lane" descends from "jail," and "on a certain summer morning" dangles beneath the main line. The temporal modifier "not less than two centuries ago" must find its proper place, as must the participial phrase "all with their eyes intently fastened on the iron-clamped oaken door."

The completed diagram resembles a medieval cathedral, with its main spire reaching heavenward while flying buttresses and delicate arches support the structure from all sides. It demonstrates how Hawthorne's sentence, for all its complexity, is not a chaotic jumble but a precisely engineered edifice where every word serves its purpose in relation to the whole.

And what of Poe, whose serpentine constructions mirror the labyrinthine terrors of his tales? Consider this opening from "The Fall of the House of Usher": "During the whole of a dull, dark, and soundless day in the autumn of the year, when the clouds hung oppressively low in the heavens, I had been passing alone, on horseback, through a singularly dreary tract of country; and at length found myself, as the shades of the evening drew on, within view of the melancholy House of Usher."

The diagram of such a sentence becomes a veritable haunted house of grammar, with corridors that twist and turn, rooms that open unexpectedly into other rooms, staircases that lead to terrifying vistas. The main clause—"I had been passing alone, on horseback, through a singularly dreary tract of country"—forms the foundation, but from it rise the spectral shapes of temporal clauses, prepositional phrases, and participial constructions. "During the whole of a dull, dark, and soundless day" hovers at the beginning, while "in the autumn of the year" depends from "day," and the clause "when the clouds hung oppressively low in the heavens" attaches to "day" as well.

The conjunction "and" bridges to the second main clause, with "at length" modifying "found," while the temporal clause "as the shades of the evening drew on" interrupts between verb and complement. The completed diagram would resemble the House of Usher itself—complex, foreboding, yet possessed of a strange and terrible beauty, where every part connects according to inviolable laws.

The benefits of such practice extend far beyond grammatical fluency. To diagram a sentence is to cultivate a habit of mind that is analytical, precise, and unafraid of complexity. These are the same habits that underpin scientific inquiry, mathematical reasoning, and ethical debate. The student who masters the diagram becomes adept at seeing relationships, at breaking down problems into their constituent parts, at distinguishing between essential structures and peripheral elements. They learn that no problem is too complex to be understood if approached methodically, no text too difficult to be analyzed if one has the proper tools, no argument too convoluted to be evaluated if one can identify its underlying structure.

Moreover, diagramming teaches a form of intellectual discipline increasingly rare in our age of instant gratification. Unlike the digital grammar checker that simply identifies errors to be automatically corrected, diagramming requires careful analysis and precise execution. It develops what philosopher Matthew Crawford calls "cognitive self-reliance"—the capacity to think through problems independently rather than outsourcing mental labor to technological systems. The student who can diagram a complex sentence has developed not only a grammatical skill but an intellectual virtue: the ability to approach complexity with both patience and precision. He has learned to analyze without being overwhelmed and to see structure within apparent chaos.

This virtue becomes increasingly valuable in an information environment too often characterized by obfuscation. The seasoned diagrammer develops an eye for the hidden architecture of language that makes him more resistant to rhetorical sleights of hand. He becomes more capable of recognizing when impressive-sounding language conceals faulty reasoning or inadequate evidence. He begins to see through the fog of verbal imprecision that envelops political discourse and corporate communication, demanding clarity when others offer confusion.

Deceptive rhetoric thrives in the absence of grammatical awareness. The citizen untrained in the parsing of sentences becomes the unwitting victim of calculated ambiguities, unable to identify the missing agent in the passive construction or to distinguish between the genuine accident and the deliberate obscurity. But the student who has spent hours with ruler and pencil, mapping the architecture of language, is given the opportunity to develop an instinctive resistance to such manipulations. He has learned to see language not merely as a vehicle for self-expression but as a system of relationships that form the structure of thought itself.

This structural understanding of language represents another dimension of diagramming's subversive potential given today's dominance of algorithmic thinking. Modern computational approaches to language often treat it primarily as a collection of data points, as raw material for pattern recognition, as input for statistical analysis rather than as the embodiment of human thought and meaning. The grammar checker identifies errors without understanding significance; the predictive text feature suggests words based on probability rather than purpose; the translation software converts between languages without grasping the nuanced relationships that diagramming makes visible. These technological approaches offer convenience, but they cannot provide understanding, the deep comprehension of how language works that diagramming develops.

The student who has mastered sentence diagramming possesses something that no algorithm can replicate: insight into the architecture of thought itself. Yes, the sentence diagramming student develops the ability to identify parts of speech but more importantly the capacity to see how they relate to create meaning. He slowly develops the wisdom to understand why certain structures serve certain purposes better than others. This understanding cannot be programmed because it is not merely about following rules but about grasping the principles that give those rules their purpose and power.

When language is treated as data to be processed rather than meaning to be understood, or manipulated for effect rather than shaped for clarity, the practice of sentence diagramming offers a quiet affirmation of human understanding over statistical analysis. It resists the reduction of words to mere data points. The diagrammer learns that language is a human achievement, not a pattern of frequencies. This resistance works by cultivating capacities that technology cannot imitate, for example, the ability to recognize underlying concepts that give grammar its purpose rather than merely its rules. The student who learns to diagram sentences gains more than technical skill; he acquires an architectural vision, a way of seeing how the elements of language fit together to form meaning, well ordered and beautiful.

Yes, there is indeed something profoundly beautiful about a well-diagrammed sentence in which visual harmony reflects the intellectual elegance of carefully articulated thought. Let us, then, reclaim the art of sentence diagramming not from nostalgia for educational practices of the past but from recognition of its enduring value for developing minds capable of precision, clarity, and depth in both thought and expression. Let us teach our students not merely to follow grammatical rules but to understand the principles that give those rules their purpose, not just to correct errors but to grasp the architectural relationships that make language both powerful and beautiful, not merely to express themselves but to do so with the conscious control that comes from structural understanding rather than mere intuition or imitation.

In this simple act of drawing lines and branches on paper, of mapping the hidden architecture of language, lies a profound educational truth: that understanding emerges not from superficial familiarity but from deep structural analysis. The patient and precise vision fostered by sentence diagramming is more than an educational tool; it is a cultural necessity. It reminds us that language, at its best, is not only a means of communication but the very architecture of thought, whose full complexity and beauty are revealed through the seemingly simple yet profoundly illuminating art of the diagram.

Recommended Further Reading

1. *Sister Bernadette's Barking Dog: The Quirky History and Lost Art of Diagramming Sentences* by Kitty Burns Florey. A charming exploration of

the history and practice of sentence diagramming in American education, offering both personal reflection and historical context for this uniquely American pedagogical tool.

2. *Grammar by Diagram: Understanding English Grammar through Traditional Sentence Diagramming* by Cindy L. Vitto. A thorough guide to the Reed-Kellogg system of diagramming with clear explanations of how this visual representation reveals the structure of English sentences.
3. *Sentence Diagramming: A Step-by-Step Approach to Learning Grammar Through Diagramming* by Marye Hefty, Sallie Ortiz, and Sara Nelson. A practical workbook that demonstrates how diagramming can be used as a step-by-step approach to understanding grammatical relationships.
4. *The Art of Grammar: A Practical Guide* by Alexandra Y. Aikhenvald. A work that explores how grammatical systems reflect patterns of human thought, offering insight into why diagramming sentences reveals cognitive structures.
5. *The Language Instinct* by Steven Pinker. Provides fascinating insights into the innate structures of language and how they reflect human cognition, giving diagramming a scientific foundation.
6. *Grammar and the Teaching of Writing: Limits and Possibilities* by Rei R. Noguchi. Examines the relationship between grammatical knowledge and writing ability, with insights into how diagramming might bridge theoretical understanding and practical application.
7. *The Grammar of Our Civility: Classical Education in America* by Lee T. Pearcy. Places grammatical instruction, including diagramming, in the broader context of classical education and civic formation.

Chapter 3

The Subversive Art of Logic

How formal reasoning cultivates resistance to propaganda and emotional manipulation

Modern education faces a striking contradiction: while "critical thinking" is invoked endlessly in mission statements and curriculum guides, the very discipline that cultivates this capacity most directly has been abandoned. Formal logic—the systematic study of valid reasoning—has largely vanished from classrooms, replaced by vague exhortations to "think critically" without being given the tools to do so. Stripped of this training, students are left vulnerable to manipulation and propaganda, unable to evaluate arguments or distinguish sound reasoning from rhetorical illusion. The progressive educator, confronted with this contradiction, responds with a sort of cheerful bewilderment. "But surely," he protests, "we can teach students to think critically without subjecting them to the tedious formalities of syllogisms and truth tables! Surely critical thinking is a natural capacity that needs only encouragement, not a technical skill requiring systematic instruction!"

This response, delivered with the unshakable confidence of one who has never examined his own assumptions, reveals the profound confusion at the heart of modern pedagogy.

Logic, properly understood, is not merely one subject among many but the very grammar of thought itself. Logic is to thinking what grammar is to language; it is not an arbitrary set of

Logic, properly understood, is not merely one subject among many but the very grammar of thought itself.

rules imposed from without but the discovery of inherent structures that make the enterprise possible. To attempt to teach critical thinking without teaching formal logic is like attempting to teach writing without teaching grammar, or mathematics without teaching arithmetic. It is to expect students to construct an edifice without first providing them with bricks.

Consider the simple syllogism, the basic unit of deductive reasoning first formalized by Aristotle. "All men are mortal; Socrates is a man; therefore, Socrates is mortal." In this seemingly elementary structure lies a pattern of reasoning so fundamental that it shapes our thought whether we recognize it or not. The syllogism does not create logical relationships; it reveals them. It shows us that certain conclusions follow inevitably from certain premises, not because of convention or preference but because of the nature of reality.

Yet how many students today could identify a syllogism, let alone determine whether it is valid or invalid? How many could distinguish between a valid argument with false premises and an invalid argument with true premises? How many have been taught that an argument can have the correct answer but still be logically flawed, or that an argument can be logically perfect yet lead to a false conclusion if it begins from false premises?

These distinctions, elementary to any student of formal logic, are exactly the tools needed to navigate the treacherous waters of modern discourse. Without them, our students are like sailors without compasses. They are at the mercy of every rhetorical current and persuasive wind. They may occasionally arrive at truth, but they do so by accident rather than by design, and they have no reliable means of distinguishing between sound reasoning and mere sophistry.[1]

The absence of logical training is especially pernicious because it creates the illusion of rationality without its substance. Students learn to use the language of reason, to speak of "evidence" and "conclusions," to pepper their essays with "therefore" and "thus," without mastering the discipline of reason itself. They become skilled imitators of logical reasoning,

1 Sophistry, derived from the Greek "sophistēs" (wise or skilled person), represents the dark mirror of genuine logical reasoning. While logic seeks truth through valid argument, sophistry employs seemingly plausible but fundamentally deceptive reasoning to win debates regardless of truth.

reproducing its gestures and phrases while lacking the disciplined thinking that gives them meaning.

Meanwhile, the forces of manipulation and deception operate with increasing sophistication. Political rhetoric and media narratives, for example, seem engineered to bypass rational faculties and appeal directly to unconscious biases. In the absence of logical training, citizens are defenseless against these manipulations. They mistake repetition for evidence, assuming that frequently heard claims must be true. They confuse correlation with causation and accept appeals to authority as definitive proof. Such citizens are easily persuaded by irrelevant arguments and convinced by reasoning that proves nothing at all. This vulnerability is not accidental but systemic. The teaching of formal logic has been deliberately marginalized, relegated to specialized courses in philosophy departments or eliminated entirely from curriculum requirements. This marginalization serves the interests of those who benefit from a populace unable to detect logical fallacies or evaluate competing truth claims. A citizenry trained in logic is inherently resistant to propaganda; a citizenry trained merely to repeat fashionable opinions is not.

A citizenry trained in logic is inherently resistant to propaganda; a citizenry trained merely to repeat fashionable opinions is not.

Of course, this is nothing new. It is not merely a product of our modern age; it is an unfortunate by-product of human nature. The original Sophists of ancient Athens, for example, were professional teachers of rhetoric and persuasion. They were roundly criticized by Plato because they taught methods of convincing others without regard for whether the conclusions reached were true or false. In our modern context, sophistry manifests whenever persuasive techniques—emotional appeals, verbal sleight of hand, strategic ambiguity, or impressive-sounding but meaningless jargon—substitute for sound reasoning. The citizen untrained in logic remains vulnerable to these manipulations, impressed by rhetorical flourish while blind to fundamental flaws in argumentation. Sophistry's enduring power lies not in its logical validity but in its psychological effectiveness.

Consider the most common logical fallacies that pervade our public discourse. The ad hominem attack, rejecting an argument based on irrelevant characteristics of the person making the argument, has become so normalized that it passes without comment; a proposal on tax policy, for instance, might be dismissed simply because "it comes from a billionaire." The appeal to emotion (pathos), substituting sentiment for evidence, dominates advertising and political rhetoric alike: a car commercial tugs at nostalgia rather than showing reliability, while a campaign speech stirs fear or pity instead of offering evidence. The false dichotomy appears whenever a debate is framed as "either you support this law or you don't care about safety," as though no alternative approach could exist. The circular argument (petitio principii), assuming what should be proven, underlies many ideological positions: "this policy must be right because it is just, and it is just because it is right." The slippery slope (*argumentum ad consequentiam*) asserts without evidence that one action (or decision) will inevitably lead to another consequence and then another, and so on, straight to the abyss; such fallacious argumentation justifies resistance to even modest reforms.

A student trained in formal logic immediately recognizes these fallacies not as persuasive arguments but as logical errors. Such a student—the *classical* student, for example—possesses an intellectual immune system capable of resisting rhetorical infections. Without this training, however, students are susceptible to every fallacy, particularly those that appeal to their existing beliefs or emotional preferences. They become, in effect, logically immunocompromised, unable to distinguish between sound reasoning and its counterfeit.

But the subversive potential of logic extends beyond the detection of fallacies to the cultivation of intellectual virtues. The study of formal logic instills habits of mind essential to the pursuit of truth: precision in defining terms, care in drawing distinctions, patience in following extended arguments, honesty in evaluating evidence, and humility in recognizing the limits of one's knowledge. These habits, once formed, transfer to every domain of inquiry, creating not merely better students but more thoughtful human beings.

Logic also inoculates against the intellectual laziness that characterizes much of contemporary discourse. It demands that arguments be evaluated on their merits rather than their popularity, that evidence be *examined* rather than assumed, that conclusions follow from premises rather than from preferences. This systematic approach provides an integral alternative to the intellectual shortcuts that dominate social media, where complex issues are reduced to slogans and tribal affiliation determines which facts are even acknowledged.

Perhaps most subversively of all, logic insists upon the possibility of objective truth, the understanding that some statements correspond to reality while others do not, regardless of how sincerely they are believed or how fervently they are asserted. This insistence challenges the relativism that has become a disturbing dogma in most educational settings, where "your truth" and "my truth" are treated as equally valid, regardless of their relationship to evidence or their logical coherence—unless "your truth" is not politically expedient or otherwise unpopular.

Logic recalls us to the solidity of reality, even as fashions of opinion shift and swirl. It is a kind of anchor, holding fast when cultural currents tug us toward confusion. Truth does not splinter into separate worlds simply because we multiply our interpretations, nor does reality dissolve when we prefer illusion. Even as many today proclaim the "death of truth," logic stands as a quiet revolution, a reminder that beneath all the noise of rhetoric and trend there is still something firm to be known, and that our minds, rightly trained, are capable of grasping it. Yet logic, for all its rigorous formality, is not the enemy of creativity; it is its necessary foundation. The greatest creative minds—whether in science, philosophy, art, or literature—have been disciplined thinkers capable of organizing ideas into coherent structures. Einstein's theories, Shakespeare's plays, and Bach's fugues all exhibit a profound logical architecture beneath their creative brilliance. Logic does not constrain genuine creativity; it enables it, just as the laws of physics do not constrain but enable flight. Nor is logic, properly understood, a cold, mechanistic process divorced from human concerns, as some will have it. On the contrary, it is a profoundly human discipline that reflects our unique capacity for rational thought. To engage in logical reasoning is to participate in a tradition that stretches back to Aristotle and forward to the present, a tradition concerned with the most fundamental questions of human existence: What is true? What can we know? How should we live?

The teaching of formal logic thus represents a radical affirmation of human dignity. It is an acknowledgment that students are not merely objects to be conditioned or consumers to be satisfied but rational beings capable of pursuing truth through disciplined thought. It treats them not as passive receptacles for information but as active minds capable of evaluating claims, detecting errors, and reaching sound conclusions. This respect for students' rational capacities is a far cry from educational approaches that appeal primarily to emotion, that reduce learning to entertainment, or that substitute affirmation for challenge. Logic demands intellectual effort, but it does so out of respect for the students' potential rather than disdain for their capabilities. It assumes that young minds are capable of rigorous thought and worthy of intellectual challenges.

In this sense, logic is inherently democratic, offering tools of analysis available to anyone willing to master them, regardless of background or beliefs. It provides a shared method for evaluating competing claims and a mutual commitment to following evidence wherever it leads. This common ground is not only valuable for education but vital for society. The teaching of logic remains quietly subversive because it unsettles assumptions that many take for granted about truth, knowledge, and the purpose of education. It demands that ideas be measured against evidence rather than accepted uncritically and that learning cultivate disciplined thought instead of mere self-expression. Logic has been pushed to the margins not because it fails, but because it challenges intellectual complacency and exposes the subtle ways ideology can manipulate belief. The revival of formal logic instruction thus represents a recovery of the essential intellectual tools needed in a complex world. Students who master the syllogism, who can identify logical fallacies, who understand the difference between inductive and deductive reasoning, who recognize necessary and sufficient conditions, possess resources for intellectual independence that no amount of information, however abundant, can provide. In the end, logic is not merely a subject but a discipline in the fullest sense of that term—a training of the mind that builds intellectual virtue and equips students for the lifelong pursuit of truth. It is not an optional supplement to a classical education but an important part of its essential foundation. To teach logic is to perform an act of intellectual liberation. It is to provide students with tools of discernment that no algorithm can circumvent and no propaganda can overcome.

The subversive art of logic thus stands as a bulwark against the currents of unreason that threaten to overwhelm our common life. It offers not merely techniques for better arguments but a vision of human beings as rational creatures capable of distinguishing truth from falsehood, valid reasoning from mere persuasion or outright manipulation. This vision is a radical affirmation of human dignity and potential. Let us then reclaim this ancient discipline as an essential resource for the present, as a living tradition of rational inquiry. In the careful analysis of premises and the rigorous evaluation of inferences lies more than a method of thought; there lies a path to intellectual freedom at a time that is increasingly characterized by mental bondage.

Recommended Further Reading

1. *Prior Analytics* by Aristotle. The foundational text of formal logic, introducing syllogistic reasoning and establishing logic as a discipline.
2. *Socratic Logic* by Peter Kreeft. Connects logical thinking to the Socratic method, showing how formal logic relates to the philosophical tradition of questioning assumptions.
3. *Logic: Or The Right Use of Reason in the Inquiry After Truth* by Isaac Watts. A clear, systematic presentation of classical Aristotelian-Thomistic logic that connects logical principles directly to right reasoning in everyday life.
4. *De Interpretatione* by Boethius. Preserved and transmitted Aristotle's logic to the Latin-speaking West. His translations and commentaries were used for centuries in medieval universities.
5. *Logic: The Art of Defining and Reasoning* by John A. Osterle. A classical approach to logic that emphasizes its practical application in everyday reasoning and its role in developing mental discipline.
6. *Crimes Against Logic* by Jamie Whyte. A witty exploration of logical fallacies in contemporary discourse, demonstrating how illogical thinking undermines rational debate.

7. *The Art of Logic: How to Make Sense in a World That Doesn't* by Eugenia Cheng. Teaches how to find clarity without losing nuance, carefully examining the complexities of politics, privilege, sexism, and dozens of other real-world situations.

Chapter 4

The Subversive Art of Studying Latin

Why an ancient language offers timeless tools for intellectual precision

Latin, a subject so often dismissed as obsolete in the modern curriculum, continues to endure in classical education, not so much as a triumphant survivor, but more like a relic species thought long extinct, quietly flourishing in some forgotten valley, unaware of its own supposed irrelevance. Its presence is less a matter of academic stubbornness than of quiet fidelity, like stumbling upon a monastery where monks still illuminate manuscripts by candlelight—as a living tradition, serenely indifferent to the invention of the printing press, electric light, or the digital screen.

Beneath this enduring practice lies a modern conviction, strange yet widespread, that the study of Latin, that ancient and allegedly dead language is a waste of valuable educational time. The modern mind, equipped with spreadsheets and driven by standards, tends to ask only what a subject can *do*. It is not, we are assured by practical-minded educators, a spoken language in the modern world. It allegedly provides no immediate advantage in the global marketplace. It appears on no list of "twenty-first-century skills" demanded by employers. It occupies precious educational hours that might be devoted to coding, entrepreneurship, or other pursuits with clear economic utility. By such utilitarian reckoning, Latin seems indefensible.

The truth, however, attested by both historical example and contemporary experience, is that Latin, with its emphasis on precision and structure, provides not merely an adequate but an ideal preparation for the development of the intellect. The student educated in this ancient language develops those capacities most valuable in any intellectual endeavor: analytical thought, creative synthesis, intellectual versatility, and the ability to navigate complexity with both precision and imagination.

The irony, of course, is that this is not a new discovery; it is an ancient wisdom, temporarily forgotten in our rush toward specialization. Latin persists not as a historical curiosity or academic fossil but as a living educational tradition that continues to attract devoted teachers and eager students. This persistence suggests that Latin offers something that our obsessively practical age needs but cannot produce on its own terms. It provides a value that transcends utility without being useless, appearing impractical because it serves purposes deeper than mere practicality. Latin seems irrelevant to contemporary concerns specifically because it addresses perennial human needs rather than the momentary cultural preoccupations that dominate our attention.

Let us begin with the most shocking claim of all: to study Latin is to study six languages at once. It is the generous mother of the Romance languages—Spanish, French, Italian, Portuguese, Romanian—all of which draw about 90 percent of their vocabulary from her treasury. To learn Latin is to discover a golden skeleton key, unlocking the grammar and lexicon of half a continent's tongues. Yet this claim, astonishing as it is, still underestimates Latin's power. Latin does not merely open other languages. It unlocks our own. English, that magpie language of borrowed words, wears a Latin cloak so comfortably we hardly notice it. Over 60 percent of English vocabulary—especially our more dignified, polysyllabic words—flows directly from Latin roots. When students learn *ducere* ("to lead"), they begin to see the connection between a duke, an educator, and an aqueduct. The child who learns *scribere* will never again confuse description with prescription, nor manuscript with inscription. Latin is like turning on a light in a room where we have long stumbled in the dark.

What Latin offers is nothing less than a complete rebuke to the fragmentary nature of modern education, with its tendency to separate subjects into disconnected domains, to privilege process over content, to value skills in isolation from the knowledge that gives them meaning and purpose. The study of Latin is inherently integrative, simultaneously developing linguistic precision, historical awareness, logical rigor, and literary sensitivity. The student who declines nouns, conjugates verbs, translates Cicero, and scans Virgil is not merely acquiring a language but entering an intellectual tradition that unites grammar and rhetoric, history and philosophy, logic and poetry in a single course of study.

The student who declines nouns, conjugates verbs, translates Cicero, and scans Virgil is not merely acquiring a language but entering an intellectual tradition that unites grammar and rhetoric, history and philosophy, logic and poetry in a single course of study.

Consider the simple act of declining a Latin noun. The English speaker, accustomed to relying primarily on word order, encounters in Latin a fundamentally different way of structuring thought, where the relationship between words is indicated not by their position but by their form. The nominative "*puer*" (boy) becomes the accusative "*puerum*" when it serves as the direct object, the genitive "*pueri*" when it indicates possession, the dative "*puero*" when it acts as the indirect object, each form indicating the word's function in the sentence's architecture.

This systematic alteration of form to indicate function teaches the student something profound about language itself: that the seemingly natural patterns of one's native tongue represent particular conventions rather than universal necessities. The English speaker who masters Latin declensions has not simply learned a new set of words but has experienced a different way of thinking, a cognitive flexibility that no amount of theorizing about linguistic diversity can provide without the actual experience of navigating an alien grammatical structure. The student begins to see language not as a transparent medium for expressing preformed thoughts but as a structure that shapes the possibilities of thinking itself.

Moreover, the precision required by Latin translation develops intellectual virtues increasingly rare in our age of algorithmic assistance and digital shortcuts. The student confronting a Latin sentence cannot rely on spell-check, grammar-correction tools, or predictive text; he must attend carefully to each word's form, analyze its grammatical function, discern its relationship to other words, and reconstruct the thought it expresses in a different linguistic medium. This process demands what philosopher Matthew Crawford[2] calls "attentiveness"—the capacity to observe closely, to analyze systematically, and to construct meaning from elements that initially appear disconnected or obscure.

This attentiveness extends to encompass historical context, philosophical concepts, rhetorical techniques, and literary allusions, all of which are necessary for accurate translation of texts embedded in a cultural world very different from our own. The student translating Cicero's orations must do more than render words from one language into another. To follow his thought, the student has to enter Cicero's world—his political struggles, his philosophical inheritance, his strategies of persuasion, and the assumptions he shared with his Roman audience. Latin, studied in this way, becomes a discipline that unites what modern education often divides. It forms a habit of mind that sees connections where others see only fragments, and that approaches knowledge not as scattered skills but as a single, living tradition. This integration resists the fragmentation that marks much of modern education, where subjects are cut off from one another and skills are taught without regard for the ideas that give them meaning. In such an environment, language is stripped from thought, and both are severed from the historical setting that once grounded them. The Latin student comes to see that language lives within the culture that speaks it and that thought itself is carried and shaped by the forms of expression available to it. Literary works, likewise, do not float free but arise from particular moments and respond to them. What begins as a study of ancient Rome thus becomes a lesson in how understanding always depends on context, a principle that holds true across every field of study and in every age.

Consider the famous opening of Caesar's *Gallic Wars*: "*Gallia est omnis divisa in partes tres.*" The student translating this seemingly simple sentence—"All Gaul is divided into three parts"—must attend not merely

2 Crawford explores this concept extensively in his work *Shop Class as Soulcraft: An Inquiry into the Value of Work* (2009) and further develops it in *The World Beyond Your Head: On Becoming an Individual in an Age of Distraction* (2015), where he examines how skilled practices demand and cultivate forms of attention that digital technologies often undermine.

to vocabulary and syntax but to geography (what constitutes "Gallia"?), history (why is Caesar writing about Gaul?), politics (what were Rome's interests in this region?), and rhetoric (why begin with this particular observation?). The sentence cannot be accurately understood without this contextual knowledge, which itself requires integration of multiple disciplines that modern education tends to treat as separate domains.

But this sentence means something deeper still. It does not mean merely that Gaul was divided. It means that reality has order, and that order can be named. Latin teaches us to name that order—to see the parts, yes, but also the whole. This necessity for integration reveals another dimension of Latin's subversive potential: its challenge to the modern separation of education into specialized domains with their own methodologies, vocabularies, and assumptions. The Latin student discovers that understanding requires not merely expertise in a particular subject but the capacity to connect knowledge across domains: to see, for example, how language, history, philosophy, and literature inform and illuminate one another. This discovery stands as a quiet rebuke to the fragmentation of modern intellectual life, suggesting that true understanding emerges not from specialized expertise alone but from the integration of diverse forms of knowledge into coherent understanding.

The study of Latin also subverts contemporary education's emphasis on immediate, visible results achieved through efficient methods. Learning Latin is inherently slow. It demands sustained devotion measured not in days but years. The student advances step by step, carrying forward the fruit of earlier effort, and learns that progress comes less through bursts of intensity than through steady practice that forms both memory and mind. This slowness is an essential quality of an education focused on depth rather than speed. In this slow unfolding the work of translation becomes less about racing toward results and more about entering into a deeper, more enduring possession of knowledge. Latin focuses on lasting development rather than immediate outcome.

This sustained focus required by Latin study becomes another form of resistance. It is the quiet insistence that some forms of learning cannot be rushed without being fundamentally altered, recognizing that certain intellectual developments require patience, and that education sometimes proceeds most effectively not by slowing down. The earnest Latin student learns not merely a language but a willingness to progress gradually through sustained attention rather than scattered focus.

The study of Latin unsettles the belief that the present age is sufficient unto itself. It reminds the student that time is not a straight march toward perfection but a dialogue across centuries. In turning to an ancient language, one begins to see that earlier ages carry insights and achievements that can still instruct, that the past is not some shadow behind us but a source of wisdom capable of shaping our lives now. In this way, the Latin student encounters not merely an ancient language but the living thought of minds separated from us by millennia yet still grappling with perennial human questions in ways that remain profound, challenging, and illuminating.

When the student encounters Cicero, Virgil, or Lucretius in their own words, the experience is one of genuine dialogue. These voices, though ancient, speak with an immediacy that belies the assumption that their concerns belong only to the past. Duty, fate, and mortality remain as pressing now as they were then, and the act of reading them in Latin allows the student to enter into living conversation with questions that continue to resist easy answers in every age.

The student of Latin thus develops not merely linguistic skills or knowledge of historical facts but a particular orientation toward knowledge itself, one that values depth over novelty. This orientation subverts many dominant educational trends with their emphasis on perceived immediate "relevance." Underlying this subversion is a fundamental recognition of classical education: that thinking itself is a techne, an art with its own standards and methods. This comes into view most clearly in the cultivation of the trivium, the set of arts that form the groundwork of liberal learning. Taken together, they form a lifelong discipline, each part reinforcing the others and all of them directing the mind toward ordered thought and genuine understanding. Grammar, the first of these arts, trains students in the precise use of language, in particular, the proper relationship between words in complex expressions. This grammatical discipline may appear pedantic to modern sensibilities, with their emphasis on self-expression and creative freedom, but grammar reflects a profound insight: that precision in language is inseparable from precision in thought. The mind cannot think clearly what the tongue cannot express accurately. Intellectual discipline begins with linguistic discipline.

Consider the simple grammatical distinction between an adjective and an adverb—a distinction that many modern students, products of educational systems that have abandoned formal grammar, cannot reliably make. This seemingly minor point of linguistic precision has profound implications for clarity of thought. The difference between "He acted badly" and "He is bad" is not merely grammatical. The distinction between a particular deed ("He acted badly.") and an essential character ("He is bad.") has both moral and philosophical import. The student who cannot distinguish between these formulations cannot think clearly about the fundamental difference between judging behaviors and judging persons, a distinction central to both ethical reasoning and everyday human interactions.

Latin, with its insistence on grammatical precision, requires and develops exactly this sort of mental clarity. To translate Latin well is to be attentive to both vocabulary and structure—the structure of the language and the structure of thought itself. While the modern student is encouraged to skim, to scan, to extract the "gist" of a text without attending to its details, the Latin translator must carefully identify what is being said and how it is being said. Latin cannot be skimmed, googled, or guessed. It must be puzzled out, piece by piece, like a mathematical theorem or a musical score.

It also turns out that much of what we call "science" is simply Latin wearing a lab coat. From Homo sapiens to magnum opus, from cortex to corpuscle, the terminology of biology, anatomy, physics, and astronomy is a litany of Latin. This is not an accident. The modern sciences were born at a time when educated men spoke Latin across Europe, from the halls of Padua to the Royal Society in London. Learning Latin today is thus an entry into the very vocabulary of the cosmos. One cannot study the parts of the human body, the branches of a tree, or the particles of the atom without paying tribute to the language that named them.

And so it happens—strangely, gloriously—that the very subject deemed irrelevant by the architects of modern schooling turns out to be a mighty enhancer of standardized test scores. Students of Latin consistently outperform their peers on the SAT and ACT, not because Latin is a test-prep course, but because it is something far better: a mind-prep course. In fact, among law school applicants, those with the highest LSAT scores and GPAs are not the finance majors or political scientists. They are the classicists.[3] Studying Latin demands sustained attention, drawing the student into careful reflection on each word and phrase. This engagement deepens understanding and comprehension while simultaneously cultivating the capacity to reason with clarity and precision. In this way, it prepares the intellect more broadly and enduringly than any narrow focus on examination techniques could achieve.

Yet these practical benefits, real though they are, still miss the deepest significance of Latin study. Latin teaches not merely a certain kind of intelligence but a certain kind of freedom. The world now defines freedom as the absence of obstacles, while Latin suggests it is the mastery of them. The student who studies Latin therefore discovers a liberty that comes not from release but from restraint. To make sense of a Latin sentence is to submit to a discipline older than oneself, and in that submission, to rise above the tyranny of impulse. It is a study that slows the mind so that it may become sharp, that narrows the attention so it may see farther. The one who translates Latin learns not simply how to read another tongue, but how to govern his own. And in an age when minds are scattered by screens and numbed by novelty, such governance is no small thing. It may be the last rebellion left.

Ironically, the supposed uselessness of Latin is arguably its most powerful use. It reaches beyond the urgency of the hour and reminds students that not all knowledge expires at the next update. Latin asks questions that our culture has nearly forgotten and offers answers that demand careful attention and courage. It draws the mind into reflection, guiding students to linger over words and ideas until understanding takes root. In its study, clarity emerges as a steady light illuminating the present from a wider, more

---

3 According to a study by Professor Derek T. Muller analyzing data from the Law School Admission Council for 2013 law school applicants, classics majors had the highest average LSAT scores (159.8) and GPAs (3.477) among all majors. Derek T. Muller, "The Best Prospective Law Students Read Homer," *Excess of Democracy*, April 7, 2014, https://excessofdemocracy.com/blog/2014/4/the-best-prospective-law-students-read-homer.

discerning perspective. The discipline shapes thoughtful human beings, capable of inhabiting both mind and world with intention and care. If this purpose feels unusual today, it reveals more about our fleeting notions of education than it does about the enduring power of the language itself.

Recommended Further Reading

1. *Ad Infinitum: A Biography of Latin* by Nicholas Ostler. Traces Latin's journey from ancient Rome through medieval Europe to its continued significance in the modern world, illustrating why it remains relevant.
2. *The Latin Language: A Historical Outline of Its Sounds, Inflections, and Syntax* by Charles E. Bennett. A classic work on the development of Latin that showcases the language's internal logic and systematic structure.
3. *Climbing Parnassus: A New Apologia for Greek and Latin* by Tracy Lee Simmons. A passionate defense of classical language study as fundamental to intellectual formation and cultural literacy.
4. *Latin Alive! The Survival of Latin in English and the Romance Languages* by Joseph B. Solodow. Explores how Latin continues to shape modern language and thought, with implications for contemporary education.
5. *The Latin-Centered Curriculum* by Andrew Campbell. Argues for Latin as the core discipline that unites the liberal arts and develops intellectual precision.
6. *Lingua Latina Per Se Illustrata* by Hans Ørberg. A revolutionary approach to teaching Latin that demonstrates its internal coherence and systematic structure.
7. *The Idea of a University* by John Henry Newman. Contains influential arguments for the place of Latin in higher education as essential to intellectual formation.

Chapter 5

The Subversive Art of Annotation

How engaging with texts creates readers who resist passive consumption

Some people imagine that books should live untouched, as if the words themselves were fragile relics rather than instruments of thought. Pages are to be turned with the utmost delicacy, margins left forever blank, sentences unmarked, paragraphs spared any sign of the reader's hand. The adherents of this doctrine speak with horror of dog-eared pages and broken spines. This superstition, and it is nothing more than superstition, becomes all the more remarkable when one considers that books themselves are nothing but marks made upon pages. The author is permitted—nay, expected—to fill the virgin whiteness with his thoughts, but the reader must keep a respectful distance, receiving the text in passive silence. It is rather like inviting a man to dinner but forbidding him to speak, or showing him a garden but prohibiting him from walking its paths.

And yet, there is a rebellious tribe among us who practice a different sort of literacy, one that refuses this artificial division between author and reader. These literary insurgents arrive at the text not as humble supplicants but as active interlocutors, pen in hand, ready to converse with the author across time and space. They practice the ancient art of annotation, the glorious tradition of marking up texts with questions, observations, arguments, and asides—and in doing so, they transform reading from a passive activity into an active engagement. They talk back to the author. They argue. They question. They applaud. They object. They make the book not merely something they have read but something they have thought with.

This practice, when examined closely, represents nothing less than a revolution in the relationship between reader and text. The annotator asserts the radical principle that reading is not merely reception but response, not consumption but conversation. The margin becomes a sort of intellectual frontier, a place where minds meet on equal terms, where authority derives not from publication but from insight, not from reputation but from reason.

Consider the simple underline, that most elementary form of annotation. When a reader draws a line beneath a sentence, he performs an act of selection, saying in effect: "This, among all the words on the page, matters most. This I shall remember. This I shall consider further." This seemingly modest gesture contains within it an implicit challenge to the author's own hierarchy of emphasis. The reader may underline not what the author considered most important but what resonates most powerfully with his own interests, experiences, or concerns. The underline is the reader's declaration of intellectual independence, a small rebellion against the author's intention, a quiet insistence on the reader's right to determine significance.

Or consider the question mark, that elegant curve that transforms certainty into inquiry. When a reader places a question mark in the margin, he disrupts the author's confident assertions, introducing doubt where the text presumes conviction. This punctuation of skepticism transforms the monologue of the text into a dialogue between minds. The author says, "It is so." The reader asks, "Is it really?" And in that simple query lies the seed of all intellectual progress.

The marginal "No!" perhaps accompanied by a vigorous underline or even multiple exclamation points represents a more dramatic confrontation. Here the reader directly contradicts the author, challenging not merely emphasis or raising questions but actively disputing claims. This negation is not mere dismissal; it is engagement at its most intense, a mind refusing to surrender its judgment even to the most eloquent persuasion. The author makes his case; the reader considers it and renders his verdict. This is not disrespect but the highest form of respect: treating the author not as an infallible authority but as a fellow thinker worthy of serious critical attention.

Marginalia represent, in this light, the democratization of the page. The white space surrounding the text becomes a commons where reader and author meet as equals, where authority derives not from the printing press but from the quality of thought. The annotator asserts, through each mark upon the page, that reading is not a passive receiving of wisdom from on high but an active collaboration in the creation of meaning.

This democratic dimension of annotation explains why the practice has so often been regarded with suspicion by institutions concerned with preserving their authority. When medieval monks annotated religious texts, they were not merely taking notes but engaging in a potentially subversive dialogue with tradition. When Renaissance scholars marked up classical texts, they were asserting their right to question ancient authorities rather than merely transmit their wisdom intact. When Enlightenment readers scribbled in the margins of political treatises, they were practicing the very sort of critical thinking that would eventually challenge monarchy itself.

The history of marginalia is, in this sense, a history of intellectual emancipation. It traces the long, halting movement from a world where truth was delivered from above to one where it emerges through critical engagement, from a world where authority resided in texts to one where it resides in the dialogue between text and reader. The annotator stands in this noble tradition, not merely consuming culture but participating in it, not merely receiving wisdom but testing it. Yet annotation is more than a political act; it is a cognitive one. The mind that engages with a text actively—questioning, connecting, challenging—processes information differently than the mind that merely receives it. The annotator does more than absorb a text; in reading, the mind reshapes it, connecting its meaning into what is already known, drawing subtle connections, and discerning both its power and its limitations. Through this active engagement, understanding grows not only in breadth but in depth, and the text becomes part of a living conversation rather than a fixed object on a page. Consider the reader who, encountering an idea in one book, writes in the margin a reference to another book where a similar or contradictory idea appears.

This simple cross-reference creates a connection that exists nowhere in either text alone. It is a new synaptic pathway in the collective brain of human knowledge, a link forged by the reader's own synthetic thinking. Or consider the reader who, encountering a passage of particular beauty or insight, draws a star beside it, perhaps adding the note "Brilliant!" or "Remember this!" This act of appreciation is also an act of curation, a judgment that this passage, among all the words on the page, deserves special attention. The annotator becomes both audience and critic, evaluating the text according to standards that may differ from those of professional reviewers or academic authorities.

The habit of annotation transforms the very experience of reading, making it impossible to remain a passive recipient of information. The annotator approaches the text with pen in hand, ready to respond, to question, to connect. This stance of active engagement becomes, over time, an intellectual disposition. It is a habit of mind that refuses to accept claims without examination.

This disposition provides a much-needed alternative to the passive consumption of information that characterizes most of contemporary media—and not just social media. The unannotated text and the unexamined sound bite, for example, tend to slide through the mind without resistance, leaving behind impressions rather than understanding or knowledge. The annotator, by contrast, demands that information justify itself before being accepted. With information more abundant than ever, this capacity for critical engagement becomes not essential. The student who cannot distinguish between valid and invalid arguments (see chapter 3), who cannot identify logical fallacies, who cannot connect new information to existing knowledge, drowns in the ocean of information that should nurture learning. Annotation provides a life raft in this flood, a means of navigating the torrent by actively processing rather than passively receiving.

Yet despite these cognitive benefits, the practice of annotation has been largely abandoned in modern education. Students are often actively discouraged from writing in books, either because the books are rented and must be returned unmarked or because marking books is seen as damaging rather than enhancing them. Even when physical annotation is permitted, the emphasis on reading quickly, on "covering" material rather than engaging with it deeply, militates against the practice.

Digital reading has further marginalized annotation, even when the student is not engaged in the practice of doomscrolling.[4] While e-readers and PDF viewers typically offer highlighting and note-taking features, these tools are often clumsy, and the resulting annotations are hidden away in separate files rather than integrated with the text. The physical separation of text and response reinforces the notion that annotation is secondary, an optional add-on rather than an essential dimension of reading itself.

This marginalization of annotation represents a profound loss, of both a useful study technique and of a way of relating to texts that has been central to intellectual life for centuries. The great minds of the past were almost invariably annotators. Galileo's marginalia, particularly in works like *On the Sphere and Cylinder* by Archimedes, include diagrams, calculations, and skeptical comments that show him testing ancient theories against his own observations, an early sign of the empirical method he would champion. In Darwin's annotated copy of *Vestiges of the Natural History of Creation* by Robert Chambers, he underlined passages and wrote probing notes that both challenge and build upon the author's proto-evolutionary ideas, revealing his methodical shaping of what would become *On the Origin of Species*. Thomas Jefferson's annotations in Enlightenment works like Locke's *Two Treatises of Government* and Montesquieu's *Spirit of the Laws* often include underlined assertions and terse marginal affirmations or objections, suggesting a deep intellectual engagement that would later inform the Declaration of Independence and his views on limited government. Marginalia were not incidental to their intellectual development but central to it, the visible traces of minds actively engaging with the ideas that would transform their fields.

To revive the practice of annotation is thus to reclaim the tradition of active intellectual engagement championed by classical education. It

---

4 Doomscrolling refers to the compulsive act of continuously scrolling through negative news or social media content on a smartphone, often late into the night. The term gained popularity during the COVID-19 pandemic, highlighting how digital media consumption can fuel anxiety, pessimism, and a sense of helplessness in modern life.

is to insist that reading is not a passive receiving of information but an active making of meaning, not a solitary activity but a dialogue across time and space. The practical implementation of this revival is straightforward enough. Students should be encouraged—indeed, required—to write in their books, to underline key passages, to question dubious claims, to connect new information to existing knowledge. They should be taught specific annotation strategies: using different symbols for different types of reactions, writing summaries in their own words, noting connections to other texts or to personal experience, identifying areas of confusion or disagreement.

But beyond these specific techniques lies a more fundamental shift in how we conceive of reading itself. The annotator approaches the text not as a sacred object but as a human communication, not as a final authority but as a provisional contribution to an ongoing conversation. This approach treats the text with respect, not the superficial respect of leaving it unmarked but the deeper respect of engaging with it seriously, of considering its claims carefully, of testing its insights against experience and other knowledge.

This serious engagement produces a transformed relationship between reader and text. The annotated book becomes a record not merely of the author's thoughts but of the reader's responses, a visible trace of the dialogue between minds that constitutes true reading. The margins fill with questions, observations, connections, and objections, transforming the book from a monologue into a conversation, from a product into a process. In this transformation lies the subversive potential of annotation. The annotator refuses to be a passive consumer of culture, insists on participating in the creation of meaning, and claims the right to question even the most authoritative texts. These constitute a quiet revolution in the relationship between individuals and the sources of knowledge that shape their understanding.

The annotated book becomes a record not merely of the author's thoughts but of the reader's responses, a visible trace of the dialogue between minds that constitutes true reading.

To teach annotation is to promote a habit of mind that honors the authority of the writer without surrendering one's own judgment. It trains the reader to enter a conversation with care and courage, to weigh words thoughtfully, and to respond with insight rather than deference. In this practice, the act of reading becomes an engagement of the whole mind and a cultivation of discernment. The revival of annotation thus represents a radical assertion of human agency in the face of forces that tend to reduce us to mere consumers of information. Let us then reclaim the margins, not as empty spaces to be preserved but as fertile fields to be cultivated as frontiers of thought.

Recommended Further Reading

1. *How to Read a Book* by Mortimer J. Adler and Charles Van Doren. The classic guide to analytical reading that advocates marking up texts as an essential part of active engagement with ideas.
2. *Marginalia: Readers Writing in Books* by H. J. Jackson. A comprehensive examination of the history and significance of marginalia, exploring how readers across centuries have engaged with texts through annotation.
3. *Used Books: Marking Readers in Renaissance England* by William H. Sherman. Investigates how Renaissance readers interacted with their books through marginalia, showing annotation as a form of intellectual engagement and resistance.
4. "A Weapon for Readers" by Tim Parks (2014 essay in the *New York Review of Books*). A meditation on how annotation transforms the reading experience from passive consumption to active dialogue.
5. *The Footnote: A Curious History* by Anthony Grafton. Chronicles how scholarly annotation evolved as a form of intellectual authority and dialogue across time.
6. *S.* by J. J. Abrams and Doug Dorst. A novel that incorporates fictional marginalia as part of its narrative structure, celebrating annotation as storytelling.
7. *The Gutenberg Elegies: The Fate of Reading in an Electronic Age* by Sven Birkerts. Examines how digital technologies have changed our relationship with texts, with insights on the value of deep, annotative reading.

Part II

Subversive Acts of Engagement

Chapter 6

The Subversive Art of Slow Reading

Why patient reading develops counterculturally deep attention spans

There is a certain kind of modern person who, having spent the morning scrolling through six hundred digital headlines without reading a single article, the afternoon skimming fourteen email newsletters without absorbing a single argument, and the evening watching thirty-second video clips without completing a single thought, will look at you with perfect seriousness and declare that he "doesn't have time to read books." This remarkable creature—let us call him Digital Man—exists in a state of perpetual motion yet perfect stillness, consuming vast quantities of text while somehow remaining untouched by the transformative power of reading. He has perfected the art of gathering information without acquiring wisdom.

The irony, of course, is that this very busy nonreader often consumes the equivalent of several novels each week in the form of social media posts, news snippets, corporate memoranda, and digital ephemera. The issue is not the quantity of words his eyes encounter but the quality of attention he brings to them. He has become a master of what might be called "anti-reading." Allow me to define this as the practice of engaging with text in a manner specifically designed to prevent deep understanding and critical reflection. He skims, he scans, he skips, he samples. He does everything with text except surrender to it.

This curious inversion, whereby those who constantly consume words claim they have no time to read, reveals something profound about our relationship with text in the digital age. We have developed a form of engagement that resembles reading in its external movements while emptying it of its internal substance. The fingers scroll, the eyes move, the words register, but the mind remains untouched, skittering across the surface of meaning like a water strider on a pond, never breaking the tension, never sinking into the depths below.

To read slowly in an age of digital skimming is to engage in a kind of cultural insurrection, to reject the values of speed and efficiency in favor of depth, reflection, and transformation.

Against this backdrop of fractured attention and superficial engagement, the practice of slow reading emerges not merely as an alternative approach to text but as a radical act of resistance. To read slowly in an age of digital skimming is to engage in a kind of cultural insurrection, to reject the values of speed and efficiency in favor of depth, reflection, and transformation. To read slowly is to insist, against the prevailing winds of techno-capitalism, that some things cannot and should not be optimized, streamlined, or accelerated—that understanding, wisdom, and insight emerge not from velocity but from patience.

Consider what happens when one reads a complex text slowly and deliberately. The experience bears almost no resemblance to the frantic information-processing that characterizes digital consumption. The slow reader does not extract data points or scan for keywords; he enters into a relationship with the text, allowing it to unfold at its own pace, to reveal its meaning gradually, to work upon his consciousness in ways that may not be immediately apparent. He does not impose his agenda on the text but allows the text to impose its agenda on him. He surrenders not his critical faculties but his impatience, his need for immediate relevance, his insistence that the text justify itself according to preestablished criteria of utility.

This willingness to approach a text on its own terms, to give it the time and attention it requires, allows the attentively slow reader to become a kind of conscientious objector in the war against sustained attention, refusing to treat words as mere instruments for the efficient transfer of information, insisting instead on their power to elevate the quality of thought itself.

The practice of slow reading begins with a recognition that all texts are not created equal, that some demand and reward a depth of engagement that others do not. The slow reader distinguishes between the online news article that can be scanned for its essential facts, the technical manual that can be consulted as needed, and the literary or philosophical work that must be entered into as one might enter a cathedral—with an expectation of transformative encounter.

For such texts—whether Dante's *Divine Comedy* or Dostoevsky's *The Brothers Karamazov*, Plato's *Republic* or Augustine's *Confessions*—a speedy efficiency is not just inappropriate but actively counterproductive. These works were not written to be skimmed; they were written to be inhabited. Entering them is a gradual process in which the language seeps into the imagination and, over time, both the arguments and the characters take shape with a depth that only sustained attention can uncover. To read such texts quickly is to fail to read them at all.

This distinction between different types of texts and different modes of reading represents another way in which slow reading subverts the dominant paradigm of our digital culture. Where technological interfaces flatten all writing into sameness—an endless scroll of uniform type stripped of context—slow reading restores shape and proportion. Not everything deserves the same level of attention; not all texts reward the same depth of engagement. To pretend otherwise is not democratic but delusional.

The slow reader adapts his approach to the text before him, giving each the attention it deserves. He might glance quickly at the morning news or move briskly through a professional journal, yet pause over a personal letter with greater care. But when he turns to the great works of literature, philosophy, history, or theology, he adopts a different posture altogether—one of deliberate slowness, not because the reading is hard, but because the work invites him to receive its riches in their fullness.

Consider Augustine's opening words in *Confessions*: "You have made us for yourself, O Lord, and our heart is restless until it rests in you." A hurried reading misses its weight. To linger here is to sense the tension between yearning and fulfillment, to hear the undertone of prayer, and to recognize how a personal cry becomes a universal truth about the soul. Or take Homer's description of dawn in the *Odyssey*: "Rosy-fingered Dawn appeared and touched the sky." At first glance, it may seem merely a recurring epithet. Read slowly, though, it becomes a window into the poem's rhythm, a reminder of the world's daily renewal, and a moment when myth and natural beauty touch. What seems formulaic opens into poetry that shapes the reader's sense of time itself.

This intentional approach eschews the implicit message of digital interfaces, which treat all text as functionally equivalent: as information to be processed rather than as an encounter to be experienced. This flattening of textual hierarchy represents a profound loss, not merely of critical distinction but of appropriate response to the different types of claims that different texts make upon us.

The second element of slow reading's subversive character lies in its refusal to treat time as the enemy of understanding. Our digital culture operates on the implicit assumption that speed is an unqualified good, that faster is always better, that waiting is always wasteful, that delay is always inefficient. The ideal reader, in this unfortunate paradigm, is one who extracts the maximum amount of information in the minimum amount of time.

The slow reader rejects this assumption, recognizing that some forms of understanding emerge only through patience, that some insights reveal themselves only after prolonged engagement. The slow reader knows that the value of reading cannot be measured by words per minute or facts acquired per hour, that the most important effects of engagement with a profound text may reveal themselves not during the reading itself but hours, days, or even years later, as the words continue to work upon the mind. Patient willingness allows

The slow reader knows that the value of reading cannot be measured by words per minute or facts acquired per hour, that the most important effects of engagement with a profound text may reveal themselves not during the reading itself but hours, days, or even years later, as the words continue to work upon the mind.

meaning to emerge in its own time rather than according to predetermined schedules of efficiency.

The third element of slow reading's subversive nature lies in its insistence on the irreducibly embodied character of genuine understanding. Despite the pretensions of technological interfaces to provide direct access to disembodied information, reading remains a physical activity. Beyond the visual processing of symbols it demands the engagement of the whole person—eyes, hands, posture, breath, and nervous system. The slow reader recognizes this embodied dimension of reading and works with it rather than against it.

This recognition manifests in a variety of practices that digital reading tends to eliminate or minimize. The slow reader may annotate the text, writing in the margins, underlining key passages, placing asterisks beside important points. He may read aloud, allowing the physical vibrations of speech to enhance understanding and memory. She may pause to reflect, to connect what she has read with her own experience, to argue silently with the author.

Such practices remind us that reading is never a simple act of decoding symbols on a page. It is a dialogue between text and reader, shaped by memory and imagination. For this reason, the cultivation of slow reading is not some optional skill but a cornerstone of classical education. To guide students into habits of patience and attentiveness is to form them as thinkers who do not mistake information for understanding. They learn that truth is discovered through engagement and that the greatest works must be taken slowly if they are to be truly received. Classical education, at its heart, insists that books are not consumed like fast food but entered like enduring friendships—demanding time and shaping the soul.

The digital interface, on the other hand, presents itself as a transparent window onto pure information, concealing its own materiality, its own shaping influence on the content it displays. It encourages the user to forget the mediated nature of the encounter, to believe that he is engaging directly with content rather than through a highly engineered and profoundly non-neutral technological system. Slow reading, by contrast, acknowledges and works with the materiality of textual encounter. The physical book, with its weight and texture, its fixed pagination and spatial stability, affords engagement that digital interfaces typically minimize or eliminate. The slow reader uses these affordances to leave traces of her own thinking alongside the author's words.

Digital texts often present information as immediate and effortless, but this ease comes at a cost. Words scroll past so quickly that comprehension struggles to keep pace, and the body's natural rhythms of attention are ignored. Links and other digital digressions interrupt the flow of thought and meaning seems to exist independently of the reader's effort. In this environment, understanding is both shallow and fleeting, as if it could be absorbed without reflection. Slow reading responds to these conditions by restoring the awareness that reading is an embodied process. True comprehension emerges only when the reader pauses, reflects on difficult passages, and allows the text to unfold over time. In doing so, the act of reading becomes a deliberate—and fruitful—encounter.

The fourth element of slow reading's subversive potential lies in its cultivation of attentional independence, defined as the capacity to direct and sustain attention according to one's own purposes rather than in response to external stimuli. Our digital communications environment is engineered to capture and direct attention through a constant stream of notifications, alerts, updates, and novel stimuli. It creates what some researchers have called an "attentional commons,"[5] a shared space of mental focus that is increasingly colonized by commercial or political interests.

The slow reader stages a kind of attentional secession from the digital commons, withdrawing from the competitive marketplace of stimuli to direct focus toward a single text for an extended period. This subversive act represents a reclamation of cognitive sovereignty; it is a refusal to surrender mental direction to external forces. Unlike the digital consumer whose attention flits between headlines and advertisements in response to engineered stimuli, the slow reader decides where to direct attention and for how long.

---

5 The concept of "attentional commons" is developed in Matthew Crawford's work *The World Beyond Your Head: On Becoming an Individual in an Age of Distraction* (2015), where he explores how our attention has become a resource that is increasingly harvested and commodified in the modern digital economy.

The contrast is readily apparent: One mind is colonized, shaped by constant external demands; the other governs itself, attending to what matters rather than what is imposed. The digital consumer bends to the "tyranny of the now," her attention guided by endless notifications and the demands of others rather than by her own judgment. The slow reader, however, establishes personal rhythms of engagement. She is able to determine individual priorities of focus and better resist the perpetual pull of novelty. This independence of attention constitutes a form of cognitive freedom increasingly rare in our digital environment. It allows the mind to dwell on a single thought until its meaning unfolds, tracing an argument with care until its logic is understood. It also permits the reader to enter a narrative world so fully that the story inhabits the mind, uninterrupted by the constant demands of the outside world. Such freedom is more than a convenience; it cultivates the inner life and fosters a power of thought that the pace of modern life all too often denies.

This dimension of slow reading reveals its political character as a form of resistance to forces that would commodify attention and redirect it toward commercial or political ends. To read slowly is to assert that one's mental focus belongs to oneself rather than to the attention economy, that the direction of one's thoughts should be self-determined rather than machine-mediated, that the rhythm of engagement should follow the natural contours of understanding rather than the artificial urgencies of digital capitalism.

The fifth and perhaps most profound element of slow reading's subversive nature lies in its implicit challenge to the concept of efficiency as applied to intellectual and spiritual development. Our digital culture operates on the assumption that reading, like all other activities, should be optimized for maximum efficiency. The goal is to extract the most information in the least time with a minimum of effort. This assumption may make sense for certain types of reading, as mentioned previously—scanning a manual for specific instructions, reviewing a document for key data points, or catching up on current events. But it becomes actively destructive when applied to texts whose purpose is, for example, to transform the reader's perspective or to enhance moral perception.

These transformative purposes cannot be achieved efficiently for the simple reason that transformation is not a matter of transferring information but of fostering integration. A profound text does not just add new data to the reader's existing mental framework. It actually reshapes the way the reader sees and interprets the world. When reading Plato's *Republic*, for instance, one does not merely learn about justice but is compelled to reconsider the nature of society and the self. Encountering Dostoevsky's *Crime and Punishment* challenges the reader to consider conscience, guilt, and moral responsibility in ways that linger long after the final page. Such shifts cannot be hurried without distortion; they unfold according to their own rhythm, as understanding deepens through struggle, reflection, and gradual assimilation.

The slow reader recognizes that profound texts like these transform the mind and refuses to sacrifice this depth for the sake of efficiency. This recognition challenges a culture organized around speed and productivity, asserting that the most important processes of human development—intellectual, moral, spiritual—follow rhythms that cannot be optimized without being distorted. Some forms of growth demand patient attention. In this light, slow reading is not merely an alternative method but a countercultural practice, a deliberate refusal of values that shape our approach to time, knowledge, and focus.

Slow reading is not a matter of personal taste; it is a quiet rebellion against the empire of distraction. The reader who lingers over a single volume, turning pages deliberately while the digital world clamors outside, enacts a form of defiance as profound as any revolutionary manifesto. Classical schools that cultivate this practice are providing training grounds for a distinctive form of intellectual freedom.

Recommended Further Reading

1. *Reader, Come Home: The Reading Brain in a Digital World* by Maryanne Wolf. Examines how our reading habits are changing in the digital age and what's at stake for deep literacy.
2. *Slow Reading in a Hurried Age* by David Mikics. Offers practical approaches to cultivating the habit of slow, thoughtful reading in a world that discourages it.

3. *The Lost Art of Reading: Books and Resistance in a Troubled Time* by David L. Ulin. Explores personal and cultural dimensions of deep reading as a counterforce to information overload.
4. *The Pleasures of Reading in an Age of Distraction* by Alan Jacobs. Makes a case for reading driven by delight rather than duty as the most sustainable approach to deep literacy.
5. *The Art of Slow Reading: Six Time-Honored Practices for Engagement* by Thomas Newkirk. Offers practical strategies for developing patient, attentive reading habits that foster deeper understanding.
6. *Slow Philosophy: Reading Against the Institution* by Michelle Boulous Walker. Advocates for slow, careful reading as resistance against institutional pressures toward speed and productivity.
7. *The Attention Merchants: The Epic Scramble to Get Inside Our Heads* by Tim Wu. Chronicles the history of how our attention became commodified and how we might reclaim it.

Chapter 7

The Subversive Art of Memorization

Why training the memory builds intellectual sovereignty

An interesting notion has taken hold in our time: that the human mind improves not by remembering but by forgetting. That we become freer by becoming emptier. That we ascend to some higher intellectual plane by casting off the burden of remembering anything at all. This progressive orthodoxy has crept into our schools and universities with the stealth of a thief in the night, and with much the same intent: to rob us of our treasures. The modern educators, with their perpetual revolution of methods and theories, have stumbled upon the extraordinary idea that memory is a kind of medieval torture chamber from which the enlightened pupil must be liberated. They speak of memorization as if it were a rusty chain dragging behind the ankle of the otherwise sprightly intellect. "Why," they ask with an air of triumphant discovery, "should any child commit to memory what can be looked up?" Or rather, as our more progressive age would have it, what can be summoned with the mere tap of a finger upon a glowing screen.

The answer, which seems to escape these educational reformers, is almost embarrassingly simple: because what is not remembered cannot be thought about. The things we know by heart are the things that shape our hearts. The verses, facts, and formulas that we have taken the trouble to commit to memory become the substance of our thinking, the materials with which the mind constructs its cathedral of understanding. A man who must look up everything knows nothing.

There was once a race of men called the ancients, though they were not particularly old at the time, who understood this profound truth about human nature. The Greeks and Romans, those extraordinary pagans who somehow managed to create civilizations of staggering achievement without the benefit of smartphones, regarded memory as a divine gift. They spoke of Mnemosyne, Memory herself, enthroned among the immortals, revered as the mother of the nine Muses. From her womb sprang poetry, history, music, and all the arts that give shape to human culture. To invoke Mnemosyne was to call upon the wellspring of inspiration, for the ancients knew that without memory there could be no song, and no story. There could be no wisdom preserved. In their vision, memory was the fountainhead of creativity. Mnemosyne was the goddess who bore forth every form of beauty and knowledge by keeping alive what might otherwise be forgotten.

These ancients developed elaborate systems—the art of memory, they called it—to store vast landscapes of knowledge within the palace of the mind. They would populate imaginary buildings with vivid images, each one triggering the recollection of some passage of poetry, some argument of philosophy, some principle of mathematics. They understood that to know something by heart is to possess it in a way that no external device, however ingenious, can replicate.

Medieval scholars continued this tradition. They recognized that memory was a tool. To forget the past, they understood, was to sever oneself from the soil in which wisdom grows. Forgetting meant exile from the treasury of human experience, a self-inflicted poverty of mind and spirit. To remember, by contrast, was to live in continuity with those who came before. They did not merely recall facts; they remembered truths.

But modern educators have decided that all this is terribly old-fashioned. We have outsourced our memories to machines, as if the mind were merely an inefficient version of a computer. We

We have outsourced our memories to machines, as if the mind were merely an inefficient version of a computer.

have convinced ourselves that knowing where to find information is the same as knowing the information itself. It is rather like a man who, having been invited to a banquet, declines to eat but takes careful note of the location of each dish on the table, congratulating himself on his superior method of nutrition.

There is something almost comical about our modern aversion to memory. Some even fear that memorization will somehow crush the delicate flower of originality, not realizing that originality itself springs from the fertile soil of what has been remembered. The poet who has never committed a sonnet to memory is unlikely to write one worth remembering. The mathematician who disdains to remember formulas will hardly discover new ones. The historian who cannot recall dates and events is merely a fabulist.

The paradox, which would be obvious if we had not educated ourselves into a kind of voluntary amnesia, is that memory liberates rather than constrains. It frees us from the tyranny of the immediate. It allows us to see the present moment not as an isolated fragment but as part of the vast expanse of human experience. A man with a well-stocked memory is never alone; he carries with him an invisible company of the wise, the eloquent, the profound.

The neglect of memory in our educational system is nothing less than a form of intellectual vandalism. It deprives children of their rightful inheritance, leaving them stranded in the narrow confines of the present moment, without the maps and guides that might help them navigate the wilderness of experience. It is as if we deliberately withheld from them the passwords and keys that unlock the treasuries of human wisdom.

Yet there is hope. Memory is a stubborn faculty. It refuses to be completely banished. It persists, like nature reasserting itself in the cracks of a pavement, in the most unexpected places.

And so, classical education proposes a quiet rebellion, a subversive restoration of this ancient art. Let us teach our students to commit to memory the literary passages that move them, the speeches that inspire them, the principles that guide them. Let us show them that their minds are not processors of information but living repositories of wisdom. Let us remind them—and ourselves—that to remember is to resist the Great

Forgetting, the amnesia of an age that would reduce us all to consumers of the ephemeral and forgettable.

In the end, what we choose to remember defines who we are. A civilization without memory is no civilization at all. It is merely a collection of individuals adrift in time, each one condemned to reinvent the wheel, over and over again. Memory is an affirmation that the past matters, that knowledge is cumulative, that wisdom can be inherited as well as earned.

The good news and the great hope is that the art of memory, which modern education has so carelessly discarded, awaits rediscovery. It stands ready to restore depth and resonance to our thinking by reconnecting us with the great conversation of humanity across the centuries. All that is required is the courage to remember, to rebel against the orthodoxy of forgetting, to reclaim what is rightfully ours: the infinite treasure house of the well-furnished mind.

It is a curious fact, which our modern pedagogues will scarcely believe, that the human mind actually takes a peculiar delight in the act of memory which we have been so diligently taught to despise. Ask any child who has mastered the art of remembering, and you will find in them not the dull-eyed victim of rote learning that our educational theorists imagine, but something approaching the joy of a conqueror. Children, for example, still delight in memorizing the lyrics of songs. They can recite dialogues from their favorite films. They can reel off the arcane statistics of sports teams. Their minds hunger for the exercise that memory provides, even as their teachers assure them that such exercise is unnecessary. For to memorize is to conquer time itself; it is to seize some beautiful or profound utterance and to say, defiantly, "This shall not pass away; this shall remain with me always."

Consider what happens when a young person first decides to commit to memory something greater than baseball stats, something on the order of Hamlet's great soliloquy on mortality. The opening lines, so familiar even to those who have never deliberately set out to learn them, act as a doorway into a palace of thought. "To be, or not to be," says the Danish prince, and already the mind is faced with the most fundamental question of existence. The student who begins the task of memorization does not merely store these words as one might file away a document; he internalizes them. He becomes, in some curious way, both himself and Hamlet, turning over the prince's dilemma as if it were his own.

The process itself is a beautiful thing. First comes the mechanical stage, the simple repetition of words, the stumbling attempts to hold the sequence in mind. This is the part that our educational reformers—haters of memorization—find so objectionable, imagining it to be the whole of memorization. But that is only the beginning, the clearing of ground before the building of the temple. As the words become familiar, something remarkable happens: they begin to arrange themselves not just in the memory but in the understanding. The pauses, the emphases, the duh-DUM rhythm of Shakespeare's pentameter becomes a kind of heartbeat in the mind.

"To be, or not to be, that is the question . . ." The student repeats it again and again, not as a parrot might, but as an explorer charting an unknown territory. Each repetition reveals new contours of meaning, new depths of implication. "Whether 'tis nobler in the mind to suffer the slings and arrows of outrageous fortune, or to take arms against a sea of troubles, and by opposing end them." Here is philosophy, ethics, the substance of human choice distilled into poetry, the language of matchless precision and beauty.

And as the soliloquy unfolds in the memory, something even more remarkable occurs. The words, through the act of repetition, become so thoroughly internalized that they cease to be separate from the student's own thought. They become a lens through which he views his own experiences, a template against which he measures his own struggles and doubts—either now or years later. To have memorized Hamlet's meditation on death is to have gained a companion in the darkest hours of the soul, a voice that speaks with more eloquence than our own could muster.

Or take Lincoln's Gettysburg Address, that miracle of concision which says more in its few hundred words than most orators could manage in hours. The student who sets out to memorize it begins with the simple act of repetition: "Four score and seven years ago our fathers brought forth on this continent, a new nation, conceived in Liberty, and dedicated to the proposition that all men are created equal."

The rhythm of these opening words, with their biblical cadence and their measured solemnity, becomes a kind of music in the mind. The student may begin by dividing the text into manageable portions, mastering each before moving on to the next. "Now we are engaged in a great civil war, testing whether that nation, or any nation so conceived and so dedicated, can long endure." The act of dividing and conquering the text mirrors the struggle that Lincoln describes, the fight to preserve the Union.

As the memorization continues, the student finds that the address begins to organize itself in his mind according to its internal logic. The three parts—past, present, and future; the founding, the war, and the dedication—create a structure that makes the whole easier to recall. And in mastering this structure, the student absorbs both Lincoln's words and his argument, his vision of America as a nation defined not by blood or soil but by its dedication to a proposition.

The same principle applies to Poe's "The Raven," a masterpiece of melodious gloom in verse. The student who undertakes to memorize it finds that its insistent rhythm and rhyme scheme, crafted by Poe with almost mathematical precision, serves as a mnemonic device in itself. "Once upon a midnight dreary, while I pondered, weak and weary . . ." The trochaic meter pounds in the blood like a heartbeat, the internal rhymes ("dreary/weary") bind the lines together in the memory like links in a chain, as if Poe meant the poem to be memorized and recited for ages to come

The difficulty of the poem, especially its rich but archaic vocabulary, becomes, paradoxically, an aid to memorization. For the mind delights in challenges, in patterns that require deciphering, in language that rises above the banal and commonplace. To memorize "The Raven" is to master a piece of verbal music. It is to feel the rise and fall of its cadences in anticipation of the inevitable "nevermore" that punctuates each stanza like the toll of a funeral bell.

But we should not suppose that memorization is valuable only for great literature. The Constitution's Preamble, so often relegated to the status of a historical curiosity, becomes, when committed to memory, a living declaration of intent. "We the People of the United States, in Order to form a more perfect Union, establish Justice, insure domestic Tranquility . . ." Each phrase, each stated purpose, becomes a standard against which to measure the success or failure of the American experiment.

To have memorized the Preamble is to carry within oneself the foundational principles of a nation. It is to possess a compass by which to navigate the complex and often contradictory currents of American political life. And in an age when constitutional principles are too often treated as mere rhetorical flourishes or inconvenient obstacles to partisan goals, such a compass is more necessary than ever.

The methods of memorization are as varied as the human mind itself. Some find that writing out the text to be memorized, again and again, imprints it upon the memory through the connection between hand and brain. Others prefer to speak the words aloud, allowing the ear to reinforce what the eye has seen. Still others use movement, walking as they recite, allowing the rhythm of their steps to synchronize with the rhythm of the words.

There is the method of loci, beloved of the ancient orators, in which each part of a speech or poem is associated with a specific location in an imagined building. As the mind moves through this mental architecture, it encounters each memorized passage in its appointed place. The method of progressive mastery is another approach, beginning with a single line or stanza, repeating it until it is secure, then adding the next, and the next, building the structure of memory brick by brick.

But whatever the method, the goal remains the same: transforming those words into understanding. This is what our modern educational theorists, with their fetish for searchable databases and instantly accessible googled facts, fail to comprehend. They see memory as a warehouse, a static repository of information. But it is actually a workshop, a living space where knowledge is transformed and incorporated into the substance of the self.

A man who has memorized the Declaration of Independence does not merely possess a historical document; he possesses a way of thinking about liberty, about the relationship between government and the governed, about the very nature of political legitimacy.

A man who has memorized the Declaration of Independence does not merely possess a historical document; he possesses a way of thinking about liberty, about the relationship between government and the governed, about the very nature of political legitimacy. The words of the Declaration of Independence, having become part of the mental landscape of the person who memorized them, shape his perception of the world around him. They provide a framework for interpreting events, a standard against which to measure the claims of those in power. Similarly, a woman who has committed to memory the prayers or sacred texts of her tradition does not merely preserve religious formulas; she interiorizes a spiritual vocabulary, a way of addressing the divine, a method of framing her own experiences within a larger narrative of meaning.

Consider the student who has memorized "The Magnificat." As she walks through life's varied circumstances, fragments of this text naturally surface in her consciousness: "My soul proclaims the greatness of the Lord, and my spirit rejoices in God my Savior." These aren't merely words she can recite; they become an interpretive lens through which she perceives her own experiences. When facing moments of unexpected blessing, the memorized lines "for he has looked with favor on his lowly servant" might spontaneously rise in her thoughts, connecting her personal experience to a timeless pattern of divine action. The text's assertion that God "has cast down the mighty from their thrones, and has lifted up the lowly" doesn't remain an abstract theological statement but becomes a framework for understanding justice and power dynamics in her own world.

Similarly, one who has internalized the Canticle of Zechariah carries within her a particular vocabulary of redemption and promise. When she encounters darkness in her life or in society, the memorized words "to shine on those who dwell in darkness and the shadow of death, and to guide our feet into the way of peace" provide not just comfort but an interpretive framework. The imagery of dawn breaking ("the tender compassion of our God, the dawn from on high shall break upon us") shapes how she perceives moments of hope emerging from despair.

This internalization runs deeper than intellectual recall. The meter and cadence of these canticles, their rhythms and pauses, become embodied knowledge, influencing breathing patterns during prayer, shaping emotional responses, and creating neural pathways that connect spiritual concepts with physical sensations. Memorizing these texts allows one to move beyond simply rattling them off these prayers. Rather, she is able to breathe them, living within their poetic structure.

Most profoundly, these memorized texts become "thoughts to think with" — cognitive tools that operate below the level of conscious retrieval. When contemplating decisions or interpreting events, the theological framework of these canticles subtly influences the student's perception without requiring explicit recall. The Magnificat's vision of God who "has scattered the proud in their conceit" might unconsciously inform her assessment of human motivations. The promise in Zechariah's canticle to "free us from the hands of our enemies" might shape how she conceptualizes obstacles and challenges. Through memorization, these sacred texts transition from external documents to internal architecture, not things she knows but ways she knows, patterns through which she interprets all subsequent content.

This is the true purpose of memorization: to furnish the mind with living ideas, to provide the raw materials from which new thoughts can be constructed, and from which new insights can grow. A mind without memory is like a painter without pigments—capable, perhaps, of conceiving great works but powerless to execute them.

So let us reclaim this ancient art, this fundamental human capacity that our age has so carelessly discarded. Let us teach students to move well beyond googling information; let us show them how to possess it, helping them transform it into wisdom. Let us show them that the mind is not a temporary cache to be periodically cleared but a permanent treasury to be filled with the gold and jewels of human thought.

A mind furnished with the best that has been thought and said is a mind equipped for the great task of living wisely and well. It is a mind capable of resisting the tyranny of the present moment, of seeing beyond the horizon of the immediate, of recognizing in the chaos of events the enduring patterns of human experience.

Recommended Further Reading

1. *The Art of Memory* by Frances A. Yates. A seminal historical study of mnemonic systems from ancient Greece through the Renaissance, revealing how memory techniques were once considered essential to intellectual development and cultural transmission.
2. *Moonwalking with Einstein: The Art and Science of Remembering Everything* by Joshua Foer. Chronicles a journalist's journey from memory novice to USA Memory Championship competitor, exploring both ancient memory techniques and their neurological foundations.
3. *The Memory Palace: Learn Anything and Everything* by Lewis Smile. A practical guide that teaches readers how to use spatial memory techniques to memorize information efficiently, using vivid examples that demonstrate how to construct effective memory palaces for long-term retention.
4. *How to Develop a Perfect Memory* by Dominic O'Brien. The eight-time World Memory Champion shares his systematic approach to memory development, demonstrating how ordinary minds can achieve extraordinary feats of recall.
5. *Make It Stick: The Science of Successful Learning* by Peter C. Brown. Presents scientific research demonstrating why memorization and retrieval practice are essential components of durable learning.
6. *Your Memory: How It Works and How to Improve It* by Kenneth L. Higbee. A neuroscientist explains memory's biological foundations and offers evidence-based techniques for enhancement.
7. *The Memory Book* by Harry Lorayne and Jerry Lucas. A classic guide to practical memory development, presenting accessible techniques for remembering everything from names to complex texts.

Chapter 8

The Subversive Art of Poetry

How memorizing verse provides portable wisdom in an age of forgetting

Here's another curious conviction among modern educators: that forcing children to memorize poetry constitutes a species of cruelty comparable to dosing them with cod-liver oil every morning. In fact, the phrase "poetry memorization" too often conjures images of pale Victorian children standing stiffly beside school desks, reciting with mechanical precision verses they neither understand nor enjoy, while stern schoolmasters hover nearby with rulers at the ready. Thomas Hughes captured this spirit in *Tom Brown's Schooldays* (1857), where boys were drilled to recite long passages under the eye of exacting masters, their performance less an act of learning than of endurance. Likewise, Charles Dickens, in *Hard Times* (1854), satirized an education of rigid facts and joyless repetition, portraying classrooms where imagination was systematically squeezed out of children until they became little more than reciting machines. This grim caricature has so thoroughly pervaded our educational imagination that the mere suggestion of requiring students to commit poems to memory is likely to be met with no less than expressions of horror.

What makes this reaction so remarkable, aside from its disproportionate intensity, is its stunning inversion of reality. At least in today's classical schools, memorization of poetry is a gift bestowed upon students and perhaps the one educational bequest that can never be taken away since it will never cease to provide both practical utility and profound joy throughout a lifetime. To deprive children of this inheritance in the name of progressive pedagogy is rather like refusing to teach them to swim on the grounds that it requires too much effort, then congratulating ourselves on our humanitarianism as they drown.

The prejudice against poetry memorization represents one strand of a broader educational heresy, the notion that anything requiring disciplined effort must, by definition, be unpleasant and therefore should be avoided in favor of activities that produce immediate enjoyment. But this heresy ignores the fundamental distinction between the fleeting satisfaction of desires and the lasting happiness that comes from mastering something difficult. It mistakes the transient discomfort of exertion for permanent misery, failing to recognize that the greatest human satisfactions typically emerge from activities that demand a great deal of effort and perseverance amid many frustrations along the way.

The student who memorizes Blake's "Tyger," Wordsworth's "Daffodils," or Shakespeare's sonnets may indeed experience moments of difficulty and frustration during the process. That's natural. At least to those unaccustomed to the practice. But the rewards far outweigh this temporary discomfort. The child who has internalized great poetry possesses a treasure that neither economic collapse nor technological revolution can devalue. It is a permanent interior landscape of beauty and insight that remains accessible with neither an internet connection nor social validation.

Consider Walt Whitman's "Song of Myself": to commit this poem to memory is to enter the sheer expansiveness of the American voice. Its rolling free verse carries the rhythms of a continent, spilling over conventional boundaries in long, breathless lines. In Whitman, memorization preserves a language confident enough to embrace multitudes. A student who inwardly carries Whitman carries also a sense of language as a living surge, expansive and democratic in its reach.

Now turn to Emily Dickinson's "Because I could not stop for Death—". Here the power of memorization lies in compression rather than expansion. Dickinson's clipped meters and slant rhymes teach the ear to attend to nuance, while her images—the carriage ride, the setting sun, the swelling ground—transform mortality into quiet meditation. To memorize Dickinson is to internalize language in its most distilled form, where every pause and every turn of phrase holds weight. A student who inwardly carries Dickinson carries also the precision and intensity of a voice that makes eternity palpable in a handful of syllables.

Together, Whitman and Dickinson illustrate the range of what memorized poetry preserves: the overflowing and the distilled. To memorize them is to carry within oneself two contrasting yet complementary modes of expression, each revealing how language can both broaden our vision and deepen our perception.

This linguistic ecosystem, like its natural counterpart, requires active stewardship to maintain its richness and vitality, and that's exactly the approach taken by a classical education. A language that loses its poetic dimension becomes progressively impoverished, reduced to a system for conveying basic information rather than a medium capable of expressing the full range of human experience. The memorization and recitation of poetry represent a form of linguistic conservation, preserving forms of expression that might otherwise vanish from living memory.

A language that loses its poetic dimension becomes progressively impoverished, reduced to a system for conveying basic information rather than a medium capable of expressing the full range of human experience. The memorization and recitation of poetry represent a form of linguistic conservation, preserving forms of expression that might otherwise vanish from living memory.

Consider, for example, the opening lines of Keats's "To Autumn": "Season of mists and mellow fruitfulness, / Close bosom-friend of the maturing sun." The child who commits these lines to memory does not merely store information about autumn; he inherits a way of seeing, a mode of attention that reveals aspects of the season invisible to prosaic observation. He learns that a season can have a "close bosom-friend," that the sun can engage in the act of "maturing," that fruitfulness can possess the quality of "mellowness." These metaphors provide invitations into a richer perceptual world, one in which natural phenomena participate in a complex web of relationships typically filtered out by utilitarian modes of awareness.

Similarly, the student who memorizes Shakespeare's "Shall I compare thee to a summer's day? / Thou art more lovely and more temperate" inherits the tradition of contemplating human beauty in relation to nature, of recognizing both the resonances and the dissonances between the world of natural processes and the realm of human experience. The sonnet form itself, with its structured development of thought providing both regularity and surprise, becomes part of the student's cognitive repertoire, a resource for organizing perception and reflection that remains available long after the specific poem has been recited.

This linguistic inheritance is a far cry from the progressive impoverishment of language exacerbated by digital communication platforms with their emphasis on push-button immediacy and emotional reaction. The child who spends hours scrolling through social media absorbs a form of expression optimized for rapid consumption that carries no lasting significance. Because these platforms reward speed and spectacle, the language contracts into fragments—words clipped short with thought reduced to shorthand. The memorization of poetry offers a powerful antidote to this linguistic impoverishment. It places in the student's mind examples of language used with a richness of precision and beauty. It is language stretched to its full expressive capacity rather than compressed to fit arbitrary technological constraints. The memorized poem becomes a standard against which other forms of expression can be measured. It is a reminder that language can do more than convey information or provoke reaction. It can also reveal dimensions of experience invisible to prosaic perception and embody rather than merely describe the realities it addresses.

But the subversive power of poetry memorization extends beyond the preservation of linguistic resources to encompass the cultivation of memory itself. Our technological culture operates on the assumption that there is no need to commit anything to memory when it can be instantly retrieved from external storage. Why memorize a poem when you can google it? Why internalize knowledge when it can be accessed on demand? Why develop mental capacities that can be replaced by algorithmic processes?

This cynical rhetoric contains a profound error: the failure to distinguish between information storage and genuine memory. When we commit a poem to memory, yes, we store its text for future retrieval, but more importantly we integrate it into our cognitive and emotional architecture, making it part of the lens through which we perceive and interpret experience. The memorized poem becomes something we know and something we know *with*. It is a resource for making sense of the world and a touchstone for evaluating other forms of expression.

A poem that sits in digital memory, waiting to be summoned, remains outside the self: inert data rather than lived knowledge. Accessing it is a mechanical act, not a human one. Genuine memory, by contrast, shapes perception from within. It is less like consulting a file and more like vision itself—a way of seeing, not merely a record of what was once seen."

The student who has memorized Wordsworth's "I wandered lonely as a cloud" possesses something fundamentally different from the student who knows how to find the poem online. For the former, the daffodils dancing in the breeze have become part of an interior landscape, a resource for understanding both solitude and unexpected joy, a framework for perceiving the relationship between natural beauty and human emotion. The poem shapes perception itself, rendering visible aspects of experience that might otherwise remain unnoticed or unarticulated.

In this sense, poetry memorization represents a form of resistance to the externalization of memory characteristic of digital culture, a reclaiming of cognitive capacities increasingly delegated to technological systems. It asserts that some forms of knowledge should be internalized rather than outsourced or offloaded. It recognizes memory not merely as a storage system but as a fundamental dimension of the self that shapes identity and perception in ways that external information repositories cannot replicate.

The third dimension of poetry's subversive power is its gift for preserving cultural memory—the wisdom of ages woven into verse and carried from one generation to the next. Without such a thread, the fabric of tradition unravels, and each age must stumble forward as if the past had never spoken.

Memorized poetry serves as one of the most efficient and enduring vehicles for this cultural transmission. A canto of Dante, a hexameter line of Homer, or a sonnet of Petrarch can condense into a few breaths the weight of thought that pages of prose might labor to convey. Dante's "Abandon all hope, ye who enter here" strikes like a tolling bell, echoing the gravity of divine justice; Homer's "Sing, O goddess, the anger of Achilles" rolls across the mind like the surge of the sea, carrying the fury, pride, and loss of a warrior's heart; Petrarch's "I find no peace, and yet I make no war" lingers on the tongue, a soft torment of desire and restraint, shaping the rhythm of thought itself. Each line carries a world within it, a pulse of human experience memorized and transmitted, resisting both distortion and forgetting.

This capacity for efficient transmission makes poetry particularly valuable for preserving insights that run counter to prevailing cultural assumptions, ideas that might otherwise be lost through the natural tendency of each age to focus on its own preoccupations to the exclusion of alternative perspectives. In this way, memorized poetry functions as a vessel for ideas that defy the dominant currents of thought, allowing them to persist beyond the immediate biases and preoccupations of contemporary culture.

These countercultural insights, preserved in the memory when they might be forgotten in the cultural marketplace, represent a form of resistance to what C. S. Lewis called "chronological snobbery"—the assumption that the present moment represents the pinnacle of human understanding, rendering previous perspectives obsolete. The memorized poem stands as a witness from another time. It challenges the provincialism of the present with the perspective of the past, reminding us that human wisdom is not a linear progression but a complex conversation across centuries, with insights gained and lost.

In this sense, poetry memorization serves a function analogous to that of an endangered species preserved in a natural ecosystem, maintaining the diversity of cultural perspectives in the face of homogenizing forces that would reduce the rich variety of human understanding to a narrow range of currently fashionable views. Just as biodiversity represents a form of resilience in natural systems, cultural diversity provides resilience in human understanding, ensuring that alternative perspectives remain available when current assumptions prove inadequate to emerging challenges. Dante's vivid descent through the *Inferno* carries moral complexity and imaginative depth across centuries, while Langston Hughes's syncopated lines in "The Weary Blues" pulse with the rhythms of social struggle and hope, keeping alive perspectives that might otherwise be eclipsed. These voices, living inside the mind rather than on a page, form a hidden reserve of understanding, ready to temper the hubris of the present, to remind us that human wisdom is never linear, never uniform. Rather, it is a tangled, thriving web of experience that we inherit and pass on.

The fourth dimension of poetry's subversive potential lies in its inherent resistance to instrumentalization, its refusal to be reduced to a vehicle for conveying information or achieving predetermined outcomes. Poetry stands as a reminder that some forms of learning cannot be reduced to their practical applications, that education serves the cultivation of full humanity. The memorized poem resists commodification because its value cannot be adequately captured in so-called practical applications. What is the market value of having Blake's "Auguries of Innocence" inscribed in memory? What measurable objective is achieved by knowing Frost's "Stopping by Woods on a Snowy Evening" by heart? These questions miss the point in the same way that asking about the practical utility of love or the market value of friendship misses the point. They apply a category of evaluation fundamentally mismatched to the reality being assessed.

This resistance to instrumentalization makes poetry memorization deeply countercultural in our modern educational landscape, shaped as it is by economic imperatives, where the value of learning is measured primarily by its contribution to employability in the job sector. The poem committed to memory serves no obvious economic function; it cannot be monetized. It cannot be converted into market advantage. Its value lies in dimensions of human experience that economic metrics cannot capture, for example, in beauty, insight, emotional resonance, and the cultivation of interior life.

To insist upon the importance of poetry memorization is thus to assert that students ought not be reduced to future workers. We must actively recognize they are human beings whose development should encompass a whole lot more than "practical skills." It is to recognize that some of the most important outcomes of education can neither be measured nor reduced to utility. The cultivation of humanity requires attention to dimensions of experience that resist both standardization and instrumentalization.

The final and perhaps most profound dimension of poetry's subversive power lies in its capacity to preserve contemplative attention, a way of perceiving and engaging with reality increasingly threatened by the fragmented awareness characteristic of digital media. The memorization and recitation of poetry cultivate this capacity to dwell on a single text. Contemplative attention allows the student to attend to its subtle intricacies, allowing it to work upon consciousness over time. Poetry, by its nature, resists superficial engagement. Its compact language demands and rewards contemplative attention, the willingness to spend time with a text, to return to it repeatedly, to allow its complexities to unfold over time, sometimes over years and decades. The memorization of poetry intensifies this demand, requiring a depth of engagement impossible in the skimming mode. To commit a poem to memory is to focus on a single text long enough for it to become part of one's mental furniture rather than a momentary distraction.

In light of these many forms of subversion, the teaching of poetry memorization in classical schools rises as a bold act of resistance. It defies a culture that drains the vitality from language, outsources memory to machines, reduces education to utility, severs us from the inheritance of the past, and shatters the unity of our attention. To place a poem in the heart is to guard treasures the age would squander. So, let us happily reclaim the practice of poetry memorization as a revolutionary act, a deliberate preservation of linguistic resources, cognitive capacities, cultural insights, and modes of attention increasingly threatened by technological and economic forces that would reduce education to training, language to information transfer, and attention to a marketable commodity. By requiring students to commit great poetry to memory, we offer them not a burden but a gift—perhaps the one educational legacy that can never be obsolete, never be commodified, never cease to provide both practical resources and profound joy throughout the entirety of a human life.

Recommended Further Reading

1. *Poetry By Heart: A Treasury of Poems to Read Aloud* edited by Julie Blake and Andrew Motion. A comprehensive anthology specifically designed for memorization, with techniques and explanations of the benefits of learning poetry by heart.

2. *Committed to Memory: 100 Best Poems to Memorize* by John Hollander. Collects poems specifically chosen for their memorability and cultural significance, with commentary on what makes certain verses particularly well-suited for retention.
3. *Heart Beats: Everyday Life and the Memorized Poem* by Catherine Robson. Explores the physical dimension of poetry memorization and recitation, examining how embodied poetic knowledge affects cognitive development.
4. *The Memory Arts in Renaissance England* by William E. Engel. Investigates historical practices of memorization, revealing how poetry served as both art form and cognitive technology in earlier eras.
5. *Proust and the Squid: The Story and Science of the Reading Brain* by Maryanne Wolf. Investigates how different reading practices, including poetry memorization, shape neural architecture and cognitive capabilities.
6. *Poetry: Sound and Sense* by Laurence Perrine. A classic textbook that illuminates the technical aspects of poetry while exploring how sound patterns enhance memorability and meaning, making it invaluable for understanding why certain poems lodge so firmly in memory.
7. *The Sounds of Poetry: A Brief Guide* by Robert Pinsky. Former US Poet Laureate examines how memorized verse continues to shape personal and cultural identity in contemporary life.

Chapter 9

The Subversive Art of Cursive Handwriting

How physical writing connects mind and body in an age of digital disembodiment

The mention of handwriting in today's educational discourse often prompts a reaction of mild incredulity, as though one had proposed bringing back inkwells or teaching students to navigate by the stars. "But children will never need this outdated skill!" comes the assured response, typically delivered with the confidence of someone convinced he can forecast the technological future. "They'll type, or dictate, or gesture toward screens. Their fingers need not bother with loops and swirls. We must prepare them for the digital world."

This response, though possibly well-intentioned, reflects a revealing instance of what might be called the fallacy of utilitarian reductionism: the notion that an activity's worth can be measured solely by its immediate, practical applications. It's rather like arguing that children shouldn't learn to climb trees because adult life rarely calls for arboreal agility, or that musical training is frivolous unless one aspires to the concert stage. The mistake is not in recognizing the value of utility, but in defining it so narrowly that any pursuit whose benefits are subtle, cumulative, or formative is dismissed as superfluous.

So yes—the case against cursive typically rests on the seemingly unanswerable question: "When will students ever use this in real life?" The modern teacher poses this query with the air of having delivered a devastating rhetorical blow, as if the inability to identify specific post-educational applications for a skill automatically disqualifies it from the curriculum. Yet this same teacher would likely be baffled if someone applied identical reasoning to, say, algebra, asking when the average adult uses quadratic equations while grocery shopping or chatting with neighbors over the garden fence.

The truth, of course, is that education has never been and should never be merely vocational training—a series of discrete skills directly applicable to foreseeable tasks. It is, rather, the development of the full range of human capacities, many of which serve not specific practical functions but the overall formation of minds capable of thinking, creating, appreciating, and judging with both precision and depth. The value of an educational practice lies not merely in whether its specific content will be "used" in adult life but in how it shapes the developing brain, cultivates valuable cognitive dispositions, and connects the student to cultural and intellectual traditions that provide context and meaning for all other learning.

The value of an educational practice lies not merely in whether its specific content will be "used" in adult life but in how it shapes the developing brain, cultivates valuable cognitive dispositions, and connects the student to cultural and intellectual traditions that provide context and meaning for all other learning.

Cursive handwriting, viewed through this broader lens, emerges not as an obsolete skill rendered unnecessary by technology but as a practice with profound developmental, cognitive, and cultural significance. It is a physical discipline that shapes mental capacities in ways that typing, regardless of its practical utility, simply cannot replicate. Its value lies not primarily in the production of handwritten documents (though there remain contexts where this is useful) but in the neural pathways, cognitive habits, and symbolic connections it establishes in the developing mind.

Consider first the purely physiological dimension of cursive writing. Unlike the discrete, staccato movements of printing or typing, where each letter stands isolated from its neighbors, cursive requires the writer to execute fluid, continuous motions that connect letters into words and words into sentences. This continuity of motion develops fine motor control, hand-eye coordination, and proprioceptive awareness in ways that tapping keys or forming disconnected letters cannot match. The hand that guides a pen through the elegant loops of cursive engages in a dance of micro-adjustments and precise control that represents a form of physical intelligence largely absent from digital text production.

This physical dimension of cursive connects directly to its cognitive benefits, for the human brain does not operate as a disembodied processing unit but as an integrated system in constant conversation with the body. The neural pathways developed through the physical practice of cursive writing create cognitive resources that extend beyond the specific act of handwriting to influence how students read, think, and create in all contexts. Research in neuroscience has consistently shown that the brain areas activated by the formation of cursive letters overlap significantly with those involved in reading recognition, suggesting that learning to write in cursive enhances the ability to decode and comprehend text in all its forms.[6]

Moreover, the continuous flow of cursive mirrors the continuity of thought itself. Unlike the staccato action of typing, which fragments each word into isolated keystrokes, cursive writing physically enacts the connectedness of ideas, the way one thought flows into another in a continuous stream of meaning. This isomorphism between the physical act of writing and the mental process of thinking creates a harmony between hand and mind that typing, for all its efficiency, cannot replicate. The student who writes in cursive experiences thought not as a series of discrete units to be assembled but as a flowing current to be channeled, an experience much

6 A 2016 review article from PubMed Central titled "Neuroanatomy of Handwriting and Related Reading and Writing Skills in Adults and Children with and without Learning Disabilities: French-American Collaborative Perspectives" by Longcamp et al., discusses brain areas activated by cursive writing and their relation to reading. A 2023 study from *Frontiers in Psychology* by Van der Weel and Van der Meer, comparing handwriting and typing brain connectivity, though not specifically cursive. NPR reports (published May 11, 2024) highlighted research on handwriting's brain benefits, suggesting early experiences translate to long-term reading outcomes.

closer to the actual nature of human cognition than the mechanistic, atomized process of digital text production.

This connection between the physical act of writing and the mental process of thinking manifests most clearly in the relationship between handwriting and memory. Numerous studies have demonstrated that students who take notes by hand retain information more effectively than those who type, even when the typed notes are more extensive and detailed.[7] This seemingly paradoxical finding makes perfect sense when we understand that handwriting is just as much external storage as internal integration. The student who writes by hand must engage more deeply with the material, filtering the essential from the peripheral rather than attempting to capture everything verbatim. The very constraints of handwriting—its relative slowness compared to typing—become cognitive advantages, forcing a level of mental engagement that more efficient methods of text production often bypass.

Beyond these cognitive benefits lies the cultural dimension of cursive: its function as a living link to the textual inheritance of civilization. The student who learns to write in cursive gains direct access to historical documents, personal letters, and literary manuscripts that would otherwise require translation. From the Declaration of Independence to the letters of Emily Dickinson, from Lincoln's Gettysburg Address to the handwritten drafts of great novels and poems, cursive script has been the medium through which much of our cultural heritage has been transmitted. To render a generation incapable of reading these materials in their original form is to place a barrier between young minds and their intellectual inheritance, requiring mediation where direct encounter was once possible.

---

7 P. A. Mueller and D. M. Oppenheimer. (2014). The pen is mightier than the keyboard: Advantages of longhand over laptop note taking. *Psychological Science* 25(6): 1159–68. https://doi.org/10.1177/0956797614524581.

K. Kubo, T. Murayama, and K. Mogi. (2021). Advantage of handwriting over typing on learning words: Evidence from an N400 event-related potential index. *Frontiers in Psychology* 12: 672252. https://doi.org/10.3389/fpsyg.2021.672252.

F. R. Van der Weel and A. L. H. Van der Meer. (2023). Handwriting but not typewriting leads to widespread brain connectivity: A high-density EEG study with implications for the classroom. *Frontiers in Psychology* 14: 1219945. https://doi.org/10.3389/fpsyg.2023.1219945.

This severance from the textual past represents a particularly subtle form of historical amnesia, not the outright forgetting of significant events or figures but the loss of immediate access to the material artifacts through which the past speaks most intimately to the present. The student who cannot read cursive depends on transcriptions created by others, on edited and mediated versions of historical texts rather than direct encounter with the original documents. This dependence introduces a layer of separation between the student and the past, a filter through which historical understanding must be strained rather than absorbed directly.

Consider what is lost when a student cannot read the handwritten letter of a Civil War soldier to his family or the manuscript draft of a beloved poem in the personal diary of a pioneer woman on the frontier, complete with crossed-out lines and marginalia that reveal the process of its creation. These are unmediated engagements with the human experience across time. To render a generation incapable of accessing these materials in their original form is to impoverish their historical imagination.

But perhaps the most subversive aspect of cursive lies in its inherent resistance to surveillance and algorithmic manipulation. The handwritten word exists in physical space rather than digital memory. It leaves no data trail for corporations to harvest and creates no profile for algorithms to analyze. It remains stubbornly private in an age of overzealous publicity and digital ephemera. Of course, the undigitized journal written in cursive cannot be searched by keywords. The handwritten letter cannot be scanned for marketable preferences. The personal note cannot be aggregated with millions of others to predict consumer behavior.

The privacy and resistance of cursive writing preserve a kind of intellectual autonomy that has become rare in the digital age. A student who writes by hand engages a medium of expression that slips past the mechanisms of surveillance capitalism—unseen by data miners and unshaped by algorithmic design. To many, this independence appears insignificant in a culture that prizes convenience over privacy and treats efficiency as a substitute for freedom. But as our reliance on digital platforms continues to erode attention, compromise privacy, and weaken mental health, the value of a practice not mediated by corporate systems may become clearer than its detractors now admit. The capacity to think and communicate outside digital channels represents a form of intellectual resilience, a cognitive insurance policy against the vulnerabilities of technological dependency. The student who can organize thoughts on paper, communicate through handwritten notes, and process information without digital mediation possesses resources for intellectual independence increasingly rare in our screen-dominated culture. This independence stands as a quiet challenge to the assumption that digital tools are not merely useful adjuncts to thinking but its necessary and inevitable medium, that cognition itself has been irrevocably digitized, with handwriting relegated to the status of quaint historical artifact rather than living alternative.

The capacity to think and communicate outside digital channels represents a form of intellectual resilience, a cognitive insurance policy against the vulnerabilities of technological dependency.

In light of these multiple dimensions—physiological, cognitive, cultural, and political—the teaching of cursive handwriting in classical schools emerges as a deliberate preservation of forms of autonomy increasingly threatened. It represents a refusal to allow a single technological paradigm to monopolize the development of young minds. It insists that human cognition and expression are too deeply embodied to be adequately served by any single medium, no matter how efficient or advanced it may seem at a particular historical moment.

The teacher who insists on cursive is both preserving a traditional skill and cultivating a distinctive cognitive ecology, a set of neural pathways and cultural connections that might otherwise atrophy in a purely digital educational environment. The classical teacher recognizes that the medium through which students process and express ideas shapes the content of thought itself. She knows that writing by hand engages the mind differently than typing. Just as reading physical texts creates different cognitive experiences than scrolling screens so too does composing a letter involve different mental processes than crafting an email. The classical teacher resists this determinism out of a deep understanding of educational purpose, the recognition that the goal is not to train students for specific technological environments that may change dramatically over their lifetimes but to develop the full range of human capacities that allow adaptation to any environment.

The teaching of cursive thus embodies a fundamental educational principle: that the value of a practice lies not in whether its specific content will be directly "used" in foreseeable contexts but in how it connects the student to traditions that provide context and meaning for all other learning. This principle applies not only to cursive but to many elements of classical education that face similar utilitarian challenges: Latin, formal logic, Euclidean geometry, poetry memorization, and other practices whose benefits, treated elsewhere in this book, are developmental and cultural—not directly vocational.

In light of these multifaceted dimensions—physiological, cognitive, cultural, and political—the teaching of cursive handwriting emerges as a profound educational practice that develops the whole person. The elegant loops and flowing lines of cursive create neural pathways that enhance reading comprehension, develop fine motor skills, strengthen memory retention, and connect students to their cultural inheritance. Beyond these tangible benefits lies cursive's quiet resistance to digital homogenization, its stubborn materiality preserving a mode of thought and expression that exists beyond algorithmic surveillance and corporate mediation. When we insist on teaching cursive, we affirm that education serves deeper purposes than mere vocational training or technological adaptation. We recognize that some practices carry value primarily in how they shape developing minds and maintain connections to intellectual traditions that give meaning to all learning. The hand that forms cursive letters today develops capacities that will serve the mind tomorrow, reminding us that human cognition remains irreducibly embodied, stubbornly material, and fundamentally personal—a truth inscribed in every flowing stroke of a young student's pen.

Recommended Further Reading

1. *The Missing Ink: The Lost Art of Handwriting* by Philip Hensher. A personal and cultural exploration of handwriting's decline and why it matters for our intellectual development.

2. *Spencerian Penmanship* by Platt Rogers Spencer. The classic text on Spencerian script, which became the foundation for American business writing and artistic penmanship.
3. *Historical Scripts: From Classical Times to the Renaissance* by Stan Knight. A beautiful examination of handwriting as an art form throughout history with detailed visual examples.
4. *Script and Scribble: The Rise and Fall of Handwriting* by Kitty Burns Florey. A blend of memoir, history, and reportage exploring the rich heritage of handwriting and its place in human development.
5. *The Art of Cursive Penmanship* by Michael R. Sull. A comprehensive guide to cursive as an art form by a master penman, focusing on the beauty and flow of American cursive.
6. *Handwriting of the Twentieth Century* by Rosemary Sassoon. A detailed study of handwriting styles and teaching methods throughout the twentieth century with implications for education.
7. *The Pen and the People: English Letter Writers 1660–1800* by Susan Whyman. Explores the cultural and historical significance of handwritten communication in developing literacy and personal expression.

Chapter 10

The Subversive Art of Rereading

Why rereading classics develops moral imagination

In our culture today, it is assumed that once a book has been read, its value is exhausted, that it has served its purpose and need not be revisited. This belief treats books as if they are consumable goods, useful only for their novelty or entertainment. As a result, those who return to the same novel multiple times are often met with confusion or disbelief. "But you already know how it ends," someone might say, revealing an understanding of literature that equates its worth solely with plot, especially the denouement. Such a view misses the deeper and enduring value of great books, especially their ability to shape the reader's imagination and character over time.

This objection, delivered with such certainty, reveals a profound misunderstanding of what we might call the very nature of bookishness itself. It is rather like suggesting that there is no point in revisiting the Grand Canyon once you've seen it, or that attending a second performance of Beethoven's *Ninth Symphony* would be redundant, or that one should marry a new spouse every few years simply to experience the novelty of different companionship. It mistakes the superficial shock of the new for the deeper satisfactions of renewed engagement, the fleeting excitement of initial exposure for the lasting rewards of deepening relationship.

The cult of novelty in reading—the fashionable obsession with contemporary voices to the exclusion of all others—represents one of the most profound impoverishments of our intellectual landscape. For in treating books as momentary diversions to be consumed once and discarded, we rob ourselves of the deepest pleasures and most profound benefits of literary engagement: the joy of returning to a text with new eyes and building a relationship with a work that grows and deepens over time.

Consider what happens when one returns to a truly great book after an interval of years. The words on the page have not changed, but the reader has. The experiences, insights, sorrows, and joys accumulated in the interim can create new resonances with the text. They can reveal dimensions invisible to younger eyes, transform what once seemed minor into central concerns and what appeared central into mere background. The young reader who first encounters *Great Expectations* may be drawn to Pip's rise in fortune and his infatuation with Estella; the older reader returns to find greater meaning in Joe's quiet integrity or in the painful wisdom gained through disappointment and forgiveness. Likewise, the teenager who reads *The Scarlet Letter* for its drama and mystery may, years later, be struck by the depth of Hester's moral strength and the quiet tragedy of Dimmesdale's inward collapse.

This transformation of the reading experience through the changed consciousness of the reader represents one of the most powerful arguments for rereading. The great book, encountered at intervals throughout a lifetime, becomes a measure of our own development, a mirror reflecting our changing capacity to perceive, understand, and resonate with its depths. We discover, in returning to such works, not only new dimensions of the text but new dimensions of ourselves—capacities for appreciation and understanding that were not available to us in earlier encounters.

This dialogic relationship between text and reader is a far cry from the consumerist model of reading that dominates our cultural moment, the notion that books are primarily delivery systems for information or entertainment, to be processed efficiently and discarded once their immediate utility has been extracted. In that model, returning to a book already read represents a failure of efficiency. But if we understand reading as a relationship rather than a transaction, then rereading emerges not as redundancy but as renewal.

The analogy to human relationships is instructive here. No one would suggest that having met a person once, there is no value in further encounters; that having conversed with a friend for an hour, all possible exchanges have been exhausted; that having lived with a spouse for a year, the relationship has yielded all its potential insights and satisfactions. We recognize intuitively that human connections deepen through sustained engagement and that intimacy requires not novelty but recursive attention. Why, then, do we fail to extend this same understanding to our relationship with books?

The answer lies partly in the commodification of reading that characterizes our cultural moment: the transformation of literary engagement from a relationship to a transaction. In an age defined by what everyone now seems to call FOMO (fear of missing out), the prospect of reading the same book twice appears as an opportunity cost: time that could have been spent adding another title to the list of works one can claim to have "covered" or "consumed."

This consumerist approach to reading manifests in the breathless language of literary recommendation: "You must read *The Goldfinch*!" "Have you read *Gone Girl* yet?" "I just devoured *The Hate U Give* in a single sitting!" The metaphor betrays the attitude—reading is cast as an act of consumption and conquest, as though books were dishes to be swallowed rather than voices to be heard. In this sense, literature is treated much like disposable entertainment, not unlike the way we speak of movies or streaming series: "I binged *Outer Banks* last weekend." "What's next on your Netflix queue?" Books are reduced to just another tray on the endless buffet of content: piled high, quickly consumed, and just as quickly replaced. The re-reader, in this context, is cast as the eccentric, irrationally devoted to that which has already been sampled. Yet this apparent eccentricity conceals a profound wisdom: the recognition that some books are not meant to be "devoured" but savored.

This quality of inexhaustibility distinguishes the truly great book from even the "good" one. The good novel, for example, may provide some modicum of healthy entertainment in a single reading, yet the "great" book reveals new dimensions with each return. The good book may impress us with its craftsmanship, its narrative efficiency, or perhaps its stylistic grace; the great book transforms us through repeated engagement, altering not merely what we know but how we see, not just what we think but how we think it.

Consider the experience of reading Dostoevsky's *The Brothers Karamazov* at different stages of life. For the high school–age reader, the novel may appear first and foremost as a drama of passion, rebellion, and philosophical daring. Ivan's fiery atheism and relentless questioning of God's justice can feel electrifying, while Dmitri's reckless impulses and Alyosha's purity of faith embody the intensity of youthful extremes. The story is alive with scandal and ideas that push against boundaries, the very things that awaken a young reader's desire for discovery.

The middle-aged reader, however, begins to see the novel differently. The focus shifts from the brilliance of ideas to the persistence of guilt amid the tangled web of human weakness. Where once Ivan's intellectual rebellion seemed exhilarating, it may now feel anguished, even dangerous, as the consequences of ideas bleed into lives and relationships. Dmitri's flaws no longer read as reckless romanticism but as painful reminders of how passion unchecked can ruin both oneself and others. Alyosha's steady witness begins to shine less as naive simplicity and more as hard-earned clarity amid chaos.

For the older reader, the book opens up still deeper registers. The novel evolves into a meditation on the possibility of redemption in a broken world. Characters once dismissed as minor or secondary, like the suffering Father Zosima or the humble servant Grigory, emerge with profound dignity. The older reader is more attuned to the quiet moments of grace scattered throughout the novel, the fleeting glimpses of love and compassion that endure even in the face of despair.

As obvious as it may be to point out, the words on Dostoevsky's page never change; the reader does. Each return to the novel unlocks new resonances because life has enlarged the reader's own capacity to hear its music. In youth, the novel dazzles with its storm of ideas; in midlife, it confronts with its moral weight; in old age, it consoles—or unsettles—with its recognition of mortality. In this way, *The Brothers Karamazov* does not so much yield its meaning once and for all as it continues to meet us where we are, deepening alongside our own experience of being human. This transformative potential of rereading emerges from the layered nature of great literature, especially its capacity to address diverse aspects of human experience within a single narrative frame. The casual reader, encountering such a text only once and then moving on, may catch the surface narrative. He may follow the plot but overlook its philosophical weight. He may register the events but miss the deeper patterns that give them meaning. By contrast, the re-reader approaches the text with the surface already familiar and the basic outline of the plot already known. This foreknowledge does not diminish the experience but enhances it, allowing attention to shift from "what happens next" to "why it happens" and "what it means," from narrative progression to thematic development. The second or third or tenth reading permits a kind of perspicacity, a perception of multiple dimensions simultaneously, impossible in the first encounter. This perspicacity represents a form of literary understanding qualitatively different from the simple comprehension of plot or the recognition of character. It is a mode of perception that sees through and beyond the immediate narrative to other important narrative dimensions, for example, the philosophical, psychological, and spiritual. The reader who develops this capacity through repeated engagement with great texts acquires not merely knowledge of particular works but a distinctive way of seeing. The re-reader develops a literary sensibility that carries over into engagement with all texts.

Here lies the educational significance of rereading, its function as a formative discipline. The student who is encouraged to return to great texts develops cognitive habits fundamentally different from those fostered by perpetual novelty. Where the cult of the new promotes variety over mastery, the practice of rereading cultivates the capacity to perceive patterns and relationships invisible to the casual glance.

These attendant qualities—patience, attentiveness, and pattern recognition—represent forms of cognitive resistance to the superficial engagement encouraged by digital media and contemporary culture more broadly. The re-reader learns to value depth over novelty, to find interest in the familiar, to discover that understanding emerges from sustained attention to worthy objects. This disposition runs directly counter to "the attention economy of digital capitalism,"[8] which profits precisely from the restless movement of consciousness from one novel stimulus to another,

8 Jenny Odell. *How to Do Nothing: Resisting the Attention Economy*. Melville House, 2019.

never lingering long enough for genuine understanding to develop.

In this light, the classical school's insistence on returning to great texts rather than constantly updating the curriculum emerges not as a failure to keep pace with contemporary trends but as a deliberate cultivation of an alternative relationship to knowledge, culture, and attention itself. The student who reads *The Odyssey* three times over the course of his education, who encounters Shakespeare's sonnets in multiple contexts, who revisits Plato's dialogues with increasing sophistication, cultivates a mode of engagement characterized by patience and cumulative understanding.

In this light, the classical school's insistence on returning to great texts rather than constantly updating the curriculum emerges not as a failure to keep pace with contemporary trends but as a deliberate cultivation of an alternative relationship to knowledge, culture, and attention itself.

This layering of multiple encounters, each building upon and enriching the previous ones, differs fundamentally from the eternal present of contemporary media consumption, where each text, image, and video tends to replace those that came before, creating a kind of cult of erasure. Through a classical education the re-reader, by contrast, builds an internal literary landscape. In this landscape, texts speak to one another. Earlier readings inform later ones, and understanding emerges from the complex interplay of accumulated literary experience.

This interplay extends beyond individual texts to encompass the dialogic relationship between works, the ways in which books speak to one another across time and space. The reader who has returned multiple times to Shakespeare finds echoes of his patterns in Faulkner. The student who has deeply engaged with Austen perceives her influence in Barbara Pym; the one who knows Dante intimately recognizes his presence in T. S. Eliot. This intertextual awareness, a perception of literature as a conversation rather than a collection of isolated works, emerges naturally from the practice of rereading, which treats books as enduring presences in an ongoing cultural dialogue.

The re-reader thus develops a relationship to culture fundamentally different from that fostered by the cult of novelty. He perceives the intricate web of influence, response, adaptation, and challenge that constitutes cultural tradition. This perception places newer works in proper cultural and literary context, allowing for a more sophisticated appreciation of both innovation and continuity.

This contextualized understanding represents another dimension of rereading's subversive potential in our historical moment. Amid what some scholars have called "presentism"—the tendency to view the past exclusively through the lens of current preoccupations, to judge historical texts by contemporary standards without understanding their context—the practice of rereading fosters a more nuanced relationship to the past. The reader who has returned many times to *Huckleberry Finn* or *Wuthering Heights* or *The Merchant of Venice* develops the capacity to engage with the complexities of historical difference. He becomes able to recognize both the distance and the connection between past and present. He is more able to resist the twin temptations of uncritical veneration and anachronistic dismissal.

This nuanced historical awareness resists the simplistic judgments that dominate much of contemporary cultural discourse. Too often, authors and literary traditions are sorted into binary categories of "approved" or "problematic." There is a rush to condemn or to canonize without first understanding. Moral posturing takes the place of genuine engagement. The re-reader responds differently. Accustomed to discovering new dimensions in familiar works, he approaches cultural questions with patience and attentiveness. He is willing to dwell with complexity rather than reduce it to simplicity. He accepts ambiguity rather than demanding certainty. He seeks dialogue rather than pronouncing judgment.

In all these ways the practice of rereading stands as a form of resistance to the frenetic habits encouraged by digital distraction. It is not a retreat from the challenges of our time, but an alternative way of confronting them. It does not reject the present, but cultivates a more nuanced relationship with it—one shaped by deep engagement with the past and open to the genuine possibilities of the future. This resistance is not primarily political. Rather, it is a deeper challenge to assumptions about human flourishing, cultural inheritance, and the nature of understanding itself. The re-reader asserts that some texts reward lifelong engagement, that understanding emerges through patient attention, that cultural tradition represents a living, ongoing conversation to be entered, and that the past speaks both to its own time and ours, though in ways that require effort and attention to discern.

In this light, the classical school's commitment to the great books as living texts to be engaged repeatedly throughout a lifetime of learning, emerges as one of its most radically countercultural features. Classical education does not fetishize "relevance." It does not pressure students and teachers to keep pace with rapidly changing technologies and social conditions. Instead, it calls for the deliberate return to texts that have endured for generations or centuries, representing a profound challenge to the assumptions of perpetual acceleration and obsolescence that dominate contemporary culture.

This challenge does not imply a rejection of the genuinely new or a blanket dismissal of contemporary literature. The classically educated reader remains open to the possibility that great works are being written in our own time. It recognizes that new voices may speak with an authority and insight comparable to those of the established canon. But this openness is grounded in a deep engagement with the best that has been thought and said in the past, an engagement that provides standards of comparison, contexts for evaluation, and the capacity to distinguish between lasting significance and passing fashion.

The re-reader approaches contemporary works with the measured appreciation of one nourished by tradition. The re-reader does not anxiously seek the next sensation but is patiently attentive to genuine achievement, not swayed by marketing campaigns or social media buzz but guided by cultivated judgment and deep familiarity with the full range of literary possibility. This grounded openness represents an authentic engagement with the contemporary.

In the end, the truly contemporary mind is not the one that knows only the present moment but the one that perceives that moment in historical context, that understands both what changes and what endures. It recognizes both the uniqueness of our time and its continuities with the past.

This historically informed consciousness emerges not from a superficial sampling of texts from different periods but from deep engagement with works that have demonstrated their capacity to speak across time, works that reveal different dimensions to readers in different eras, that communicate to generations yet unborn.

The great paradox of rereading is that it leads to a more authentic engagement with the present. The classically educated re-reader who has returned multiple times to Homer or Tolstoy or Steinbeck brings to contemporary literature a depth of literary experience for comparison and context that the perpetual consumer of novelty can never develop. Such a reader perceives both what is said and what remains unsaid.

A book that can be read only once is rarely worth reading at all. The ones that invite us back a third, a fifth, even a tenth time are of a different order. They hold not only entertainment or information but also the possibility of wisdom. Such books do more than fill an idle hour; they shed light on the present moment. They offer not escape from ourselves but a way of knowing ourselves more deeply. They extend our vision beyond the narrow boundaries of daily life and open, for a moment, onto the larger landscapes of human experience and possibility—landscapes that form both our inheritance and our hope.

Recommended Further Reading

1. *The Art of Being Human* by Michael S. Rose. A guide to rereading classic works that help us learn from the past to inform present decisions about modern threats like genetic engineering, transhumanism, and totalitarian rule while maintaining our humanity in a dehumanizing world.
2. *The Pleasures of Reading in an Age of Distraction* by Alan Jacobs. A celebration of reading for delight rather than utility that explores how returning to beloved books enriches our intellectual lives.
3. *The Art of Slow Reading: Six Time-Honored Practices for Engagement* by Thomas Newkirk. Offers concrete strategies for developing the habit of patient, attentive reading that allows for deeper textual understanding.

4. *Lost in a Book: The Psychology of Reading for Pleasure* by Victor Nell. Explores the profound psychological benefits of immersive reading and returning to cherished texts throughout life.
5. *Reading Reconsidered* by Doug Lemov, Colleen Driggs, and Erica Woolway. Offers practical approaches to teaching students to reread texts carefully for deeper understanding and appreciation.
6. *The Anatomy of Influence: Literature as a Way of Life* by Harold Bloom. Explores how repeated encounters with canonical works shape our literary sensibilities and intellectual development.
7. *The Practice of Reading* by Denis Donoghue. Examines how different approaches to reading, including rereading, inform our relationship with literature and culture.

Part III

Subversive Acts of Mind

Chapter 11

The Subversive Art of Thinking

How sustained contemplation challenges the culture of distraction

Consider the paradox: At a time when "critical thinking" has become the most celebrated aim of our educational system, trumpeted in school mission statements, curriculum guides, and pedagogical manifestos—true thinking has nearly vanished from our classrooms. We have accomplished the remarkable feat of reducing "critical thinking" to a slogan, a catchphrase, a marketing term—everything except the actual act of thinking critically. It is rather like a society that endlessly celebrates the virtues of breathing while simultaneously removing all the oxygen from its buildings, or the restaurant that praises the healthful benefits of nutrition while serving only pictures of food on its plates.

The modern world is filled with men who cry "Think for yourself!" while carefully telling you *what* to think. They insist upon freedom of thought with the same breath they use to declare which thoughts are permissible. This contradiction would be merely amusing if it were not so destructive to the fundamental purpose of education. For the cry of "conspiracy theorist!" has become the universal cudgel, wielded with ruthless efficiency against any who dare question the manufactured consensus. The label itself performs a kind of magic, transforming a person engaged in the ancient art of inquiry into a figure of ridicule who may be dismissed without the inconvenience of addressing their actual arguments.

This is not an accident but the inevitable fruit of an educational system that has exchanged the pursuit of truth for the maintenance of conformity.

For what passes as "critical thinking" in our modern educational temples is not the patient, disciplined, open-minded pursuit of truth through careful reasoning, but a form of ideological conditioning in which students are taught not how to analyze and evaluate arguments but how to recognize and repeat the approved opinions on a narrow range of contemporary controversies.

The typical lesson in "critical thinking" now consists of presenting students with a social or political issue about which there is substantial disagreement among reasonable people, then guiding them toward the single acceptable conclusion while maintaining the fiction that they have reached this view through independent analysis. It is a process not of developing intellectual autonomy but of ensuring ideological conformity. And it is done, most remarkably, in the name of teaching students to "think for themselves"—a phrase that would be darkly comic if it were not so damaging to the same capacities it claims to promote.

What makes this situation particularly perilous is that we live in an age that demands more genuine thinking than ever before. Our citizens are bombarded daily with claims and counterclaims, with statistics and studies, with experts and counter-experts, with news and "fake news." The world has never been more complex, never more filled with information requiring careful evaluation. Yet at this present moment, when the need for actual critical thinking has never been greater, our educational system has largely abandoned the teaching of those intellectual disciplines that would develop this capacity.

The tried and true tools of freedom—history, literature, logic, and rhetoric—have been discarded in favor of a bland, prepackaged curriculum of obedience. Students are no longer taught to evaluate ideas on their merit; they are taught to memorize the ideas of others. The goal is no longer wisdom but conformity. It values compliance over understanding.

Consider the modern history classroom, where primary sources have largely vanished, replaced by textbooks that present simplified narratives with predetermined interpretations. Rather than examining the Federalist Papers directly and debating Madison's arguments about faction and representation, students receive predigested summaries that extract "key points" while stripping away the nuance and complexity that might invite genuine questioning. The teaching of American history has become particularly emblematic of this approach, where events are no longer presented as complex human dramas with multiple causal factors and competing interpretations, but as morality tales with clear heroes and villains, designed to inculcate specific emotional responses rather than analytical thought.

In literature classes, the close reading of texts has given way to the application of fashionable theoretical frameworks. Instead of encountering Shakespeare's *Macbeth* as a profound exploration of ambition, moral corruption, and the human capacity for self-deception, students are taught to view it through contemporary ideological lenses—to search for evidence of patriarchal oppression, colonial attitudes, or other preselected fashionable social themes. The text—even a great text—is reduced to a specimen to be dissected according to existing taxonomies. The questions are no longer "What does this mean?" or "Why did the author make this choice?" but "How does this text reinforce or challenge current social theories?"

As mentioned in an earlier chapter, the abandonment of formal logic in education represents perhaps the most devastating loss to our intellectual tradition. When students receive no training in logical thinking, they become particularly vulnerable to manipulation. The teacher who presents climate change or immigration policy as having only one defensible position—framing support as the sole compassionate stance or opposition as the only rational view—exploits this vulnerability masterfully. Without understanding how to identify an ad hominem fallacy, students cannot recognize when their peers dismiss an argument by attacking its source rather than its substance. Lacking familiarity with post hoc, ergo propter hoc reasoning, they cannot discern when politicians falsely attribute positive economic trends to their own policies simply because one followed the other. Never having learned about the appeal to authority, they accept statements from experts uncritically, unaware that expertise in one field grants no special authority in another. The student confronted with emotional appeals about "saving the children" or "defending our values" possesses no analytical framework to separate sentiment from substance, no intellectual discipline to distinguish between valid concerns and manipulative rhetoric. This inability to evaluate claims independently transforms education from liberation into indoctrination, replacing the pursuit of truth with the absorption of approved opinions, regardless of which political or social perspective those opinions represent.

Not unrelated, the study of rhetoric has suffered a profound transformation in modern education, stripping it of its classical purpose as the art of effective and ethical communication in service to truth. Visit any contemporary high school speech class and you'll likely find students learning to craft persuasive presentations on topics they've been assigned rather than those they've thoughtfully chosen through personal conviction. A student might argue passionately for stricter gun control laws on Monday, only to advocate with equal fervor for Second Amendment rights on Tuesday. The content matters less than the performance. This approach teaches rhetoric merely as technique, divorced from any commitment to truthful expression.

Consider the typical AP composition course, where students engage in what educators call "rhetorical analysis," but which amounts to little more than technical dissection. I observed this firsthand when visiting a prestigious high school where seniors were analyzing Martin Luther King Jr.'s "Letter from Birmingham Jail." Rather than grappling with the moral force of King's arguments or evaluating the truth of his claims about justice and civil disobedience, students focused exclusively on cataloging his use of allusion, metaphor, and emotional appeal. When one student attempted to discuss whether King's natural law arguments were philosophically sound, the teacher redirected the conversation: "We're not here to evaluate content—just identify rhetorical strategies." This absurdist approach transforms one of the most profound moral documents of the twentieth century into merely a showcase of persuasive techniques.

The College Board's official AP Language and Composition exam reinforces this separation of rhetoric from truth. The rhetorical analysis section asks students to explain how authors build arguments through stylistic choices but never requires them to assess whether those arguments stand on solid factual ground. A student could perfectly analyze how a climate change proponent constructs an apparently logical argument while remaining entirely unconcerned with whether the underlying claims contradict scientific consensus. This strange separation became starkly evident in a classroom where students received high marks for analyzing how effectively a pharmaceutical company's publicity materials built consumer trust—without ever investigating whether the company's claims about drug efficacy were supported by clinical trials.

Oxford Dictionary's selection of "post-truth" as 2016's Word of the Year punctuated this troubling educational trajectory. The term's definition—"relating to circumstances where objective facts are less influential in shaping public opinion than appeals to emotion and personal belief"—describes what students practice in these composition courses. They learn to craft arguments not by marshaling evidence and reasoning toward truth, but by strategically deploying language to elicit desired emotional responses. A valedictorian I once interviewed candidly admitted that his award-winning essay on environmental protection contained statistics he suspected were exaggerated, "but they created the emotional impact I needed." When our educational system rewards such calculated manipulation rather than truthful communication, we shouldn't be surprised when public discourse degenerates into competing narratives untethered from factual reality.

Cicero's ancient conception of the ideal orator as "a good man speaking well," one whose rhetorical skill grows from and serves moral character, finds little place in this instrumentalized approach. Quintilian's understanding of rhetoric as fundamentally ethical, as the discipline that enables citizens to advocate for justice and defend truth against falsehood, has been replaced by a technical conception of rhetoric as simply "what works" to produce desired outcomes. When persuasion becomes severed from truthfulness, words become weapons rather than bridges, and public discourse degenerates into sophisticated manipulation rather than genuine communication aimed at shared understanding.

The result is a populace ill-equipped to grapple with the complexities of the modern world, blank slates onto which the trending ideologies of the day are scrawled with neon markers. They march, zombielike, in lockstep with the latest causes, virtue-signaling their righteousness without the faintest whisper of genuine thought. We see this in the sudden appearance of Ukrainian flags on social media profiles and storefronts across America, adopted by individuals who, if asked, could not explain the historical relationship between Ukraine and Russia, the significance of NATO expansion, or the complex ethnic dynamics of the region—or whether Ukraine is or ever was a democracy. We witness it in the coordinated posting of black squares on Instagram to signal solidarity with racial justice movements, a gesture requiring no actual sacrifice, no genuine engagement with complex policy questions of criminal justice reform, economic inequality, or historical redress. Perhaps most telling were the "Science Is Real" yard signs that proliferated during the pandemic. One such sign was prominently displayed at a neighbor's house—the same neighbor who, when someone mentioned emerging research questioning the efficacy of cloth masks for preventing viral transmission, accused them of "anti-science thinking" and "dangerous misinformation." The irony was palpable. The yard sign portrayed science as a catechism of fixed conclusions rather than what it actually is: a method of systematic inquiry characterized by hypothesis testing, rigorous experimentation, and constant revision of theories in light of new evidence.

This fundamental misunderstanding was evident in heated school board meetings[9] across the United States, where some parents invoked "following the science" to oppose school reopenings, even as emerging epidemiological data from European countries, such as Germany and Norway, indicated minimal COVID-19 transmission in educational settings.[10] When public health experts or board members attempted to highlight this evidence, they often faced fierce resistance and were accused of endangering children. The "science" being followed seemed resistant to new data or nuanced interpretation.

What ties these examples together is their common substitution of signal for substance. The modern educational system has produced minds that respond to complex issues not through independent analysis but through social conformity. Students develop a fundamental intellectual dependency when history becomes reduced to simplistic narratives rather than taught as the complex drama of human experience across time. This dependency deepens when literature serves merely as a vehicle for predetermined interpretations instead of an exploration of the richness and contradictions

9 M. Goldberg. (March 31, 2021). "'Follow the science,' they said . . ." *The New York Times*.

10 C. Vardavas, K. Nikitara, A. G. Mathioudakis, M. Hilton Boon, R. Phalkey, J. Leonardi-Bee et al. "Transmission of SARS-CoV-2 in educational settings in 2020: A review." *BMJ Open* 12(4): e058308, 2022. doi:10.1136/bmjopen-2021-058308.

of human nature. The abandonment of logical reasoning further weakens intellectual autonomy, leaving students unable to evaluate claims on their merits. When persuasive communication becomes divorced from truth-seeking, the final foundation of independent thought crumbles away. In this educational environment, students learn to navigate challenging questions by checking which position will generate social approval from their peer group. They develop a reflexive orientation toward consensus rather than evidence, creating citizens uniquely vulnerable to manipulation—unable to distinguish between widespread belief and well-founded conclusion.

The modern educational system has produced minds that respond to complex issues not through independent analysis but through social conformity.

This is not freedom. This is not progress. This condition represents a profound distortion of genuine education—a state more accurately described as mass conformity disguised as enlightenment. When universities proudly announce record-breaking consensus on controversial social issues, they inadvertently reveal not intellectual achievement but the collapse of independent thought. The modern student learns to live comfortably with cognitive dissonance, simultaneously proclaiming devotion to diversity while enforcing rigid homogeneity of opinion.

Consider how this manifests in classroom discussions where certain conclusions are treated as foregone before evidence is examined. A teacher begins a unit on economic inequality with the unexamined premise that disparities represent only injustice rather than also the complex interplay of choice, circumstance, ability, and opportunity. Students learn quickly which perspectives merit exploration and which trigger immediate disapproval. The socialization process completely overshadows educational development, producing graduates skilled in signal-sending but impoverished in genuinely principled judgment.

True liberation begins elsewhere, not with correct opinions but with the recovery of one's full intellectual capacities to properly observe, analyze, and judge. The student who learns history as a complex terrain of human choices made under constraints, who approaches literature as a window into the unchanging dilemmas of human existence, who practices logical analysis of arguments regardless of their source, who masters rhetoric as the art of truthful persuasion—this student develops genuine intellectual independence. Classical education does not promise comfortable certainty but offers something far more valuable: the capacity to navigate uncertainty with both clarity and courage, to stand firm against the currents of fashion when evidence and principle require it.

The classical approach to thinking stands as a most viable alternative to this modern counterfeit. It begins with the recognition that thinking is not a natural capacity that emerges spontaneously but a disciplined art that must be practiced, refined, and systematically developed (see the earlier chapter on logic). Just as one cannot become a concert pianist merely by sitting at a keyboard and expressing one's musical feelings, one cannot become a clear thinker merely by having and expressing opinions. Both require instruction, imitation of masters, knowledge of principles, and extensive practice. They require a progressive development from basic competence to genuine mastery through sustained engagement with the discipline.

Perhaps the most revolutionary aspect of classical education's approach to thinking is its insistence on the connection between thought and reality. Modern education too often treats thinking as a game played with conceptual tokens, a manipulation of ideas detached from any necessary connection to the actual world. But classical education insists that true thinking begins with careful observation of reality itself, with seeing what is actually there rather than what one expects or wishes to see, with attending to the details and distinctions present in the world rather than imposing preconceived categories upon it.

This discipline of observation stands at the heart of both scientific and humanistic inquiry in the classical tradition. The student of natural science learns not merely to memorize formulas but to observe phenomena carefully, to discern patterns, to test hypotheses against evidence rather than against prevailing opinion. The student of literature learns not merely to deploy fashionable theoretical frameworks but to attend closely to the text itself, to notice the author's actual words and choices rather than reading through the lens of contemporary preoccupations. In both cases, the emphasis falls on reality as the standard against which thinking must be measured—on the world *as it is* rather than *as we might wish it to be.*

The reality principle poses a fundamental challenge to many contemporary educational practices. Modern education often substitutes ideological frameworks where careful observation should prevail, places theoretical constructs ahead of empirical evidence, and promotes approved narratives rather than fostering genuine inquiry. This approach undermines the essential understanding that reality exists independently of our theories about it, contradicting the notion that reality is merely a social construction, that facts should be subordinate to perspectives, or that truth is simply whatever those in power declare. Instead, this principle asserts that authentic thinking must begin with humble attention to objective reality, even as we acknowledge that our understanding remains partial and our knowledge provisional.

This emphasis on reality as the starting point for thought connects to another distinctive feature of classical education's approach: its recognition that thinking is not merely an individual activity but a participation in an ongoing conversation across time. The classical student learns to think not in isolation but in dialogue—with peers, with teachers, with the great minds of the past whose works constitute what Matthew Arnold called "the best that has been thought and said in the world."[11] This dialogical dimension of thinking provides both the freedom to develop one's own understanding and the responsibility to engage seriously with other perspectives.

The great books curriculum that forms the backbone of many classical education programs embodies this dialogical approach to thinking. Students engage not merely with contemporary voices but with thinkers from across the centuries, not merely with those who share their cultural assumptions but with those who challenge and expand them, not merely with simplified summaries but with original texts that demand careful reading and thoughtful response. This engagement across time develops not merely knowledge of particular ideas but a distinctive quality of mind, one capable of seeing beyond the limitations of the present moment, of

11 Matthew Arnold. *Culture and Anarchy: An Essay in Political and Social Criticism.* Smith, Elder & Co., 1869.

recognizing both the wisdom and the blindness of earlier thinkers, of distinguishing between the essential and the accidental in human thought.

This historical consciousness represents another form of resistance to the presentism that dominates much contemporary education, with its implicit assumption that the current moment represents the pinnacle of human achievement and that the past exists primarily as a record of errors to be avoided rather than wisdom to be recovered. The classical student, however, encounters the living thought of minds separated from us by millennia yet still engaging perennial human questions in ways that remain both challenging and illuminating. Socrates's explorations of justice, Aristotle's analysis of happiness, Dante's vision of the afterlife, Shakespeare's probing of ambition and conscience, Austen's examination of moral discernment, Dostoevsky's exploration of freedom and responsibility: these are all common examples of living engagements with fundamental questions that continue to shape human experience across time and culture.

This discovery challenges the progressive narrative that treats current concerns as naturally more important than perennial questions. It suggests instead what philosopher Hans-Georg Gadamer called a "fusion of horizons."[12] This engagement between past and present creates a powerful dialogue where each realm enriches our understanding of the other. When we immerse ourselves in ancient texts, they cast our contemporary assumptions into sharp relief, revealing their contingency rather than their inevitability. Simultaneously, our modern questions illuminate classical works in unexpected ways, drawing out meanings their original authors may never have anticipated but which nonetheless reside within the text's deeper structures. This conversation across time grants us something far more valuable than mere historical facts; it provides us with genuine perspective. By stepping outside our historical moment through sustained engagement with the past, we gain critical distance from our own cultural assumptions, allowing us to see them not as universal truths but as particular ways of understanding reality that might have been otherwise. The past can then be understood as much more that a collection of information

12 Hans-Georg Gadamer. *Truth and Method.* Translated by Joel Weinsheimer and Donald G. Marshall, 2nd rev. ed., Continuum, 2004.

about bygone eras. It can be seen as a mirror in which we glimpse ourselves anew, suddenly aware of intellectual habits and cultural frameworks we had previously accepted without question.

Where the modern student often encounters education as a series of disconnected subjects—history in one room, literature in another, mathematics in a third—the classically trained mind perceives the profound unity underlying these artificial divisions.

The student of classical education is also primed to develop a distinctive quality of mind that transcends fragmented specialization. This integrated intellect perceives the world with unusual clarity, seeing past the provincialism of the present moment to discern deeper patterns that connect seemingly disparate fields of knowledge. Where the modern student often encounters education as a series of disconnected subjects—history in one room, literature in another, mathematics in a third—the classically trained mind perceives the profound unity underlying these artificial divisions. Such a student recognizes how Euclidean geometry informs Renaissance painting, how ancient rhetoric shapes political discourse, how philosophical questions echo across centuries in new guises. This integrated understanding proves particularly valuable when confronting complex problems that refuse to respect our arbitrary academic boundaries. While contemporary education often produces graduates who know more and more about less and less, classical education cultivates thinkers who can synthesize insights from multiple traditions, recognize essential principles amid accidental details, and move with confidence across intellectual landscapes that would paralyze more specialized minds.

This refusal to partition the intellectual world into hermetically sealed compartments is at the heart of classical education's approach to thinking. The classical student does not languish in disciplinary silos. He finds himself exploring geometry shortly after parsing Latin verbs, contemplating Aristotelian ethics immediately before analyzing poetic meter. This cross-pollination cultivates a mind attuned to patterns across different domains. It allows insights from one field to inform solutions in another and encourages the simultaneous consideration of multiple perspectives when tackling complex problems. Even in computer science, for instance, the most groundbreaking algorithms emerge not solely from raw computational prowess but from a synthesis of logic, mathematics, and even the humanities. This integrative capacity becomes increasingly valuable amid the corporate world of accelerating specialization, where experts in different fields often lack the common language and conceptual frameworks necessary for meaningful collaboration. The classically educated thinker serves as a kind of intellectual translator. He is able to bridge these specialized domains and recognize common patterns beneath different terminologies. He is able to facilitate the cross-pollination of ideas that drives genuine innovation. This is not a rejection of specialization—depth of knowledge in particular fields remains essential for solving complex problems—but a recognition that breadth of understanding is equally necessary for putting specialized knowledge to effective use.

But perhaps the most subversive aspect of classical education's approach to thinking lies in its moral dimension: Authentic critical thinking moves beyond a technical skill to a moral activity. It is not just a means to solve problems but a way of orienting oneself toward truth, goodness, and beauty. This moral dimension manifests in the development of intellectual virtues like honesty, humility, courage, and perseverance—qualities of character that shape how one uses one's intellectual capacities, that govern whether one's thinking serves truth or merely self-interest.

This emphasis on intellectual virtue provides contrast to the amorality that characterizes much contemporary thinking, with its focus on advancing agendas rather than pursuing wisdom. The classical approach insists that how we think is as important as what we think about. It insists that the development of intellectual character is as essential as the acquisition of intellectual skills and that the purpose of thinking is ultimately to live well.

This moral dimension of thinking extends beyond the individual to the social and political realm, where the capacity for reasoned deliberation, evidence-based judgment, and thoughtful engagement with diverse perspectives forms the foundation of democratic citizenship. The classical education of the mind is thus simultaneously an education for freedom—not the shallow freedom of doing whatever one wishes, but the deeper freedom that comes from the development of the capacities necessary for self-governance, both individual and collective.

The citizen who cannot recognize fallacies and rhetorical manipulations is not truly free. Rather, he is vulnerable to control by those who master these arts. The person who has not developed the intellectual virtues of honesty, humility, courage, and perseverance will use whatever thinking skills he possesses not in service to truth but in service to his own interests or prejudices. The society whose members have not learned to engage in reasoned deliberation across differences cannot sustain the delicate balance of liberty and community that democracy requires.

Classical education's approach to thinking represents a quiet revolution against contemporary trends that would reduce thinking to mere technical proficiency—at best. It stands in contrast to educational models that prioritize agenda advancement over truth-seeking and that encourage conformity rather than authentic inquiry. Far from retreating from modern challenges, classical education offers a more thorough preparation for addressing them. It provides a more coherent framework for its integration; instead of denying technological realities, it presents a more human-centered methodology for engaging with them.

In the end, the question is not whether education will change in response to changing circumstances—it surely will and always has—but whether those changes will be guided by substantive understanding of human flourishing or merely by the technological and ideological currents of the moment. Classical education's approach to thinking represents a principled commitment to the development of those intellectual capacities and virtues that remain essential for human flourishing in any age: the capacity to perceive reality clearly, to reason soundly, to communicate effectively, to integrate knowledge coherently, to judge wisely, and to act virtuously on the basis of that judgment.

Let us, then, resist both the modern counterfeit of "critical thinking" that serves ideological conditioning rather than intellectual liberation, and the cynical dismissal of thinking itself as merely a mask for power struggles. Let us reclaim the classical arts of grammar, logic, and rhetoric as living disciplines essential for clarity, precision, and effectiveness in thought and communication.

Recommended Further Reading

1. *Rhetoric* by Aristotle. The foundational text of Western rhetorical theory that serves as a counterpart to Aristotle's work on logic and dialectic.
2. *De Oratore* by Cicero. This dialogue on rhetoric by the Roman statesman and orator Cicero expands on Greek rhetorical traditions while adapting them to Roman contexts.
3. *Novum Organum* by Francis Bacon. Discusses intellectual errors he calls "Idols of the Mind," which prevent clear reasoning and encourage groupthink.
4. *Being Logical: A Guide to Good Thinking* by D. Q. McInerny. Offers a straightforward introduction to logical thinking principles for everyday reasoning.
5. *The Closing of the American Mind* by Allan Bloom. A provocative critique of modern education and its failure to cultivate genuine critical thinking.
6. *Sophie's World* by Jostein Gaarder. An engaging introduction to philosophy through narrative that encourages questioning fundamental assumptions.
7. *The Abolition of Man* by C. S. Lewis. A profound examination of how education shapes the capacity for critical thinking and moral reasoning.

Chapter 12

The Subversive Art of Geometry

Why studying mathematical beauty reveals the ordered structure of reality

Our society widely believes that mathematical and literary thinking are opposites. This false dichotomy suggests that numbers and metaphors belong to different brain hemispheres and different types of people. We confidently label individuals as either "math people" or "humanities people," as if they possess fundamentally different cognitive abilities and belong in separate intellectual domains. This misconception has become so entrenched in our educational system that we treat it as an obvious truth.

What makes this dichotomy so remarkable is not its pervasiveness but its profound wrongness. It fails to recognize the aesthetic foundations of mathematics. It cannot hear the mathematical music that flows through poetry. It remains blind to the reality that geometry embodies one of beauty's purest expressions. Geometry transcends mere calculation with spatial elements; it represents the contemplation of order in its highest form. The geometric mind explores harmony and discovers patterns that unify disparate elements of reality into coherent wholes. This discipline cultivates perception of proportion, symmetry, and elegance—the same qualities that form the foundation of aesthetic judgment across all human creative endeavors.

Consider the simple circle, defined by the elegant constraint that all points on its circumference stand at exactly the same distance from its center. This single definition contains a perfection of form that has captivated human attention across cultures and centuries. The circle serves as a visual embodiment of unity, completeness, and harmony throughout human history. It appears prominently in the sacred art of major civilizations, becoming central to temple and cathedral architecture. The circle shapes garden designs and city plans with its perfect geometry. Religious and philosophical traditions worldwide have adopted it as a core symbol. Far beyond a mere mathematical construct, the circle functions as a metaphysical statement. It is a visual representation of perfect equality without hierarchy. It is a representation of completion that neither lacks nor exceeds what is necessary.

Or consider the regular polyhedral, those five platonic solids whose faces are identical regular polygons, arranged with perfect symmetry in three-dimensional space. Their discovery by ancient geometers represented not just a mathematical achievement but a philosophical revelation, a glimpse into what Plato called the eternal Forms that underlie the apparent chaos of material existence. These figures—the tetrahedron, cube, octahedron, dodecahedron, and icosahedron—appeared to the Greek mind as manifestations of an underlying cosmic order, an intelligence permeating the universe and accessible to human reason through the disciplined study of geometry.

This vision of geometry as a pathway to metaphysical understanding persisted through centuries of Western thought, from Pythagoras's discovery that musical harmony could be expressed in precise mathematical ratios to Kepler's search for the geometric patterns underlying planetary motion, from the medieval cathedral builders who embedded sacred geometry in their soaring structures to the Renaissance artists who rediscovered the divine proportions of the golden section. Throughout this long tradition, geometry was understood not only as a practical tool or abstract mental exercise but as a discipline that trained the mind to perceive the order, harmony, and beauty inherent in the structure of reality itself.

The modern reduction of geometry to a collection of formulas and proofs, to be memorized without understanding and applied without appreciation, represents a profound impoverishment of this rich heritage. When we teach students to calculate the area of a circle without helping them perceive its perfect symmetry, or to measure the angles of a triangle without marveling at the fact that they always sum to exactly 180 degrees, we deprive them of more than mere mathematical understanding. When we manipulate the equation of a parabola without noticing the elegant curve it traces through space, we fail to cultivate their aesthetic sensibility. True education in mathematics nurtures the capacity to recognize, appreciate, and create ordered beauty—a sensibility that extends to all domains of human experience. This aesthetic dimension of geometric understanding undermines the utilitarian approach that dominates contemporary mathematics education, with its emphasis on "practical applications" and standardized test performance. The utilitarian preparation for "tech careers" treats geometry as a means to an end. It reduces it to a set of tools valuable primarily for their usefulness in solving practical problems or accessing more advanced mathematical concepts. It asks "What can geometry do?" rather than "What is geometry and how does it define or describe the world around us?"

Yet the power of geometry to shape the mind lies in its union of logical precision with aesthetic harmony. The student who works through the steps of a geometric proof experiences the satisfaction of reaching a correct answer, yes. But the deeper pleasure lies in observing how one truth invariably follows from another and how complexity arises from simplicity through the precise logic of geometric reasoning. This experience cultivates a distinctive quality of mind, one that combines careful attention with an awareness of larger patterns, rigorous reasoning with a sense of synthesis, and precision with an appreciation for elegance and proportion. It shapes a mind capable of moving seamlessly between analysis and insight, perceiving both the smallest details and the harmonious whole, and recognizing the quiet beauty inherent in the order of things. Consider, for example, the classic proof that the sum of the angles of a triangle equals 180 degrees. The student begins by drawing a line parallel to the base of the triangle through its apex, creating alternate interior angles equal to the two base angles. Since a straight line represents 180 degrees, and since the apex angle plus the two alternate interior angles form this straight line, the three angles of the triangle must together equal 180 degrees. What appears at first as a mysterious property of triangles, that their angles always sum to the same value regardless of the triangle's size or shape, emerges through this proof as a necessary consequence of more fundamental principles, revealing an underlying order not immediately apparent to the senses.

This is the gift of geometry to the education of the mind. It teaches us to look beyond the surface and glimpse the hidden order beneath. It discloses connections that seemed invisible, binding the arbitrary into necessity. It reveals how complexity unfolds from the simplest of principles, how beauty emerges from structure. It trains a mode of perception that seeks to transform observation into understanding. This mode, once developed, extends beyond geometry itself to inform how the student approaches literature, history, art, nature, and human affairs more broadly.

The mind trained in geometric thinking learns to look for underlying patterns and principles that explain diverse phenomena through the cultivation of an eye for order and a sense of proportion. This capacity represents a form of intelligence distinct from both rote calculation and unbounded creativity. It is a disciplined perception that discerns structure and order without reducing complexity to an oversimplified uniformity.

In literature, a geometric sensibility reveals itself in the way a reader attends to the hidden architecture of a work. A student who has learned to see the elegant inevitability of a circle, or the way the angles of a triangle necessarily cohere, begins to notice how writers shape their creations with comparable order. In Shakespeare's *King Lear*, for example, the division of the kingdom at the play's opening establishes a structural symmetry that echoes through the tragic unraveling, each act reflecting the consequences of that first imbalance. In Austen's *Pride and Prejudice*, the gradual unfolding of Elizabeth and Darcy's relationship has the precision of a well-constructed proof: every misunderstanding and reversal fits into a larger design, so that the resolution feels not arbitrary but necessary. To recognize such patterns is not to reduce literature to algorithm, but to see how proportion and harmony give narrative its distinctive power—how beauty emerges when every part belongs to the whole.

In art, a mind trained by geometry learns to discern more than surface beauty; it becomes attentive to the hidden proportions that lend a work its lasting power. Vitruvius, in outlining the ideal education of an architect, insisted that geometry was indispensable, for only through proportion could buildings be raised in harmony with the Roman orders. That same sense of proportion distinguishes the Pantheon's measured columns from a simply functional colonnade, or Raphael's *School of Athens* from a crowded sketch. The artist who understands proportion creates equilibrium in a canvas or sculpture but by outright necessity, arranging each element so that tension and balance coexist in a dynamic whole. Across the centuries, geometry has guided artists in different forms: the golden section shaping classical temples, the mathematical ratios of musical scales determining consonance, Brunelleschi's discovery of perspective providing Renaissance painters with a new visual order, and the rib vaults of Gothic cathedrals channeling mathematical ingenuity into soaring stone. Again and again, geometry appears as an inner law of form, the principle that transforms matter into art. In ethics and politics, geometric understanding manifests in the recognition that human affairs, no less than mathematical objects, exhibit patterns of proportion and balance that constitute their health or dysfunction. The student of geometry learns to see that justice, oft-represented as a well-formed triangle, exhibits certain necessary proportions; that social harmony, like musical harmony, depends on precise relationships between parts; that political stability, like architectural stability, requires balanced tensions rather than the elimination of all opposing forces. This geometric sensibility does not reduce ethical questions to mathematical formulas but it does recognize that similar principles of order, balance, and proportion operate in both domains, though with appropriate differences in application.

In each of these areas, geometric thinking contributes by fostering a kind of vision trained to discern recurring principles that give shape and coherence to the world. This way of seeing, known to the ancient Greeks as *mathesis*, reflects a disciplined sensitivity to patterns that lie beneath the surface of what may at first seem random or chaotic. In ancient and medieval contexts, *mathesis* (which can be translated as "learning") came to denote a particular kind of disciplined, often mathematical or scientific understanding: knowledge that perceives intelligible structure and order within the world. It is *mathesis* that enables the mind to grasp the ways in which individual elements fit into larger unities and to understand how the most intricate forms can emerge from the interplay of the simplest conceptual foundations.

This *mathesis* is a form of intelligence increasingly rare in our specialized age, where technical expertise in narrow domains often substitutes for the broader capacity to recognize similar principles operating in different contexts. The student educated solely in the humanities may develop sensitivity to human complexity without the disciplined perception that geometry cultivates. Similarly, the student trained only in technical subjects may acquire procedural mastery but without the appreciation for harmony and proportion that geometric understanding fosters. Only the integration of these complementary modes of thought, the precise and the poetic, produces the fully educated mind capable of perceiving both the structure within beauty and the beauty within structure.

The classical approach to geometry embodies this integration. Yes, formulas need to be memorized and procedures must to be followed, but more importantly, this approach represents a disciplined exploration of intellectual beauty through logical means. The tradition of geometry has long served as a school of both rigor and beauty. In *The Elements*, Euclid begins with the humblest of definitions—a point, a line, a circle—and through patient deduction builds a vast edifice of theorems whose necessity feels at once logical and almost artistic. Centuries later, Descartes transformed the study of space by wedding algebra to geometry, so that curves and shapes could be translated into equations, and equations back into figures. In the nineteenth century, mathematicians began to imagine worlds where Euclid's fifth postulate no longer held, discovering non-Euclidean geometries that shattered the illusion of absolute necessity and opened new vistas for thought. Each stage reveals something essential: geometry disciplines the mind to precision while at the same time awakening it to elegance, to the surprising ways truth can be both necessary and contingent. In this tradition, "the proof" stands as the distinctive form of geometric discourse. The proof is a structured argument that demonstrates that something is true and, more importantly, *why* it must be true. It reveals the necessary connections between premises and conclusion. Likewise, it reveals how complex truths emerge from simpler ones through logical progression. The experience of working through such proofs, of seeing how each step follows necessarily from those before, of discovering that what appeared at first as arbitrary facts are actually necessary consequences of fundamental principles. This experience shapes a mind attuned to order and coherence without sacrificing appreciation for the aesthetic unity that the Greeks called *eurythmia*.

Euclid's Proof (The Infinitude of Primes)
Proposition: There are infinitely many prime numbers.
Proof: Assume, for contradiction, that there are only finitely many prime numbers. Let's call them: $p_1, p_2, p_3, \ldots, p_n$.

Now consider the number:
$Q = p_1 \times p_2 \times p_3 \times \ldots \times p_n + 1$

This number Q is not divisible by any of the primes in our list, because dividing Q by any p_i leaves a remainder of 1.

So either Q is itself prime, or it is divisible by some other prime not on our original list.

In either case, we have found a prime number not included in our supposedly complete list.

This contradicts our assumption. Therefore, there must be infinitely many prime numbers.

The contemporary neglect of this formative dimension of geometric education represents a profound impoverishment of mathematical understanding. When geometry is reduced to a collection of formulas for calculating areas and volumes, its power to shape the mind's perception of order and beauty is lost. This neglect betrays a deeper malaise at the heart of contemporary education: a slavish devotion to utility, as if the only justification for learning were its capacity to grease the wheels of industry or pad a résumé. Geometry, in this view, is stripped of its intrinsic wonder and reduced to a mere stepping stone, either an awkward prelude to calculus or a prerequisite for engineering, grudgingly tolerated for the sake of future earnings. Its role in forming the intellect is dismissed as quaint or irrelevant. The question "What is geometry good for?" becomes not a philosophical inquiry but a demand for immediate market value, replacing the more human and more profound question of what geometry *is*, and what kind of mind it helps form.

In such an atmosphere, beauty is sacrificed on the altar of expedience, and the soul of education withers under the cold stare of economic calculation.

The irony of treating geometry as a merely practical tool is that this instrumental approach ultimately fails to achieve even its own goals. Students who never come to grasp its inner logic often falter even in the applied fields that are supposed to justify its place in the curriculum. The engineer who has not cultivated a geometric imagination struggles to devise solutions that are both efficient and elegant. The architect who does not perceive proportion or harmony can raise buildings that stand but do not endure, lacking the grace of the Pantheon or the measured rhythm of a Palladian villa. A programmer trained only in calculation may miss the deeper symmetries that unify complex systems, just as a scientist inattentive to form may overlook patterns hidden within apparent randomness. Across disciplines, the absence of genuine geometric understanding leads to a narrowing of vision: the professional becomes competent in procedure but blind to order. What geometry at its best provides is more than technique; it is an education of the imagination, forming a mind capable of perceiving harmony, proportion, and intelligible structure—the same qualities that allow technical skill to be transformed into lasting achievement. In this light, Euclidean geometry stands uniquely valuable because of its systematic progression from simple principles to complex structures through logical necessity. The student navigating Euclid's propositions develops a distinctive quality of mind: attentive and precise, yet simultaneously alive to harmony and elegance. This mind perceives what the utilitarian calculator misses: that beauty often emerges from mathematical necessity rather than arbitrary adornment. This geometric mindset represents a quiet rebellion against our age's peculiar dogmas.

While modern education busily fragments knowledge into marketable specialties, the geometer insists that order and beauty belong together, like two sides of a perfect triangle. While progressive pedagogy divorces innovation from understanding (as if one might build without foundation), geometric thinking reminds us that true creativity always builds upon disciplined comprehension. It is rather like expecting a pianist to compose sonatas without first mastering scales, or demanding architectural innovation from someone who has never studied proportion.

The progressive educator, confronted with Euclid, experiences the uncomfortable sensation of meeting something both ancient and more advanced than their latest classroom innovation. In geometry's elegant proofs lies evidence that precision and beauty are not warring opposites but necessary companions. This is a truth our utilitarian educational bureaucrats find most disturbing: that some knowledge justifies itself through the transformation of the knower.

In geometry's elegant proofs lies evidence that precision and beauty are not warring opposites but necessary companions.

To reclaim geometric education, we must return to the wisdom of the ancients, who recognized that certain intellectual virtues endure beyond every change of fashion. For Plato, geometry was not a mere instrument but a gateway to the eternal, training the mind to look beyond the flux of appearances toward the realm of necessary truth. Within the quadrivium, it stood as one of the four liberal arts that prepared the soul for philosophy, harmonizing the disciplines of number, music, and astronomy. Vitruvius, following this tradition, required the architect to be formed in geometry, since only a mind trained to perceive proportion and necessity could build according to the true principles of beauty. Such an education cultivates more than technical skill. It grants the mind the power to discern patterns that lie hidden from the untrained, to perceive both the whole and its parts, and to contemplate the harmony that unites them. The great irony of our utilitarian age is that the minds most praised as "practical" so often falter because they lack geometric sensibility. They suffer from an absence that no amount of specialized training can remedy. They have been taught everything except how to see mathematically, which turns out to be essential for seeing clearly at all.

Recommended Further Reading

1. *Euclid's Elements* by Euclid (translated by Thomas Heath). The foundational geometric text that demonstrates how complex truths emerge logically from simple axioms.

2. *The Beautiful and the Sublime* by Edmund Burke. Explores aesthetic perception and how mathematical principles underlie our experience of beauty.
3. *Beauty for Truth's Sake* by Stratford Caldecott. Examines how the quadrivium (geometry, arithmetic, astronomy, and music) integrates beauty and truth.
4. *Modern Art and the Death of a Culture* by Roger Scruton. Analyzes how the loss of geometric sensibility has affected artistic expression and cultural understanding.
5. *Mathematics and the Imagination* by Edward Kasner and James Newman. Reveals how mathematical thinking cultivates creative insight across disciplines.
6. *A Mathematician's Lament* by Paul Lockhart. A passionate critique of how modern education strips mathematics of its inherent beauty and aesthetic wonder.
7. *The Geometry of Art and Life* by Matila Ghyka. Illuminates how the golden ratio and geometric harmonies appear throughout art history and natural forms.

Chapter 13

The Subversive Art of Storytelling

How narratives shape moral understanding in ways information cannot

Somewhere amid the chrome gleam of PowerPoint virtue slides and the faint hum of climate-controlled classrooms lined with motivational posters, there spreads a peculiar delusion perfectly adapted to the technocratic metabolism of our age. The fantasy is that goodness can be downloaded like firmware into the juvenile mind, installed via "character education programs" and "social-emotional learning modules" packaged in pastel colors and metrics-friendly charts, as if the human soul were a motherboard awaiting the right update.

Vision statements proliferate like weeds in administrative landscapes, all committed to "respect," "empathy," "accountability," though few could trace these words beyond the committee meeting that birthed them. Moral development, in this LED dream, is reduced to a system: measurable, efficient, noninvasive. No need for saints or heroes, no need to watch your father fail nobly or your mother forgive undeservedly. Just tick the rubric and proceed. And somewhere in this machinery of good intentions, the shape of moral reality—its jaggedness, its beauty, its tragic proportions—is flattened into something safe.

What makes this confusion so remarkable is its perfect contradiction of what human beings have known for millennia: that moral understanding emerges through narrative encounter, through stories that engage both the intellect and the imagination of the developing child. The ancient Greeks understood this when they raised their young on Homer's tales of courage and folly. The medieval mind grasped it when illuminating biblical parables for the unlettered masses. Even the austere Puritans recognized it when penning allegorical tales for their children's moral formation. It is only we, in our technological sophistication, who have managed to forget this most elementary wisdom about how human beings come to understand what it means to live well.

Moral imagination begins in the quiet hush before bedtime, when a child listens with wide eyes as a wolf with iron lungs menaces a house of straw. It is in these humble tales of talking animals and enchanted strangers that the child first learns what the world is really like in its moral shape. The wolf is not just a beast; he is malice itself, relentless and real, and the brick house is not just a shelter, but the fortress built by foresight and labor. A single pea beneath a tower of mattresses becomes a parable of hidden truth and deep feeling, suggesting that sensitivity is not weakness but a rare and royal gift. And the ragged boy who offers his crust of bread to a beggar unknowingly entertains a power beyond his comprehension, as kindness reveals itself to be a magic stronger than spells. In these stories, virtue glows with the golden light of enchantment, and vice shows its teeth as a threat with eyes and a name. Here, before reason fully wakes, the child learns to see good and evil as realities to be loved or feared.

The power of these tales lies in the integrity of the story itself: how events unfold, how characters confront challenges, how choices lead to consequences. A child enters these stories as a fellow traveler, experiencing the trials and triumphs alongside the characters. Through repeated encounters with virtue and vice, the child begins to internalize a vision of the moral life. Yes, these stories quietly shape the imagination, offering a world that is intelligible and rich with meaning, where actions matter and character counts. Their ethical force seeps in through immersion, gradually forming habits of perception and judgment that guide the child's understanding of right and wrong.

Consider the sublime architecture of E. B. White's *Charlotte's Web*, that masterpiece of children's literature that has shaped generations of young minds. At first glance, the novel seems little more than a child's story of barnyard animals. Yet beneath its plain surface unfolds a drama of friendship and sacrifice. Wilbur's terror before the inevitability of death awakens in the reader a sympathy that is anything but childish, and Charlotte's quiet labor of weaving words into her web transfigures the ordinary into the miraculous, revealing language itself as a means of redemption. Even Templeton, drawn reluctantly into the story, embodies the crooked usefulness of selfish creatures within a larger providence. And Fern, who begins as the guardian of her beloved piglet, gradually learns that innocence cannot be preserved unchanged, but must give way to the responsibilities of maturity. The child who weeps at Charlotte's death has already begun to receive a moral education. In that sorrow, she has glimpsed the mystery of sacrifice and the quiet nobility of giving oneself for another. She has encountered the beauty of friendship that is not based on advantage or gain, but on love and loyalty. She has begun to sense, perhaps for the first time, that dignity dwells even in what seems smallest and most easily overlooked. The lesson is not confined to the barn spider alone, but extends more deeply, teaching her to glimpse the hidden worth that abides within every human soul.

Charlotte's Web does not preach these truths; it embodies them. White's novel creates in Charlotte a character whose actions reveal friendship's deepest essence. "I am not entirely happy about my diet of flies and bugs, but it's the way I'm made," says Charlotte. "A spider has to pick up a living somehow or other, and I happen to be a trapper. I don't want to eat flies and bugs, but I have to, and what's more, I rather like it." Here White suggests, with remarkable subtlety, the tension between necessity and choice, between what we must do by nature and what we choose to do by character.

This distinction between narrative understanding and abstract instruction also lies at the heart of C. S. Lewis's *Chronicles of Narnia*, a series that has initiated countless children into moral and spiritual understanding through the adventures of ordinary children in an extraordinary world. *The Lion, the Witch and the Wardrobe*, the first book in the classic series, begins in the simplicity of children's play, with Lucy's stumbling into an old wardrobe. Yet that small doorway opens upon a vast architecture of meaning. The endless winter under the White Witch is an image of the soul frozen by tyranny and despair. The children's gradual recognition of Aslan's majesty parallels the awakening of conscience to the presence of transcendent good. Most profoundly, the great lion's willing death upon the Stone Table—mocked and bound in humiliation—becomes the story's pivot, where sorrow and apparent defeat transfigure into the triumph of new life. Children encountering these pages learn, even before they have words to name it, that sacrifice can be redemptive and that joy is not the denial of grief but its fulfillment. "You would not have called to me unless I had been calling to you," says Aslan to the Pevensie children who have summoned him. In this single line, Lewis addresses one of the most profound theological and philosophical questions: the relationship between divine initiative and human response. Yet he does so in a way that even a child can grasp intuitively, if not analytically. This is the unique power of narrative to convey truths too complex for abstract explanation.

The moral education provided by such narratives operates at levels both conscious and unconscious. The child who thrills to the adventures of the four Pevensie children is simultaneously absorbing a vision of courage, sacrifice, forgiveness, and redemption that will shape their moral imagination long before they have the vocabulary to articulate these concepts. The story provides a whole moral landscape of both virtue and vice. Lewis creates a world ordered by moral logic, a place where every action carries weight and every choice reveals its consequence, so that character and destiny are shown to be inseparably bound together.

This same vision of moral order, though expressed with a gentler and more playful touch, also appears in Kenneth Grahame's *The Wind in the Willows*, a story whose lighthearted exterior conceals deeper moral insights. Toad's reckless pursuit of motorcars, for example, becomes more than a comic episode—and it is indeed funny! Those memorable scenes reveal the dangers of unchecked impulse and the chaos that follows when desire overwhelms reason. Rat and Mole's journey into the Wild Wood, Badger's quiet strength in offering refuge, and the friends' determined effort to restore order to Toad Hall all offer a vision of the moral life that is learned through shared experience. The young reader absorbs lessons about courage, hospitality, loyalty, and justice that no worksheet on "character traits" could possibly convey.

The scene where Mole, homesick and tearful, suddenly catches the scent of his abandoned underground house, and Rat, though eager to reach their destination, insists on helping Mole find his way home, contains more wisdom about true friendship than volumes of ethical theory. "What lies over there is good and what lies the other side of the parish boundary is in some strange way evil," intones the scholarly Rat, expressing the universal human sense that there is something sacred about home, something that calls for reverence and loyalty beyond mere sentiment. This is moral education at its most profound. Couched in joyful entertainment, the novel cultivates the formation of a heart that recognizes and responds to goodness when encountered.

Even some of the simplest stories written for the youngest readers have a remarkable power to begin shaping the moral imagination from the earliest years of life. Take, for example, Beatrix Potter's *The Tale of Peter Rabbit*, a deceptively gentle tale in which a young rabbit defies his mother's clear instructions and barely escapes the dangers of Mr. McGregor's garden. Yes, Potter's tale offers a clear moral lesson in the wisdom of heeding a mother's warning. But Beatrix Potter's brilliance lies in her ability to portray Peter as more than a naughty rabbit. He is endearing even in his folly, and his disobedience arises not from malice but from that familiar human instinct to imagine that rules are meant for others, not for oneself. As the young reader accompanies Peter through his frightening misadventure—caught in the gooseberry net, frantically searching for an exit, fleeing the shadow of Mr. McGregor—he does more than observe the consequences of poor choices; he *feels* them. What emerges is an interior knowledge: that obedience, far from being a restriction, is often a path to peace and safety.

Potter does not moralize. She does not preach. She simply tells a compelling story in which moral cause and effect are woven into the narrative itself. When Peter, having lost his new clothes and shoes in the garden, is sent to bed with chamomile tea while his siblings enjoy blackberries and milk, the child reader experiences vicariously the natural consequences of Peter's poor choices.

As the child matures, stories take on greater complexity, reflecting the challenges and contradictions of moral life. Literature offers a kind of moral apprenticeship, where readers enter into the struggles of others and, in doing so, begin to sharpen their own judgment. When a teenager accompanies Huck Finn through his moment of crisis, torn between the rules he has been taught and the sense of right that grows in him, the reader is sharing in the weight of that decision, testing his own instincts, feeling the tension between obedience and conscience. Though the narrative is fictional, the experience is real enough to leave a mark. It prepares him, quietly and gradually, to recognize those moments in his own life when moral clarity will require courage, even at the cost of approval.

Likewise, in *Crime and Punishment*, the reader is drawn into the troubled mind of Raskolnikov, not to weigh abstract arguments about right and wrong, but to endure with him the haunting aftermath of his terrible choice. As his isolation deepens and his sanity frays, the reader feels the cost of his crime—especially in the erosion of his humanity. The slow movement toward confession and the quiet hope of redemption do not arrive as neat conclusions, but as hard-won revelations. In entering into this narrative realm of a story well told, the reader comes to see that moral transgressions carry consequences that no rationalization can erase, and that true restoration demands a fair amount of humility and not a little suffering.

This engagement of the whole person in moral exploration explains why the storytelling of literary narratives proves so much more effective than abstract instruction in shaping ethical understanding. Moral action in real life emerges from the integration of cognition, emotion, imagination, and will—the same integration that narrative engagement fosters.

The moral efficacy of narrative explains why all religious traditions place stories at the center of their ethical teaching. The Hebrew Bible, for example, conveys its moral vision less through abstract maxims than through the drama of human lives placed before God. When Abraham walks up the mountain with Isaac, he embodies the terrifying trust that obedience can require, a trust that strains the limits of human understanding. When dream coat Joseph embraces the same brothers who betrayed him, the narrative reveals forgiveness not as a principle to be debated but as a lived reality that restores broken kinship. When David confesses his sin with Bathsheba, the story shows repentance as more than remorse. It becomes the doorway to renewal, even for a king. In these ways, the Scriptures teach by showing how faithfulness and failure unfold in the lives of real people, making their moral truth unforgettable.

Similarly, in the New Testament, it is instructive to note that Jesus teaches primarily through parables. The Good Samaritan exemplifies compassion across social boundaries. The Prodigal Son's father illustrates the nature of mercy. The Rich Fool demonstrates the emptiness of material acquisition without spiritual purpose. These parables work so powerfully because they engage the moral imagination rather than making a blind appeal to the analytical intellect. They invite readers to inhabit a vision of reality.

Yet if one seeks the fullest expression of literature's power—outside of Holy Writ—to shape the moral imagination, one must turn to the plays of William Shakespeare. For centuries, his tragedies and comedies alike have stirred hearts and deepened understanding of the human soul. It is no accident that Shakespeare's works appear—always and without exception—on the reading lists of authentic classical schools, even as these plays are being excised from many high school and college curricula. The Bard's plays represent the pinnacle of the literary art: a mirror held up to nature, capturing the full range of human experience.

Julius Caesar, for example, offers a searching meditation on political loyalty, civic duty, and the tragic consequences of noble intentions gone astray. Brutus, torn between his devotion to Caesar as a friend and his fear of Caesar's rising power, persuades himself that assassination is the only path to preserve the Roman Republic. His choice, however, sets in motion not stability but civil war, as the conspirators' act unleashes a tide of violence they cannot control. Students reading the play see how Brutus's self-deception—his belief that murder can be justified for the common good—leads ultimately his own destruction. The tragedy lies not only in Caesar's death but in the collapse of Brutus's own moral compass, as his reasoned idealism blinds him to the darker passions his actions will provoke. The play thus serves as a grave warning: when virtue is severed from prudence, and when loyalty to principle ignores the complexity of human ambition, even the best of intentions may lead to ruin.

Much Ado About Nothing, one of the Bard's most popular comedies, illuminates the moral imagination through its interplay of wit, misunderstanding, and eventual reconciliation. Through the sparring of Beatrice and Benedick, students see the power of truth-telling and loyalty in a world often muddled by deception and pride. Claudio's rash judgment and his painful repentance present a vision of sin and forgiveness, while the play as a whole reminds us that joy and virtue need not be strangers, and that folly can be redeemed by love rightly ordered. *The Tempest*, one of Shakespeare's final works, offers a vision of mercy that crowns justice. Prospero, betrayed and exiled, holds in his hands the chance to avenge—but chooses instead to forgive. In this, he models a moral maturity that transcends vengeance. The play, which explores the use and abuse of power, ends not in triumph or tragedy, but in reconciliation, teaching that greatness lies not in domination, but in self-mastery.

One of the most striking illustrations of Shakespeare's power to form the moral imagination comes in the "Seven Ages of Man" monologue from *As You Like It*:

> All the world's a stage,
> And all the men and women merely players;
> They have their exits and their entrances;
> And one man in his time plays many parts,
> His acts being seven ages. At first the infant,
> Mewling and puking in the nurse's arms;
> And then the whining school-boy, with his satchel
> And shining morning face, creeping like snail
> Unwillingly to school. And then the lover,
> Sighing like furnace, with a woeful ballad
> Made to his mistress' eyebrow. Then a soldier,
> Full of strange oaths, and bearded like the pard,
> Jealous in honour, sudden and quick in quarrel,
> Seeking the bubble reputation
> Even in the cannon's mouth. And then the justice,
> In fair round belly with good capon lin'd,
> With eyes severe and beard of formal cut,
> Full of wise saws and modern instances;
> And so he plays his part. The sixth age shifts
> Into the lean and slipper'd pantaloon,
> With spectacles on nose and pouch on side;

His youthful hose, well sav'd, a world too wide
For his shrunk shank; and his big manly voice,
Turning again toward childish treble, pipes
And whistles in his sound. Last scene of all,
That ends this strange eventful history,
Is second childishness and mere oblivion;
Sans teeth, sans eyes, sans taste, sans everything.

In just a few lines, Shakespeare distills the entire arc of human life, from infancy to death, with poignant clarity and emotional depth. The speech, delivered by the melancholic Jaques, offers a profound philosophical reflection on the stages of life through a mirror in which the reader sees the dignity and frailty of the human condition. Each age—"the whining schoolboy," "the lover, sighing like furnace," "the soldier, full of strange oaths," and so on—depicts recognizable truths about ambition, love, pride, and eventual decline.

This passage expands the moral imagination by prompting students to view life as a meaningful whole rather than a series of disconnected moments. It evokes both humility and compassion: humility, because it reminds us that all glory and strength are fleeting; compassion, because it invites us to see others not only as they are now, but as they once were and one day will be. The monologue cultivates a deepened awareness of mortality, maturity, and the common humanity we share. In the classroom, it becomes more than poetry. It becomes a meditation on what it means to live wisely and to grow old with grace.

In a classical education, especially in the twenty-first century, when the forces of ideological novelty and moral confusion are particularly strong, it is vital to choose works of children's literature with care, knowing that these stories help shape the child's moral imagination at a formative age. The narrative mode of moral development, which unfolds through stories and characters, undermines the informational model so dominant in contemporary education. That model falsely assumes that moral understanding consists chiefly in learning rules, grasping principles, and practicing decision-making strategies, as though virtue could be mastered like algebra.

It treats character formation as an academic exercise, reducible to measurable skills and cognitive tasks. But children are not formed by slogans or procedures; they are formed by the worlds they inhabit through the imagination. That is why it matters so deeply which stories they are given. Many of the finest books from the twentieth century are rich in imagination and serious in theme without being "preachy." They still speak to children with clarity and power. Such works should be selected for their enduring literary and moral worth, not because they are new. Not because they are politically fashionable or tailored to advance some current social agenda.

The formative power of narrative, for example, offers a compelling explanation for why oppressive regimes so often fear great literature. Stories have the unique capacity to cultivate inner moral vision, one that cannot easily be overwritten by propaganda or ideological coercion. This is why totalitarian regimes have historically silenced writers and banned books: the Soviet Union exiled or imprisoned authors like Aleksandr Solzhenitsyn for exposing the moral rot beneath the regime; Nazi Germany burned books and censored writers like Thomas Mann and Erich Maria Remarque; Communist China continues to suppress works by Liu Xiaobo and many others who advocate for freedom of conscience. A child who has entered the world of *The Lion, the Witch and the Wardrobe* has encountered a vision of justice and sacrifice that resists the lie that "might makes right"— that strength alone determines right. The reader who has accompanied Frodo on the long journey to Mount Doom has been immersed in a truth deeper than ambition: that true greatness lies in humility and self-restraint. The adolescent who has stood beside Atticus Finch has already begun to internalize a quiet, principled resistance to prejudice and the pressure of the crowd. Such stories do not merely entertain; they plant within the soul a standard of goodness that can withstand distortion. When external voices attempt to shift moral horizons, these inwardly formed imaginations are more likely to stay oriented toward what is true, just, and good.

The moral imagination shaped by great stories functions beneath the surface of conscious choice or learned behavior. It becomes part of the soul's vision, informing how we perceive the world: what captures our attention, what stirs our admiration or our disdain, what we come to regard as beautiful, noble, or worthy of sacrifice. Such formation does not begin with rules or arguments; it begins with seeing rightly. The interpretive lens forged through narrative influences how we make sense of others, of suffering, of joy, of our duties and desires. A child who has wept over the worn, loved skin of *The Velveteen Rabbit* enters the world with a sense of love that endures and transforms, quite unlike the child whose moral sense has been shaped by hollow spectacles crafted only to promote consumption. The adolescent who has walked the wooded paths of Prince Edward Island with Anne Shirley understands friendship not as convenience or self-promotion, but as a deep and sustaining companionship, something far richer than what is typically modeled on the curated performances of TikTok. Through such stories, the moral imagination is not only awakened; it is trained to see with clarity and to love what is good.

> *The moral imagination shaped by great stories functions beneath the surface of conscious choice or learned behavior. It becomes part of the soul's vision, informing how we perceive the world: what captures our attention, what stirs our admiration or our disdain, what we come to regard as beautiful, noble, or worthy of sacrifice.*

The classical tradition recognizes that moral education begins with what the soul learns to love. More than just "knowing what is right," it is a matter of developing a deep-seated attraction to what is good. This formation takes place through immersion in a culture that orients the heart. Children and adults alike are shaped by the stories they dwell in, by the lives they hold up in admiration, by the quiet, persistent images of human flourishing that surround them. Philosopher Iris Murdoch described this process as a kind of sustained looking—an act of "selfless attention" that gradually draws us toward the good.[13] As we fix our gaze on what is noble and worthy, our vision becomes clearer, our loves more rightly ordered, and our moral sense more fully alive.

---

13 "The moral life . . . is something that goes on continually. . . . It is a selfless attention to the world and the patient reordering of our inner landscape." Iris Murdoch. *The Sovereignty of Good*. Routledge and Kegan Paul, 1970, p. 55.

This expansive vision proves particularly vital in an age dominated by what philosopher Charles Taylor calls "the ethics of authenticity"[14]—the modern ideal of self-creation, self-expression, and self-fulfillment that has largely replaced traditional moral frameworks in contemporary culture. While this ideal contains genuine insights about human dignity and development, it often lacks substantive content about what constitutes a good life or a noble character beyond the imperative to "be yourself" or "follow your passion." Narrative provides precisely the substantive content that the ethics of authenticity requires to avoid collapsing into self-indulgence or trivial self-expression. It offers visions of human possibility that expand rather than limit the self, ideals of character that fulfill rather than constrain authentic development, models of excellence that inspire rather than restrict self-creation.

This is why classical education surrounds children with narratives that embody virtue and present compelling visions of goodness. It recognizes that we become virtuous by developing moral character, those stable dispositions of judgment, and action that enable us to respond appropriately to the complex moral situations we encounter throughout life. This may seem quite obvious, but alas modern educational approaches often—*usually*, quite frankly—neglect this formative dimension of moral education. We are told instead that the soul of the child can be shaped by the same machines that churn out vapid amusements and pixelated distractions, as though a child's moral compass could be calibrated by the indifferent flicker of a screen. It is an age of contradiction: where the heart is starved of virtue, yet the air is thick with the hum of entertainment that promises to fill it. Here, in the world of social media, where one's "likes" and "shares" are the measure of worth, morality is reduced to popularity, and decency to convenience. On Instagram, the "influencers," modern jesters of our age, dangle before us the fleeting joys of vanity, while the deepening wrinkles of the soul are ignored. It is a world where appearances are polished to a mirror-like perfection, and any thought of a deeper truth, truth that might bind a man to higher duties, is relegated to the shadows.

---

14 Charles Taylor. *The Ethics of Authenticity*. Harvard University Press, 1992.

Then we turn to the virtual world of the violent role-playing video game, where the adolescent mind becomes enraptured, drawn into the labyrinths of violence, conquest, and greed. Here the hero does not struggle for virtue, but for a higher score, or the next level, or perhaps just for the brutal annihilation of some faceless foe. Whether it is the latest war game where the destruction of life is reduced to a calculation of points, or the fantasy worlds where betrayal and murder are simply steps along the way to power, these games feed a different beast altogether, a beast that devours the sense of justice and spits out an amoral chaos. The child who grows accustomed to these landscapes will find it difficult to discern the difference between a well-lived life and the aimless wandering through a maze of unearned victories and hollow rewards.

The tragedy is that this modern edifice of "entertainment" claims to offer a kind of education, a moral instruction, if you will, that is a mere shadow of the true thing. It is no longer virtue that is honored, but vice—vice engaged in for personal gain. Where the child of old learned from the ancient epics the meaning of honor, of sacrifice, of the sacredness of the human soul, today's child learns only how to accumulate followers, to collect likes, and to "level up." The classic stories, once so revered, have been replaced with narratives that drain the heart and leave only the hollow pursuit of the momentary thrill. In the face of such hollow pursuits, how can we be surprised when the moral imagination withers, and the concept of right and wrong becomes as fluid and inconsequential as the next viral trend?

The classical tradition, by contrast, recognizes that moral formation occurs even without our conscious intention. Children's imaginations are shaped by the stories they encounter, which means that education must approach its narratives with deliberate care, selecting those worthy of attention and emulation. Moral education is not a subject to be confined to a specific time or course; it permeates all authentic learning. It manifests in every discipline, in the culture of the school, and in the daily interactions between teachers and students. We must restore to our children their rightful inheritance—compelling visions of goodness, characters to admire, and stories to engage with. These narratives are at the heart of moral education. They shape the imagination. They build character, and they develop a taste for what is truly good, beautiful, and true. This process holds the promise of not only individual flourishing but also the renewal of culture itself, creating citizens capable of sustaining the shared moral order that makes genuine community possible.

Recommended Further Reading

1. "The Moral Imagination," (essay) by Russell Kirk. Demonstrates how literature and narrative tradition sustain ethical understanding across generations.
2. *The Moral Imagination* by Gertrude Himmelfarb. Examines how Victorian literature cultivated moral sensibilities through narrative rather than abstract principles.
3. *Tending the Heart of Virtue* by Vigen Guroian. Shows how children's literature shapes moral character through narrative engagement.
4. *The Child That Books Built* by Francis Spufford. A memoir exploring how childhood reading shapes moral and intellectual development.
5. *The Discarded Image* by C. S. Lewis. Illuminates how medieval literary imagination created a coherent moral universe for readers.
6. *Tenured Radicals* by Roger Kimball. Critiques how modern education has abandoned the moral formation provided by great literature and tradition.
7. *The Death of Character* by James Davison Hunter. Analyzes how modern education has abandoned moral formation in favor of values clarification and self-esteem.

Chapter 14

The Subversive Art of History

Why chronological understanding creates citizens resistant to presentism

In the modern educational establishment, a quiet but pervasive bias against the past has taken hold. This is not a conspiracy of shadowy figures scheming in secret, but a far more polite and institutional affair, carried out under the banner of progress and reform. Traditional history has gradually been displaced by something else: "social studies," a subject that favors themes like "global citizenship" and "cultural awareness." These substitutes wear the outward appearance of historical study, but they lack its substance. They are to real history what a glossy photograph of a feast is to the feast itself: visually suggestive, perhaps even appealing, but ultimately devoid of nourishment.

What makes this substitution so remarkable is that it has occurred with so little protest. It is remarkable that it has occurred with such perfect assurance that what is being done represents progress rather than decline. The modern educator, having replaced the sprawling epic of human civilization with a thin gruel of disconnected facts, contemporary grievances, and fashionable perspectives, stands back with an air of perfect self-satisfaction, as if he had not eliminated history but somehow improved it. With a straight face, he acts as if stripping away both its chronological structure and its substantive content had somehow rendered it more educational than a traditional survey of the events of history.

The curious disappearance of history from our schools takes the form of a strange and subtle emptiness: an absence dressed in the robes of presentism. One cannot open a "social studies" curriculum guide and find it filled with the drama of the past unfolded, replete with the stories of battles and laws, or kings and revolutions. Rather, one finds the murmured incantations of "skills" and "competencies." One enters the social studies classroom and witnesses exercises in comparing viewpoints as if history were a debating club for the dead. Tests no longer ask *what* happened, but how cleverly one might comment upon a source whose context has been carefully obscured. It is all very modern, and very clever, and very much like teaching a child to wield a knife with precision while keeping the cupboard bare. The outline of learning remains, but the meal is never served. One is left with the handle of history, but not its blade.

Imagine a boy standing in the middle of a museum, surrounded by artifacts whose meanings he doesn't know and whose placards he hasn't read. He sees shapes and colors, textures and shadows, and feels vaguely that they are important—but he doesn't know why. That's something like the situation of the modern student: dropped into the present like a man waking up with amnesia in a strange city, fumbling through headlines and hashtags as though they were clues in a private mystery he doesn't remember signing up for. He's told to care about this cause, fear that crisis, vote in this direction, celebrate or condemn—usually both, depending on the hour. But without a sense of how we got here, of who these people are and why they matter, it all starts to feel like noise. History used to be the story we told to make sense of our being; now it's a background hum, replaced by "skills" and "perspectives," which turn out to be just more ways of drifting. The result isn't rebellion. It's a kind of numbness. It's reflective of the Great Forgetting.

This historical amnesia is most evident in the inability to situate events and cultural movements within their proper temporal frameworks—to distinguish the ancient from the medieval, for example. Time collapses into an undifferentiated "past" distinguished from the present only by what gets articulated as its moral and technological deficiencies, a shadowy realm where everyone wore funny clothes, harbored reprehensible opinions, and died young from preventable diseases while waiting for the enlightened present to arrive and set things right.

This temporal confusion reveals itself in classroom discussions where students confidently explain that "in the olden days, women couldn't vote or own property"—a statement that, in its vague generality, obscures the vast differences between Periclean Athens, medieval France, Tokugawa Japan, Victorian England, and 1950s America. This approach treats history as a uniform expanse of undifferentiated oppression interrupted only by the occasional appearance of a heroic figure who somehow transcended the limitations of his time to embrace "contemporary values." It manifests in the bewilderment that greets simple chronological questions: Did the American Revolution occur before or after the French? Were the ancient Greeks contemporaries of the Romans? Did Columbus know about the printing press? These are not advanced historical inquiries but the basic temporal framework without which more sophisticated understanding becomes impossible.

The modern curriculum weakens students' understanding of history by replacing chronology with themes. Instead of following a clear timeline, students receive isolated case studies. History is no longer taught as a chain of causes and effects but as a series of examples chosen for their relevance to some current pet issue. A unit on immigration might mix ancient Rome, nineteenth-century America, and modern Europe, without explaining what separates these eras. A lesson on revolutions might compare distant events without addressing the specific conditions that shaped them. A study of human rights might jump from Magna Carta to the Universal Declaration, skipping the long evolution of political and philosophical ideas in between.

This thematic approach—skipping across time periods and civilizations to superficially examine selected topics—creates only the appearance of historical understanding. In reality, it fosters a form of cultural amnesia, severing students from the wisdom of the past and insulating the modern world from its influence. Ignorance of one's heritage—of the enduring truths that resurface across generations—leaves a person more vulnerable to political and cultural manipulation, more prone to uncritically embrace novelty and the fleeting trends of the present. By preventing deep engagement with history, this approach ensures that the lessons of time cannot "infect" the modern mind, leaving it unmoored and malleable.

Defenders of the fragmented approach often argue that it is impossible to "cover everything" and that teaching should favor depth over breadth. This assumes, wrongly, that the only alternative is a dry list of disconnected facts. But teaching history in chronological order does not prevent deep understanding. On the contrary, helping students build a basic timeline of human civilization should be seen as a vital goal, not a failure. The real mistake is framing the choice as one between shallow coverage and isolated depth. There is another way: a clear and connected narrative that offers both structure and meaning. It allows students to see not just what happened, but why it mattered.

The classical approach to history brings together both chronology and meaning. It treats history not as a list of facts or a set of skills, but as a story to be understood. This story has a beginning and a middle, though its end is still unfolding. It includes characters, causes and effects, and themes that change over time. It shows how conflict leads to transformation. Though the story is complex and sometimes unclear, it follows patterns that students can study, question, and understand. This narrative approach does not imply simplistic storytelling or uncritical acceptance of traditional accounts. On the contrary, it provides the necessary framework within which critical analysis becomes meaningful rather than fashionable. With this framework, students can analyze ideas in a meaningful way. They are able to weigh perspectives rather than simply absorb them, and they can test revisionist claims against the broader record instead of taking them at face value. A student grounded in the basic timeline of Western civilization, for example, can situate interpretations of the Renaissance within their proper context, approach debates over colonialism with historical perspective, and assess arguments about the Industrial Revolution with a clearer sense of cause and consequence. Without such a framework, the student is left only to echo the opinions of others. He accepts or rejects ideas without truly understanding what they mean or where they originate.

Replacing the narrative approach with thematic fragments and abstract skills does not improve historical education. It dismantles it. This shift does not lead to greater inclusion or deeper thinking. It leads to confusion and vulnerability. Without a clear timeline, solid knowledge, and an understanding of how events connect, students cannot make sense of competing ideas. They cannot judge whether a claim is traditional or new, fair or biased, Western or non-Western. Lacking this foundation, they become easy targets for ideology. They cannot place current ideas in context or see how they compare with the past. They cannot tell what is truly new and what is simply old thinking in a new form.

A lack of historical understanding leaves students vulnerable to manipulation. They often treat current controversies as entirely novel, unaware that many of today's debates echo earlier struggles. Without knowledge of past conflicts, they assume no one has faced similar challenges. For instance, students may view debates over free speech as uniquely modern, oblivious to earlier disputes during the Enlightenment or the civil rights era. They may panic over political polarization without recognizing the fierce partisanship of early America. Or they may treat questions of gender and identity as unprecedented, ignoring centuries of philosophical and cultural reflection on human nature. Lacking this broader story, students respond with a mix of overconfidence and fear, convinced they are on the "right side of history" but overwhelmed when answers prove elusive. Deprived of historical context, they lack both humility and resilience.

A lack of historical understanding leaves students vulnerable to manipulation. They often treat current controversies as entirely novel, unaware that many of today's debates echo earlier struggles.

This historical amnesia also undermines civic understanding. It deprives students of the knowledge necessary for meaningful participation in a democracy. A citizen ignorant of the Constitution's origins cannot evaluate its present application. A voter unaware of past economic reforms, like the New Deal or Reagan-era policies, lacks the context to assess today's proposals. A neighbor unfamiliar with the roots of racial and class divisions cannot help heal them. In each case, ignorance compounds confusion. Without a historical foundation, people become susceptible to simplistic answers and emotional slogans, rather than engaging in rational debate. They are easily led.

The connection between history and democracy is not accidental. Democratic societies have always valued historical education because it provides the shared literacy necessary for public life. History helps citizens engage across differences by grounding them in a common narrative. Understanding the Constitution's context allows for serious debate about its meaning. Knowledge of past civil rights movements informs today's struggles for justice. A shared historical framework allows us to distinguish real progress from recycled mistakes. Without it, democratic discourse collapses into tribalism, and reason yields to passion. We have seen this play out all too often this century.

By contrast, the classical approach to history, at least broadly understood, strengthens civic life by providing students with a chronological framework and coherent narrative. It moves beyond isolated facts or abstract analysis to tell the continuous story of human civilization, emphasizing the political, philosophical, religious, and cultural traditions that shape our world. Students learn about democracy's origins in Greece, the republican institutions and legal traditions of Rome, the rise of constitutionalism in Europe, and enduring debates over liberty and authority. This context enables them to better understand contemporary issues (now and in the future), from personal freedom to the role of government. They see how questions of liberty and equality, faith and reason, local autonomy and central control have shaped the West from its beginnings.

It is worth pointing out, however, that historical knowledge does not dictate a student's views. Rather, it equips him for thoughtful engagement. A student familiar with the history of religious liberty can evaluate its modern limits. One who understands past economic debates can assess current policies. Another who grasps the long-standing tension between individual rights and the common good can contribute meaningfully to contemporary discussions. In each case, history empowers judgment; it doesn't replace it.

But the removal of historical context from education is more than an academic failure; it is a civic crisis. When students are cut off from the past, they lose the tools to think critically about the present. Instead of becoming independent thinkers, making informed prudent decisions for themselves, they become ideological consumers, primed to absorb whatever narrative is most persuasive in the moment. Without the ability to test claims against historical precedent, they become vulnerable to media manipulation and propaganda. They become slaves to the sophists.

This erosion of historical education also erodes civic engagement. Citizens who lack a shared understanding of the past cannot fully grasp the stakes of present debates or the consequences of their choices. They become passive recipients of information rather than active participants in public life. Deprived of context, they cannot question or challenge what they're told. In the end, this trend prepares citizens not for democracy but for its imitation. Free elections and the rule of law may persist in form, but the substance gives way to oligarchic control. Power concentrates in the hands of elites who face little accountability, while citizens unarmed with the perspective history provides fail to recognize the danger. The absence of shared reference points makes genuine dialogue nearly impossible. Polarization intensifies. Public opinion is shaped not by debate but by manipulation.

This civic dimension of historical amnesia reveals that its promotion is not an educational oversight but a political strategy. The replacement of coherent historical instruction with fragmented "social studies," grievance-based content, and abstract "skills" training does more than weaken academic achievement. It cripples democratic capacity. It deprives citizens of the ability to understand their society in context, to evaluate present claims through the lens of experience, or to discern true progress from fleeting trends. The result is a population of confused consumers, easily manipulated by cultural elites, political activists, and technocratic managers who prefer power without accountability. This, increasingly, is the civic condition of our own age.

The recovery of classical historical education is no less than an effort to renew civic life by restoring knowledge essential to democratic participation. This kind of education does not offer a sanitized version of the past. Instead, it gives students the tools to see historical events in context. They learn to understand both the virtues and the vices of human history as part of a coherent story. The goal is not to impose a single view of that story. Rather, it is to equip students with the historical knowledge necessary to evaluate competing interpretations thoughtfully rather than ideologically or tribally.

This recovery begins with a simple idea that now feels subversive: that history should be taught as a chronological story, not as a set of themes or isolated case studies. Students should see the past as a continuous and understandable narrative. The recovery also insists that learning concrete historical knowledge is essential. Names, dates, events, and ideas are not trivial facts simply to be memorized—and they *should* be memorized—but the groundwork for real understanding. Finally, the classical recovery affirms a deeper purpose for studying history. The goal is not just to gather information or "practice skills." It is to develop a way of thinking that connects past and present and helps students see lasting patterns in human experience.

This classical approach to history differs fundamentally from both the uncritical traditionalism that accepts inherited accounts without question and the presentist revisionism that judges the past exclusively by contemporary standards. Such a consciousness does not seek to whitewash the past, but neither does it sneer at it. It sees the splendor of Gothic cathedrals and remembers the suffering of serfs; it hears the Declaration of Independence and does not forget the slave ships. It has the courtesy to listen before it judges, and the humility to recognize that our own moment may be no less blind than those we are tempted to condemn. For if we are the heirs of history, we are also its prisoners. We move through time with the illusion of novelty, mistaking our fashions for wisdom and our slogans for truth. But history, rightly studied, teaches the opposite of arrogance. It teaches irony. It teaches awe. It reveals how civilizations, at once noble and cruel, brilliant and broken, rise with confidence and fall with confusion. It reminds us that we are not the climax of the human story but its continuation—flawed, striving, and unfinished. To possess historical consciousness is to stand, for a moment, in the presence of time itself, and to feel both the weight of the past and the burden of the future.

To teach history as if it mattered is, in our present moment, a radical act. It flies in the face of every modern tendency to flatten time, to treat the past as a museum of curiosities or a quarry for grievances. The classical educator, then, becomes something of a heretic—insisting, almost quaintly, that events have order, that causes precede effects, and that civilization is not a series of unrelated accidents but a long and difficult conversation across generations.

This is no small rebellion. For we live in an age that exalts novelty, forgets yesterday, and mistrusts memory. Against that tide, the cultivation of historical consciousness stands firm. It teaches not simply that things happened, but that they happened to people not so unlike ourselves—people who built, believed, fought, failed, and hoped. It holds fast to the strange and stubborn belief that we cannot understand the present if we treat the past as either a golden idol or a punching bag. What is offered here is neither blind reverence for old things nor reflexive contempt for them. It is something far more difficult: the call to know before we judge, to listen before we lecture. It is an invitation to enter the story of mankind, not as detached critics or passive consumers, but as responsible inheritors. This tradition does not begin in cynicism or end in dogma. It begins in wonder. And it leads, if faithfully pursued, to wisdom.

It is no accident that the loss of historical education has coincided with the rise of civic confusion.

Let no one say that the study of history is a flight from the real world. It is, in fact, the only path back to it. Without the past, the present becomes a riddle without a key, a crisis without a context. A people that cannot remember will not know what to do next, for every current challenge is the echo of some older struggle. It is no accident that the loss of historical education has coincided with the rise of civic confusion. A mind that cannot place events in time cannot place itself in the world.

The truth is blunt: those who strip history from education do not make students freer; they make them more easily led. A young person who has never studied tyranny in Rome or revolution in France is less likely to recognize it in his own backyard. And he may mistake a slogan for a truth, or an emotional appeal for a reasoned argument, not because he is unkind or unintelligent, but because no one ever gave him the tools to tell the difference. This is why the restoration of historical knowledge is not merely a pedagogical reform. It is a public service. It is the groundwork of liberty. In a time when debate too often yields to shouting, and analysis to instinct, the ability to think historically may be our last defense against political amnesia—and the dangerous confidence it breeds.

The question, "Whatever happened to history?" is not a lament for dusty textbooks. It is a warning. For what has vanished from many classrooms is not just content, but coherence; not only facts, but the fabric that gives those facts meaning. The story has been silenced, and in its place, we have scattered episodes, moralized fragments, and exercises in self-expression. This is not education. It is confusion disguised as liberation.

The classical response is simple and severe. We must begin again. Not by adding more worksheets or changing the vocabulary, but by recovering the story itself: its shape, its sequence, its substance. Only then can we form students who are not merely skilled but rooted, who understand their place in the world because they understand that the world did not begin this morning.

Recommended Further Reading

1. *The Future of the European Past,* edited by Hilton Kramer and Roger Kimball. Critiques modern education's shift from traditional learning, including history, to politicized curricula.
2. *The Idea of Decline in Western History* by Arthur Herman. Examines how presentism distorts our understanding of historical development.
3. *The Lost History of Western Civilization* by Stanley Kurtz. Chronicles how narrative history was systematically dismantled in modern education.
4. *We Are Doomed: Reclaiming Conservative Pessimism* by John Derbyshire. Examines how historical amnesia leads to unrealistic political expectations.
5. *The Burden of Bad Ideas* by Heather Mac Donald. Shows how abandoning historical understanding undermines social institutions.
6. *Why Study History?* by John Fea. Makes a compelling case for chronological historical education as essential to democratic citizenship.
7. *The Death of the Past* by J. H. Plumb. Explores the consequences when societies lose their connection to historical consciousness.

Chapter 15

The Subversive Art of Teaching Western Civilization

How cultural inheritance equips students to evaluate competing worldviews

Consider a striking contradiction at the heart of modern education: that the children of a civilization should be raised without a coherent understanding of its own story. American students are increasingly expected to navigate the complexities of civic and cultural life while remaining largely unfamiliar with the intellectual traditions, philosophical debates, artistic achievements, and political foundations that have shaped the very society they inhabit. This prevailing notion, that Western civilization should be marginalized in Western schools, represents a form of cultural amnesia so profound that it would appear self-evidently absurd in any other context. Imagine a Chinese school system that considered the study of Chinese history an optional specialization, or a Japanese curriculum that treated Japanese cultural traditions as merely one perspective among many of equal relevance to Japanese life. The absurdity would be immediately apparent. Yet in our own educational landscape, this precise absurdity has been elevated to orthodoxy, defended with perfect seriousness by those who consider themselves sophisticated rather than confused.

What makes this contradiction of logical incoherence so remarkable is its perfect disguise as enlightened inclusivity. The marginalization of Western civilization in contemporary curricula is rarely presented as what it actually is—a severing of students from their cultural inheritance—but rather as an act of broad-mindedness. "Why focus on one tradition," the argument goes, "when we live in a global society? Why privilege Western voices when all cultures have contributed to human understanding? Why center European and American developments when the world is so much larger and more diverse?" These questions, delivered with the confident righteousness of those who believe themselves to have transcended cultural provincialism, effectively mask the radical nature of what is being proposed: that students should remain functionally illiterate in the traditions that shaped the institutions, values, and intellectual frameworks of their own society.

A generation unmoored from its own intellectual patrimony is a generation adrift, unable to understand the foundations of the very liberties it takes for granted, incapable of contextualizing contemporary debates within the larger story of human thought, blind to the hard-won wisdom embedded in institutions and practices whose origins remain mysterious.

This educational amnesia, the systematic forgetting of our cultural story, has consequences far beyond the classroom. A generation unmoored from its own intellectual patrimony is a generation adrift, unable to understand the foundations of the very liberties it takes for granted, incapable of contextualizing contemporary debates within the larger story of human thought, blind to the hard-won wisdom embedded in institutions and practices whose origins remain mysterious. It is rather like inheriting an ancient mechanism of extraordinary complexity and value while deliberately avoiding instruction in how it was built, how it functions, what purposes it serves, and how it might be maintained. The inheritor who knows nothing of the device's origins or design principles becomes entirely dependent on others for its operation, vulnerable to those who would repurpose it for ends it was never meant to serve, incapable of distinguishing between essential maintenance and destructive modification.

The simplest answer to why Western civilization should be taught—indeed, why it *must* be taught if education is to fulfill its proper function—is that Western civilization is the foundation of our intellectual and cultural heritage. Understanding it is essential for grasping the ideas, values, and institutions that shape our world today. This is not a claim of Western superiority but a recognition of historical reality: the political systems, legal frameworks, scientific methods, artistic traditions, and philosophical discourses that dominate global life emerged from this particular cultural tradition. To remain ignorant of its development is to lack the contextual framework necessary for meaningful participation in contemporary society, whether as citizen, creator, or critic.

But the answer goes deeper still. We are not only Westerners by cultural inheritance; as Americans, we are citizens of a specific nation that represents a distinct chapter in the Western story. Our founding documents, our constitutional principles, our political debates, and our social movements all emerge from and respond to the Western intellectual tradition. If education is to develop moral character and civic virtue, then students must understand the principles upon which their society is built. This includes not only celebrating the achievements of the West but also understanding its contradictions and imperfections, from historical injustices like slavery to modern challenges like censorship and propaganda. A true education does not ignore flaws but engages with them honestly, fostering informed perspectives and a deeper appreciation of the ideals that societies strive to uphold.

Unfortunately, in too many contemporary schools, the study of history and literature—Western or otherwise—has been marginalized or reduced to fragmented summaries. As mentioned in the previous chapter on history, chronology has been abandoned in favor of thematic units that jump haphazardly across time periods; sustained engagement with primary texts has been replaced by excerpts and secondary analyses; the coherent narrative of cultural development has dissolved into disconnected case studies selected for their contemporary relevance rather than their historical significance. This fragmentation leaves students with a jumble of historical trivia rather than a coherent understanding of how their civilization developed, what challenges it faced, what wisdom it accumulated, and what flaws it continues to wrestle with.

The consequences of this historical dismemberment are evident in the civic illiteracy that increasingly characterizes our public discourse. One cannot fully understand modern democratic institutions without studying the Enlightenment thinkers who shaped them. The Enlightenment itself cannot be understood without knowledge of the Renaissance, which in turn draws from the intellectual legacy of Greece and Rome. This intellectual continuum, spanning thousands of years, is critical to preparing students for civic life. Without it, they are vulnerable to oversimplifications and ideological distortions that prioritize contemporary perspectives over deep intellectual and moral development. The Latin phrase *Scientia est Libertas* ("Knowledge is Freedom") encapsulates this belief: true freedom requires knowledge of the ideas and systems that have shaped our world.

Yet the critics of Western civilization courses raise objections that must be addressed rather than dismissed. Does focusing on the Western tradition mean neglecting the rest of the world? This is a false dilemma. In fact, studying the West often highlights its intersections with other civilizations. Greek philosophy, for instance, was shaped in part by contact with Egypt and Mesopotamia. Roman expansion brought Europe into dialogue—sometimes violent, sometimes fruitful—with Persia and North Africa. The Renaissance cannot be understood apart from the transmission of classical texts preserved by Islamic scholars or the influence of trade with the East. Even the Industrial Revolution unfolded within a global network of resources, markets, and cultural exchange. Far from isolating the West, a coherent study of its history provides the framework for tracing its connections with the wider world and for making meaningful comparisons across civilizations.

Yet, while classical education values global contributions, its foundation remains rooted in the Western tradition because that is the intellectual and cultural framework students inhabit. To teach otherwise would be to sever them from their heritage, leaving them unprepared to navigate their role in its ongoing story. A powerful example of this principle comes from the study of logic. The either/or fallacy, also known as the false dichotomy, is a logical error first identified by Aristotle, a Greek philosopher who is a pillar of the Western canon. This fallacy warns against oversimplifying complex issues into false choices, such as the idea that an emphasis on the West necessarily excludes other cultures.

The study of Western civilization provides the necessary foundation of global awareness. It equips students with the historical, philosophical, and cultural literacy needed to understand their own society—its achievements and its failures, its ideals and its compromises, its continuities and its changes. This understanding does not preclude but rather enables meaningful engagement with other traditions, allowing students to approach cross-cultural study with the contextual framework necessary for genuine comprehension rather than superficial tourism.

Moreover, the Western tradition itself is not the monolithic, exclusionary narrative that its critics often portray. It includes diverse voices, competing perspectives, and internal critiques that have driven its development over millennia. The democratic ideals of Athens existed alongside the aristocratic values of Sparta; the rationalism of the Enlightenment developed in dialogue with Romantic emphasis on emotion and intuition; the traditional Christianity of medieval Europe gave way to the secular humanism of modernity through a complex process of evolution rather than simple replacement. To study this tradition is not to absorb a single perspective but to encounter a dynamic, self-critical conversation that continues to unfold.

This recognition reveals the myopia of those who would marginalize Western civilization in the curriculum: they mistake the forest for a collection of disconnected trees, failing to recognize that the Western tradition itself teaches the same skills of critical analysis, comparative evaluation, and intellectual pluralism that they claim to champion. It was Socrates who first scandalized the city by asking questions no one had thought to answer, or dared to. It was Erasmus, gentle and unflinching, who turned the tools of learning upon the sacred page—not to mock it, but to read it more truly. And it was Mill, strange defender of unpopular speech, who reminded the modern world that the pursuit of truth cannot survive without the freedom to be wrong. These were not rebels in the name of chaos, but guardians of something higher than comfort. They belonged to the only civilization in history that built its own critiques into the structure of its thought. The Western tradition, for all its faults—and they are real—taught men to doubt even what they most deeply believed, not to destroy it, but to purify it.

And so the irony grows rich: that in the name of "diversity," many now discard those virtues that once made such diversity possible. After all, what is genuine critical thinking, if not the ability to examine one's own foundations without falling through the floor? What is true "global awareness," if not the willingness to meet other traditions with both charity and clarity? The Western mind, at its best, has always done both—challenged its own idols and honored the image of truth wherever it may appear.

It is a curious fact that the loudest champions of open-mindedness so often seem hostile to the very tradition that made open-mindedness possible. It was this tradition, after all, that gave the world the Socratic method—teaching us to separate thought from feeling by submitting ideas to rational scrutiny. It was this tradition that produced the Roman legal system, where disagreement could be structured and adjudicated without collapsing into personal animosity. It was this tradition that, through thinkers like Locke and Montesquieu, taught the modern world to distinguish principle from prejudice in matters of conscience and law. And it was from within this same tradition that movements for freedom and equality arose: the abolition of slavery, the expansion of women's rights, and the defense of religious liberty were all argued on the grounds of principles first articulated in the West. To abandon this inheritance is not to become more critical, more cosmopolitan, or more free. It is to become unmoored—blown about by every fashionable wind, and congratulating ourselves on our aimlessness. The marginalization of Western civilization in contemporary education thus represents not an advance toward greater inclusivity but a retreat into a peculiar form of provincial presentism that treats the past as irrelevant except where it confirms contemporary assumptions. It reflects what C. S. Lewis called "chronological snobbery"[15]—the uncritical acceptance of the intellectual climate of our age and the corresponding dismissal of the intellectual achievements of earlier periods. This temporal provincialism is no less limiting than geographical provincialism; indeed, it may be more so. After all, while we can travel physically to other places, we cannot visit other times except through the careful study of their ideas, artifacts, and cultural productions.

The classical educator does not treat the past as a corpse to be dissected, nor as a criminal to be cross-examined, but as a guest at the

15 C. S. Lewis. *Surprised by Joy: The Shape of My Early Life.* Harcourt, Brace, 1955.

table—sometimes bewildering, often brilliant, always worth hearing out. While the modern mind is tempted to sneer at the centuries, brushing them aside like cobwebs in a well-lit room, the classical mind asks what those centuries might still whisper in the dark. It is a curious kind of arrogance that mistakes proximity in time for superiority in thought. Against this chronological snobbery, the classical tradition stands like a stone in the current, insisting that what is old is not necessarily obsolete, and what is enduring may also be essential.

For the West—yes, the flawed, wrinkled, often misquoted West—has at least done this much: it has quarreled with itself in public. It has asked whether truth exists, and how we know it. It has sought to pursue justice, not merely shouted slogans about it. It has wondered aloud whether beauty is real, and whether happiness is the goal of man or merely the bait. To shut students out of this grand, grumbling, glorious debate is not to set them free. It is to exile them to the parochial prejudices of the present, where every opinion is freshly printed and rarely questioned. A student who is never asked to argue with Augustine or puzzle over Plato may well grow up fluent in the latest hashtags but illiterate in perennial wisdom.

It is important to return to the idea mentioned already in several previous chapters, that education is not merely a transfer of information. It is an invitation to a conversation that began long before we were born and will go on long after we are gone. The society that forgets how to listen to its ancestors will soon forget how to speak to its descendants.

Teaching the intellectual patrimony of Western civilization thus stands as a quiet act of resistance against the currents of educational amnesia that threaten to sweep away our cultural inheritance. It represents not a retreat into an idealized past but a recovery of the intellectual resources necessary for addressing present challenges with depth, nuance, and historical awareness. It aims not at uncritical veneration of Western achievements but at thoughtful engagement with both the wisdom and the folly of our cultural ancestors, recognizing that we stand on their shoulders even when we transcend their limitations or correct their errors.

This engagement is not a luxury but a necessity in a world where public discourse increasingly resembles a collective form of amnesia, where "historical references" extend back perhaps a decade rather than centuries or millennia, where political debates proceed as if fundamental questions of justice, freedom, and human nature had not been explored with extraordinary depth and subtlety by generations of thinkers whose work remains available but increasingly unread. The student who knows Plato's critique of democracy brings a different perspective to discussions of populism than one whose historical horizon extends no further than the last election cycle; the citizen who understands the complex development of natural rights theory approaches constitutional questions with greater depth than one who treats founding principles as self-evident rather than hard-won insights emerging from centuries of philosophical struggle.

The teacher of Western civilization thus performs a profoundly countercultural service, preserving cultural memory in an age of forgetting and cultivating depth in a culture of superficiality. This service benefits both the individual students and the society they will help to sustain or transform, providing the historical awareness and philosophical depth necessary for thoughtful engagement with contemporary challenges. A civilization that forgets its own story forfeits wisdom—the accumulated insights, hard-won principles, and tested practices that constitute its most valuable inheritance.

Let us, then, not teach Western civilization as if it were a guilty secret or a half-forgotten rumor, but as a great inheritance—battered, certainly, and often betrayed, but still the best map we have for navigating the strange terrain of the modern world. Let us teach it not because it is flawless, but because it is ours, and because one cannot repair what one has never learned to value. Education, rightly understood, is not the programming of future employees or the smoothing-out of social attitudes. It is the awakening of understanding, and understanding is a thing with roots.

To teach Western civilization today is, in the eyes of many, a dangerous thing—and let us admit it gladly. It is dangerous in the way truth is always dangerous: it does not flatter fashion, it does not bend to trends, and it does not apologize for having shaped the world. In an age that bows to the tyranny of the novel and the now, to open Homer or Cicero or Dostoevsky or Dickens is, to be sure, subversive. It is to light a candle in a house determined to live by the flicker of a screen.

The tradition of teaching Western Civilization, though bruised and belittled, is not dead. It breathes still in the cadences of our language, the structure of our laws, the moral intuitions we cannot quite explain but dare not ignore. It is a debate—a loud, living, unfinished debate—that calls our students to spirited participation. Let them read it. Let them question it. Let them argue with it and, in doing so, understand it. That is education. That is freedom.

Recommended Further Reading

1. *How the West Won: The Neglected Story of the Triumph of Modernity* by Rodney Stark. Examines how Western intellectual traditions created the foundations for scientific, political, and social progress.
2. *Who Killed Homer?* by Victor Davis Hanson and John Heath. Argues for the continued relevance of classical education and explores why it has been marginalized.
3. *Nihilism: The Root of the Revolution of the Modern Age* by Eugene Rose. Analyzes how disconnection from cultural inheritance creates intellectual and spiritual drift.
4. *The Revolt of the Elites and the Betrayal of Democracy* by Christopher Lasch. Examines how detachment from tradition undermines democratic participation.
5. *Culture Counts: Faith and Feeling in a World Besieged* by Roger Scruton. Makes a compelling case for the enduring value of Western classics in education, defending classical education for preserving cultural heritage.
6. *Lost in Thought: The Hidden Pleasures of an Intellectual Life* by Zena Hitz. Defends the intrinsic value of engaging with the Western intellectual tradition.
7. *The Lost History of Western Civilization* by Stanley Kurtz. Chronicles the systematic dismantling of Western civilization courses in American education.

Part IV

Subversive Acts of Beauty

Chapter 16

The Subversive Art of Pursuing Beauty through the Visual Arts

How classical training restores attention and reverence

Modern thought harbors a strange assumption: that beauty is optional. In the minds of planners and policymakers, it is often treated as an embellishment, something to be considered only after function has been achieved, budgets balanced, and deadlines met. At best, it is tolerated like a decorative flourish on the margins of practicality; at worst, it is treated as a distraction, a kind of aesthetic sedition threatening the sober aims of progress. What was once held as nearly sacred—that beauty matters, that it nourishes the soul as surely as food sustains the body—has been turned on its head. To champion beauty now is to risk being labeled unserious, even regressive.

There is something quietly rebellious in defending beauty today, precisely because it confronts the dreary utilitarianism of the age. It dares to say that man is not merely a producer and consumer. It asserts that his spirit longs for what is lovely. The arch and the dome, the statue and the song, still speak with a power that spreadsheets and memes cannot match. Beauty is not a luxury. It is a signpost pointing beyond ourselves. To exclude it is not progress but forgetfulness. It is a forgetting of who we are and what we need.

Beauty has a long and illustrious history. The Greeks, who carved their temples with a meticulous devotion to proportion, understood beauty as the manifestation of a deeper order. The Romans and later the European Renaissance took up this conviction, transmuting mathematical precision into soaring domes and gilded frescoes, affirming that beauty is neither arbitrary nor subjective but rooted in discernible principles: proportion, coherence, and integrity, for starters. To create, in this tradition, was not to indulge in self-expression but to participate in a higher logic, to render visible what was already latent in nature.

Modernism, by contrast, defined itself in opposition. "Ornament is crime," proclaimed Adolf Loos,[16] and with that decree, an era set about purging embellishment, distilling form to its most brutal essentials. What was framed as a noble pursuit of honesty in design became, in practice, an aesthetic of negation. If classical architecture sought to express a vision of order and meaning, modernism rejected those same premises. Function, liberated from beauty, became a justification unto itself. The results were predictable: landscapes littered with glass-and-steel anonymity, civic spaces stripped of the humane touch with structures whose inevitable demolition elicits not regret but relief. Pervasive ugliness.

This is not simply a matter of taste. When a city forgets how to build beautifully, it forgets how to live well. A street is not just a strip of asphalt, nor is a building a container for human activity. They are stages upon which the drama of daily life unfolds. And like any stage, they shape the play. The loss of beauty in our built environment is not some incidental oversight. It is a profound disorientation of the spirit. When we cease to care whether a place is beautiful, we teach ourselves to stop seeing altogether. The windowless concrete slab, the office block without ornament, the home built with all the warmth of a shipping crate. These things do not simply offend the eye; they instruct it. They tell us that utility is all that matters, suggesting that the past has nothing to teach us. They promote the false, but commonly accepted idea, that human beings are cogs in a machine rather than creatures made for wonder. The flattening of form leads to the

16 Adolf Loos. "Ornament and Crime." *Ornament and Crime: Selected Essays*, translated by Michael Mitchell, Ariadne Press, 1998, pp. 167–76. (Loos's essay was originally published back in 1910.)

flattening of thought. A culture that builds without grace (what Vitruvius called *venustas*) will soon govern without memory and live without joy.

Even in an age that scoffs at beauty, there remain those who remember what it once meant—and what it still must mean. To champion beauty today is to reclaim what has been forgotten, and the classical approach to art education offers a path forward. It provides an antidote to the aesthetic nihilism of the present age. It is to remember that art, before it became therapy or provocation, was something more exacting and more exalting. It was a labor of the hand and the soul. The classical tradition of art instruction does not flatter the ego with abstraction or indulge the mood of the moment; it begins, instead, with the humble act of seeing.

To teach a student to draw what is truly there—to measure the angle of a brow, to trace the shadow cast by an unseen light—is to teach attention, and through attention, reverence. The vanishing point in perspective, more than a technical device, becomes a metaphor for mystery itself, directing the gaze toward the ordered vastness of space and the harmony of proportion. Raphael's *School of Athens* makes this visible: the central figures of Plato and Aristotle stand at the convergence of carefully measured lines, their placement embodying the union of philosophy and geometry, thought and form. Artists across the centuries have turned to the human body as a measure of this order, discovering in its proportions—from Polykleitos's canon to Leonardo's Vitruvian Man—a reflection of the universal. In symmetry, in the tension of balance, in the quiet arrangement of forms, the artist discovers the conditions through which beauty is revealed and endures. In such a discipline, there is no room for the tyranny of self. One learns, first and foremost, to serve what is real and to echo what is true. Only then perhaps may the artist find a voice worth hearing. Beauty is not improvised. It is discovered.

Far from stifling creativity—this always seems to be the claim—a rigorous classical training refines perception, sharpening the ability to see order in what might otherwise appear as visual chaos. Students practice copying master drawings—from Renaissance studies by Alberti and Vignola to Baroque compositions by Nicolas Poussin. Yet this exercise is not as an end in itself. More importantly, it is a disciplined means of absorbing the language of form. Students learn to analyze the anatomical precision of

Michelangelo's figures, the narrative clarity of Raphael's frescoes, and the luminous color harmonies of Titian. Through such engagement, they internalize artistic principles that later may guide their own creative endeavors.

In addition to two-dimensional studies, classical art education embraces the pursuit of three-dimensional forms, recognizing sculpture and architecture (see chapter 18) as essential disciplines that shape human experience. Students in a classical school engage in sculptural studies by modeling in clay or carving in plaster. They learn to render the human form in the round with attention to anatomical accuracy and expressive gesture. Did you know, for example, that the Greeks—recorded for us by the Roman architect Vitruvius—conceived the human body itself as a system of perfect proportions: the foot as one-sixth of a man's height, the head as one-eighth, the length of the outstretched arms equal to the body's full stature? They study the great sculptors—Phidias, Donatello, Bernini—examining how volume, texture, and movement bring life to inert materials.

Likewise, architectural and urban design studies introduce students to the timeless principles of proportion, order, and structural harmony. They explore the classical orders—Doric, Ionic, and Corinthian—learning how these elements contribute to the beauty and stability of great buildings. Through measured drawings and scale models, students develop an appreciation for the language of classical architecture and its role in shaping civic spaces. They analyze urban plans from ancient Rome to Renaissance Florence, understanding how cities can be designed with both functionality and aesthetic dignity.

Art history is not treated as a detached survey of past achievements but as a living tradition, informing contemporary work. Students are encouraged to explore the symbolic vocabulary of classical and religious art, recognizing how gesture, drapery, and spatial arrangement communicate meaning. They might study Bruegel's *Tower of Babel*, where architectural ambition becomes a cautionary tale of human pride; Giotto's frescoes, where the turn of a hand and the weight of drapery bring sacred narratives to life; or Bramante's sculptural designs, in which clarity of proportion and harmony of form reveal a vision of the human spirit elevated by order. As they progress, these students transition from imitation to invention, applying classical techniques to original compositions that uphold beauty, order, and truth. The result is not only a well-trained artist but a cultivated soul, one who approaches artistic creation with both skill and reverence.

Such an education does more than produce skilled artists. It cultivates a mode of seeing that extends beyond the canvas or drafting table. The student who learns to appreciate the harmony of a Doric column or the balance of a Raphael composition is also learning to recognize structure and meaning in the wider world. The cultivation of beauty fosters important observational skills that are increasingly scarce in an age of distraction and disposability.

The implications for society are profound. A culture that values beauty nurtures citizens who see beyond mere utility. It forms men and women who resist the reduction of life to transactions and efficiencies. Public spaces designed with an awareness of proportion and human scale invite contemplation and civic pride. Architecture that aspires to something higher than expediency fosters participation in a shared inheritance. The alternative is all too evident: the soulless expanses of suburban strip malls, the anonymous glass-and-steel towers of many financial districts, the crumbling concrete housing blocks of mid-century modernism. Such landscapes neither elevate nor endure. They signal nothing so much as the indifference of their creators, and in turn they teach indifference to those who inhabit them.

The status quo in the world of art education, at both the K–12 and collegiate levels, is quite a different story. We are told that children must be free to express themselves, although they don't seem free to learn how. Instead of drawing a tree, they are asked how a tree *feels*. Instead of learning to mix color, they are encouraged to splash it. We have replaced discipline with dabbling, and then wonder aloud why the walls are plastered with what looks like the tantrums of the subconscious. Unfortunately, many modern art educators do not instruct, but incite. They confuse chaos with creativity, and in their crusade against "rules," they forget that even rebellion needs a thing to rebel against. It is one thing to break the canon and quite another never to have read it. The old masters toiled in the shadows of cathedrals and palaces to discover the secrets of proportion and harmony; the new masters toil in faculty lounges to discover new excuses for not teaching them.

There is a deep cruelty in all of this. We are not elevating young artists; we are abandoning them. We hand them the brush and deny them the map. We flatter their instincts and starve their skills. And when they produce work that is confused, crude, and incoherent, we nod solemnly and declare it "authentic," which is modern parlance for "bad, but yours." This is not art education. It is aesthetic malpractice. It does not liberate the soul; it shrinks it. It does not form creators; it manufactures confusion. It does not lift the human spirit toward truth or beauty. Instead, it fastens it to a mirror and calls the reflection a masterpiece. The task before us is not to invent a new aesthetic but to recover an old wisdom—to see again, as our predecessors saw, that beauty is not a luxury but a necessity, as fundamental to the human spirit as light and air. And if we fail? If we persist in this denial of beauty's significance? Then we risk not only the diminishment of our man-made environment but of our own vision, until at last, having surrounded ourselves with nothing worth contemplating, we forget that we ever knew the difference.

We are not elevating young artists; we are abandoning them. We hand them the brush and deny them the map. We flatter their instincts and starve their skills. And when they produce work that is confused, crude, and incoherent, we nod solemnly and declare it "authentic," which is modern parlance for "bad, but yours." This is not art education. It is aesthetic malpractice.

Recommended for Further Reading

1. *Beauty: A Very Short Introduction* by Roger Scruton. Explores how beauty in art connects to moral and spiritual dimensions of human experience.
2. *The Visual Arts: A History* by Hugh Honour and John Fleming. Demonstrates how the greatest masterworks across cultures and centuries reveal universal principles of beauty, craftsmanship, and human meaning that transcend their historical contexts.

3. *Painting and Reality* by Étienne Gilson. Examines the metaphysical dimensions of representational art and beauty.
4. *The Elements of Drawing* by John Ruskin. A foundational text on learning to see and render the world with precision and reverence.
5. *The Shock of the New* by Robert Hughes. Provides a critical perspective on modernism's rejection of traditional artistic beauty.
6. *Beauty Will Save the World* by Gregory Wolfe. Explores how beauty in art offers cultural renewal and spiritual insight.
7. *Art Needs No Justification* by Hans Rookmaaker. Argues for the intrinsic value of beauty in art beyond utility or political purposes.

Chapter 17

The Subversive Art of Pursuing Beauty through Music

How musical training develops the soul against utilitarian reduction

Modern music education has undergone a subtle but profound distortion. It no longer begins with the pursuit of beauty or the disciplined cultivation of the ear. Instead, it fixates on technique for its own sake and treats personal expression as the highest aim. What once required patient apprenticeship has given way to a pedagogy shaped more by impulse than by insight. The language of tradition and form has been replaced by a rhetoric of feeling, as if emotion alone could sustain the weight of art. In this world, the structures that give music its meaning are dismissed as constraints, and the deep coherence of the classical tradition is set aside in favor of what is immediate and idiosyncratic. The result is not liberation, but a thinning of musical understanding It is an education that teaches students to speak before they have learned to listen.

What makes this inversion so concerning is not simply that it abandons the method by which the greatest musical minds were formed, but that it does so in the name of "creativity," even as it quietly erodes the conditions that make true creativity possible. The towering works of the Western canon did not arise from an absence of structure, nor from a naive spontaneity mistaken for genius. They came from those who steeped themselves in the grammar of music until it became second nature. These maestros knew the rules so well that their departures from them bore the mark of insight rather than ignorance. The originality of a Bach or a Beethoven was not a rejection of tradition, but a flowering of it, shaped by limits and disciplines that modern education now treats as obstacles. In seeking to free the student from form, today's pedagogy leaves him unformed.

In the long reverberations of musical tradition, where harmony once revealed a vision of divine order and composers labored to bind beauty to form, there remains an enduring conviction that music, rightly understood, speaks to the soul through structure as much as sound. To seek this kind of music today is to push back against a culture that confuses noise with authenticity and spontaneity with meaning. The classical approach does not silence emotion but gives it shape, directing passion through the channels of discipline. In a time when music is often treated as background or spectacle, the serious study of melody and form becomes an act of defiance, quietly affirming that beauty is not a by-product of one's personal feeling, but the fruit of attention, memory, and restraint.

To study music seriously is to encounter music as a language, to learn the structured articulation of mathematical and aesthetic principles that reach beyond the individual. To grasp composition is to learn a syntax that binds the impulse of inspiration to the rigor of form. Beethoven, in those maddening scrawls that covered his notebooks, did not indulge in randomness; he forged and refined, submitting raw material to an architecture of sound that demanded discipline and vision. The great composers understood music as more than pleasure. They knew that it was more than the mere manipulation of frequencies for the sake of entertainment. It was—and is—a way of knowing, a means of entering into the order of things. It is a way of drawing harmony from the seemingly chaotic.

Musical notation stands as a quiet testament to the human desire for order. It is the perennial attempt to catch the fleeting shape of sound and hold it steady across time. These marks on the page are invitations to enter into something greater than the self, to join a conversation already in motion. To learn this language is to discover the

Musical notation stands as a quiet testament to the human desire for order. It is the perennial attempt to catch the fleeting shape of sound and hold it steady across time.

grammar by which music breathes and unfolds. Through the careful study of counterpoint and harmony, students come to sense the pulse beneath the notes. They feel the tension and release that give music its depth. When this is dismissed in favor of impulse or improvisation unmoored from understanding, music becomes untethered from its past and drifts into ephemerality—heard once and then forgotten.

And what of the voice, the first and most primal instrument, the one that needs no tuning fork but the soul? To study singing in the classical tradition is to cultivate both sound and spirit. It is to discipline breath, to sculpt tone, to recognize that the voice is a bridge between flesh and the ineffable. When one sings within the classical canon, be it in a soaring polyphony of Palestrina or the molten legato of Schubert, one participates in something far older than the self. The voice moves beyond a tool for self-expression to a vessel, lifting up, bearing meaning, proclaiming that beauty is not an accident but an intention.

The history of music unfolds as a continuous act of remembrance, each memory building upon the last, forming a living chronology of styles and composers. It is a living symphony shaped by minds that saw their labor as participation in something enduring. To enter this history is to listen with humility. It is to recognize that every new composition echoes with the memory of what has come before. We are not the first to seek order in sound or to chase beauty through disciplined expression. Every phrase we encounter in music carries traces of past discovery, echoing the accumulated insights of generations. The contemplative clarity of a medieval chant, for example, reveals a devotion to God as well as to the discipline of sound itself—its monophonic lines and measured intervals training both performer and listener to dwell in stillness. Centuries later, the intricate design of a Baroque fugue, as seen in Bach's "The Well-Tempered Clavier," demonstrates a mastery of counterpoint, where independent voices intertwine in precise mathematical relationships, producing a beauty that is both intellectual and emotional. Moving into the Romantic era, the lyrical tension of a nocturne by Chopin or a song by Schumann shows how composers layered harmonic daring onto expressive melody, expanding the capacity of music to capture the nuances of human feeling. In each case, contemporary listeners and performers inherit a living dialogue, where every note and phrase resonates with the discoveries of those who came before, shaping the way we understand and create music today. These musical masterpieces are not relics for admiration at a distance, as is often the perception. They are provocations inviting us to join a musical conversation that has never ceased. In learning their language, we recover a vision of music as something that endures because it speaks to more than the moment.

The classical study of music offers more than the refinement of taste or the sharpening of technique; it offers formation. In a culture that prizes speed and spontaneity, this tradition insists on slowness through apprenticeship. It requires the quiet virtue of attention. It trains the student not only to hear but to heed, to sense the order behind the ornament. This is no invitation to self-display but to self-forgetting, for the music worth making does not orbit the ego. It arises when the player submits to the form, when the hand and ear yield to the grammar of beauty. In such study, by learning how to play, one learns how to be shaped by something older, wiser, and more lasting than the self.

Modern music education, if it may still be called education, has grown suspicious of anything older than itself. It no longer teaches a child to tune his soul to harmony but to applaud the discord he already carries. Where once a teacher might have spoken of beauty as something to be pursued with humility and rigor, today we hear only of "authenticity," as though the mere fact of feeling were enough to make a sound worth hearing. Tradition, once honored as a tutor, is now cast in the role of tyrant, blamed for shackling genius when in fact it once gave genius its wings. The classical view, by contrast, sees no quarrel between freedom and form. It knows that a melody without structure is like a sentence without grammar: something shouted, perhaps, but never truly said. Only when the student submits to the discipline of scales, the order of harmony, and the architecture of composition does he discover the strange paradox: that obedience to the old laws opens the door to new songs.

Consider what it means to train the musical ear—not simply *to hear*, but *to listen* with understanding. This faculty, so often mistaken for a gift, is more truthfully a craft. It does not arise fully formed but is shaped over time by careful attention and repeated encounters with the finest examples of musical order. The student must be taught not only to notice sound, but to discern the difference between noise and music, between what pleases by accident and what moves by design. As the ear matures, intervals begin to reveal something beyond mere sensation; they become echoes of proportion and reason. Chords take on a character of necessity, their resolutions felt as inevitable rather than convenient. And beneath the surface of each composition, the student begins to perceive a logic at work. No, it is not cold or mechanical, but organic and luminous, mirroring the structure of things far beyond sound itself.

This training of the musical ear stands at the heart of classical music education, preceding and informing both theoretical understanding and technical execution. It establishes listening as the foundation for all musical activity, ensuring that theory serves sound rather than abstracting from it, that technique serves musical expression rather than mere display, that composition emerges from deep familiarity with how tones relate rather than from arbitrary experimentation. This primacy of listening distinguishes the classical approach from methods that emphasize either abstract theory without grounding in sound or technical facility without development of discriminating ear.

As the ear grows more discerning, it becomes the guide rather than the follower of theory. The student begins to see that musical understanding is not a matter of memorizing detached rules, but of uncovering the inner logic that great composers have long obeyed. Theory, rightly taught, is a lens, revealing how the parts of music relate with a kind of necessity that is at once rational and mysterious. The triad, once a simple sound, becomes a glimpse into the order of the universe. Counterpoint reveals itself as the strange and beautiful art of allowing voices to differ without disorder. Sonata form, far from a formula, unfolds like a narrative. It is, in a sense, an argument of tones that surprises only by obeying a deeper coherence. In this light, theory ceases to be a burden and becomes the language of music itself.

The repetition of exercises becomes a kind of meditation, a slow awakening to the inner logic of music. Each motion of the hand begins to correspond with a structure the mind has already begun to grasp. The playing of scales traces the contours of melodic thought, while the shaping of arpeggios quietly echoes the architecture of harmony. Rhythms are not struck as mere pulses in time, but lived as musical breath—infusing the notes with motion and life. In this union of motion and meaning, the student's body learns to speak the language the ear has begun to understand.

In the classical approach to music education, the faculties of listening, understanding, and performance grow together as aspects of a single pursuit. Each supports and refines the others, forming a habit of mind and body ordered toward the discernment and realization of beauty. As the student listens, he begins to notice more. Patterns that once passed unnoticed now press forward with clarity. This attentiveness shapes his understanding, which in turn steadies his hand and voice. Technique becomes a mode of knowing, not through abstraction, but through the shaping of gesture to meaning. In this way, the musician is formed not by the accumulation of parts, but by the slow inward alignment of soul to sound, mind to measure, and action to the order of music itself.

In the classical approach to music education, the faculties of listening, understanding, and performance grow together as aspects of a single pursuit.

The classical approach to music education thus represents a form of resistance against what philosopher Josef Pieper called "total work"[17]—the modern tendency to value all activity, including artistic creation, primarily for its utility or productive output rather than for its capacity to embody beauty or facilitate contemplation. The classical music teacher, however, insists that music is the revelation of an ordered beauty that reflects deeper patterns of reality. The classical teacher sees music as an invitation to lasting contemplation. This insistence stands as a quiet protest against the reduction of music to both the functionalism that asks only "What use is it?" and the expressionism that asks only "How does it make me feel?"

To teach music in the classical tradition is to undertake a quiet defiance in a world that treats sound as commodity and listening as a passive indulgence. The prevailing culture encourages a relationship to music that is fleeting and unreflective, one in which feeling is provoked (or manipulated)

---

17 Josef Pieper. *Leisure: The Basis of Culture*. Translated by Alexander Dru, Ignatius Press, 2009.

rather than cultivated, and where meaning is subordinated to marketability. In this climate, the classical educator introduces a different mode of encounter, one that calls for the shaping of emotion by intellect. Rather than turning away from contemporary musical realities, this tradition equips students to meet them with discernment, drawing upon a heritage capable of forming both the hand that plays and the ear that judges. What emerges is the recovery of a richer vocabulary by which to speak musically of the present.

This recovery begins with the recognition that music involves more than personal preference or fleeting reaction; it stands as a disciplined art, governed by objective principles that can be studied and mastered. Far from being a free-form outlet of self-expression, music speaks through a language shaped by the structure and coherence of its internal logic. It engages the emotions, yes, but in a way that unveils rather than distorts the beauty and order embedded into the architecture of reality. A student formed in this tradition enters into music as a participant in something enduring. The student develops a keener eye for discernment. He learns to distinguish between what is merely new and what has true depth. He can separate flashy surface brilliance from genuine substantive expression. He recognizes when something only stirs the emotions temporarily. And he understands when something truly awakens the soul.

In our era of fractured focus, classical music education fosters a contemplative attentiveness rarely found elsewhere. Students learn to dwell with a single composition, such as Beethoven's *String Quartet No. 14 in C-sharp minor*, exploring its subtle harmonic shifts, intricate counterpoint, and emotional depth while allowing the music to gradually transform their consciousness. This deep engagement stands apart from the typical digital experience. Where online platforms push constantly toward novelty and stimulation, classical training invites patience and depth. The digital world encourages us to sample briefly before moving on—treating each musical piece as temporarily intriguing but ultimately replaceable. In fact, most listeners today never remain with any composition long enough to be genuinely changed by it. They adopt a skimming approach that reduces music to a series of fleeting impressions, each worthy of momentary interest but not sustained commitment. Classical education challenges this disposable relationship with art.

Music ought to draw the listener into a depth of experience that refuses to be grasped all at once. Its richness unfolds slowly, resisting quick consumption and requiring a kind of attention that deepens with each return. The student who enters seriously into a work finds that it begins to inhabit the mind as a lasting presence. Over time, the piece becomes familiar in the way a landscape becomes familiar—through many quiet encounters that reveal new features and hidden patterns. What begins as study becomes something more like friendship, shaped by patience and sustained reflection.

This cultivation of contemplative attention represents perhaps the most radical dimension of music's subversive potential in our digital age. It asserts that some works—those works worthy of the student's attention—deserve not merely to be consumed but to be known intimately, integrated into the structure of consciousness itself. It stands as a quiet repudiation of the assumption that all content is ultimately interchangeable, that all pieces are equally deserving (or undeserving) of sustained attention, that all musical experiences can and should be processed in the same superficial manner.

The student who has dwelt deeply with even a few works of music gains a habit of mind that stands in quiet defiance of the ambient noise of the age. Where so much of modern experience encourages hurried encounters and fleeting impressions, this formation trains the listener to remain, to attend, to let the fullness of a thing emerge in time. Such attention does more than serve musical understanding; it begins to color the way the student encounters the world itself. Rather than skimming over the surface of things, the student learns to wait for their richness to appear, to move from reaction to reflection, from distraction to wonder.

Given the many ways in which contemporary culture undermines the deeper habits of mind and heart, the teaching of music in classical schools becomes an intentional stand against the erosion of inner life. It seeks to uphold a vision of education in which memory remains active and interior, something carried within rather than stored elsewhere. Language, in this vision, is more than a tool for information. It is a vessel of meaning, shaped by history and capable of shaping the soul. Tradition, too, is regarded as a source of richness and insight that the present moment alone cannot generate. This kind of education draws from what has endured, trusting that wisdom is cumulative and that the deepest learning comes through long inheritance. This classical approach grows from the conviction that certain human powers—reflection, discernment, attentiveness—are still vital, even if they have grown rare. Music, rightly taught, keeps these powers alive.

Let us, then, approach the teaching of classical music as one might approach the lighting of a lamp in a darkened world, guided by the boldness of those who preserve truth in an age that forgets. The modern world, restless and wired, dreams of shrinking the soul to fit the screen. It treats education as a tool for productivity, language as a transaction of signals, and a child's attention as a commodity to be harvested. Yet to teach music with seriousness is to stand against this thinning of the human spirit. The child receives no burden, but a key, a means of opening doors hidden to the hurried and the distracted.

The boy who remembers the sound of a fugue and hears it again in silence carries within him a quiet abundance. The girl who holds in her memory the architecture of a chant or the joy of a sonata bears a companion that time cannot dissolve. This inner store, unaffected by passing trends or shifting fortunes, offers more than delight. It becomes a place of return in hours of loneliness, a height from which to see the world with greater clarity. In such music, rightly learned, there is a kind of homecoming—a reminder that the world possesses depths greater than appearances suggest, and that the soul stretches farther than the confines of the screen. Music, in this vision, becomes both sanctuary and summons, forming a spirit capable of wonder in a world that too often forgets how to wonder.

Recommended Further Reading

1. "*De Musica*," essay in *Moralia* by Plutarch. Examines music's moral and educational role in society, arguing that proper musical training shapes character and citizenship.

2. *On the Fundamental Concepts of Music* (*De Institutione Musica*) by Boethius. Establishes the philosophical foundation for Western music theory, connecting mathematical harmony to cosmic order.
3. *The Rest Is Noise* by Alex Ross. Chronicles how modern music education has moved away from traditional beauty toward novelty and expression.
4. *The Aesthetics of Music* by Roger Scruton. Examines how music embodies ordered beauty that transcends mere subjective expression.
5. *This Is Your Brain on Music* by Daniel J. Levitin. Details how disciplined musical training shapes cognitive development and perception.
6. *Leisure: The Basis of Culture* by Josef Pieper. Explains how musical contemplation resists the utilitarian reduction of human experience.
7. *The Responsibility of the Artist* by Jacques Maritain. Explores how musical tradition forms the artist through disciplined attention to beauty.

Chapter 18

The Subversive Art of Pursuing Beauty through Science

How wonder and observation restore meaning to scientific inquiry

Since the advent of today's technological culture, science has largely been stripped of its original spirit of wonder. What was once a deep and contemplative effort to understand the natural world has become a mechanical exercise, focused more on technique than discovery. This shift is most clearly seen in the rise of STEM education, which presents itself as a mark of progress while quietly narrowing science into data handling and job training. The result is a form of education that looks forward with confidence but sees less and less of what truly matters: the beauty, order, and meaning at the heart of nature itself.

The STEM evangelists have recast the scientist not as a wonder-struck seeker of truths hidden in starlight and cell walls, but as a sterile processor of preapproved facts. Gone is the Copernican daredevil, the Darwinian wanderer, the Faraday mystic. In his place stands a credentialed technician, spreadsheet in one hand, rubric in the other, churning data like grist in the bureaucratic mill, mistaking fluency in Python for insight into the human condition. Science, once a sustained pursuit of understanding over time, now lies flat-packed in standardized modules, bite-size for easy assessment. It is no longer an apprenticeship in humility before nature's cryptic abundance, but a competitive scavenger hunt through predigested content, timed to the second and optimized for test scores. Inquiry, once sacred, is now staged; students are shepherded through sanitized "labs" with known outcomes, lest the mess of genuine discovery derail the learning objectives or upset the grant-dependent machinery.

Thus has the experiment become an exercise, the unknown replaced with multiple choice, the hypothesis neutered, the wild curiosity of a Kepler or Curie reduced to a rubric of competencies—"can identify," "can apply," "can calculate." The noble habit of perceiving the real, of standing dumbstruck before the elegant absurdity of a universe that *is*—is traded for the dull mimicry of procedural fluency.

And what of the soul, that ancient, unruly participant in the drama of knowledge? It has no place here. The soul cannot be benchmarked. Awe cannot be graphed. Wonder doesn't fit on a transcript. So the system shaves them off, like barnacles from the hull of a vessel built not for exploration but delivery. Deliver the product. Deliver the grade. Deliver the degree. The world is not to be loved or contemplated; it is to be engineered.

This narrow view finds its most revealing expression in the popular slogan, "Follow the science," an insulting phrase that treats science as some final verdict. The absurdity of the phrase is not just semantic; it is metaphysical. To "follow the science," one must first believe it walks ahead, that it knows where it's going, that it moves with unerring direction along a linear path of truth-distribution, while we—the grateful, ignorant masses—march docilely behind, clipboard in hand, obedient to the lab-coated priesthood. But science, in its true and ancient form, does not march; it stumbles, it wanders, it questions itself, it revises with embarrassment. It lives in doubt. It *breathes* through contradiction.

Yet the phrase survived the COVID-19 scare precisely because it flatters our craving for certainty in an age allergic to ambiguity. The political manager, the educational consultant, and the pharmaceutical exec all adore this slogan because it grants their proclamations the halo of neutrality and the armor of inevitability. Once invoked, "the science" halts debate. The messy polyphony of hypotheses and counterhypotheses vanish in the glare of a single, blinding searchlight: "consensus." But consensus, in the real life of science, is but a fragile détente always on the verge of collapse beneath the weight of some heretical datum.

Even worse, the phrase performs a sleight of hand, dressing up a contested, interpretive act as something merely *received*. What was once a dialogue between thinkers becomes a directive from above. Galileo did not "follow the science." He defied it. So did Darwin, Lavoisier, Planck, and every other troublemaker who dared tug at the fraying edges of the reigning paradigm. And those paradigms never quite settle into final form, always threatening the smooth narratives crafted for textbook margins and campaign slogans.

"Follow the science," then, is not a call to intellectual rigor, but to intellectual abdication. It imagines science as monolithic and moral, as if experiments could deliver stone-etched commandments from Sinai. But the scientist is not a prophet. He is a person: situated, fallible, often wrong, occasionally brilliant. His work is not scripture. It is sediment, layers of thought and struggle and often-forgotten contradiction laid down by generations fumbling toward understanding. And so, the next time the phrase floats down from on high, accompanied by a PowerPoint and a TED Talk and a smug policy directive, recall that real science does not ask to be followed. It asks to be engaged, wrestled with, doubted, revised, and sometimes, when the data rebel and the model collapses, it must be rebuilt entirely from the rubble of its own ruined certainty.

Is it any wonder that the nation—the whole world, perhaps—so easily fell for such a ridiculous sound bite? In most of our contemporary classrooms, after all, science is reduced to a set of facts to be memorized—never mind asking questions. Students are taught conclusions, but the process by which those conclusions were reached remains obscured. The scientific method is presented as a mere collection of answers, while the deeper practices of observation, attention, and inquiry are sidelined. Students might learn about photosynthesis without ever observing it firsthand in the natural world. They study astronomy, yet rarely look up to witness the stars themselves. The periodic table is memorized, yet the dynamic reactions it describes remain out of reach. Evolutionary theory is discussed without the opportunity to examine fossils or compare anatomical structures. This approach allows for the retention of information but neglects the richer, experiential engagement that makes science a journey of discovery.

And so, there emerges an inflated reverence for Science with a capital "S," and especially its white-coated high priests in the field of medicine, whose proclamations descend from on high, bathed in institutional logos and acronyms. It's a reverence that brooks no heresy. The layperson, conditioned from adolescence to accept conclusions without question, now flinches at the thought of asking *why*, or worse, *how do you know that?* as if epistemology itself were a kind of indecent exposure. What results is a populace disturbingly pliable, no longer trusting their own eyes, ears, or even gut-level perception of observable fact if it dare contradict the dogmas that descend from national or global technocratic authorities. The spell is complete: minds schooled to accept theory as truth are rendered helpless before contradiction, mistaking skepticism for sin, and inquiry for rebellion.

The classical approach to science at least proposes a way out of the cul-de-sac of canned conclusions and institutional catechisms. It does not regard science as a static reliquary of certified truths to be recited like mantras preceding from "follow the science," but as a methodical, at times maddening, inquiry into the stubborn particulars of the world. Yes, there's information to absorb and facts to know, but these are the trail markers, not the trail itself. The classical mind is trained not to ingest, but to *behold*. The classical science student is asked to attend closely to what *is*, before it rushes to pronounce what *ought to be* believed. It does not begin with a diagram or a dataset, but with dirt under the fingernails. It begins with a shadow crossing a sundial or the sticky unfolding of a milkweed pod. Questions come before answers. Reality is observed before interpretation. It is a science that refuses to divorce itself from the actual. And in this lies its quiet subversion: Where the modern approach cultivates a docile reverence for theory, especially theory sanctified by glowing screens and international task forces, the classical method fosters independence of mind. It breeds a suspicion, not of science, but of the bureaucratic machinery that ossifies it into dogma. The classical student does more than study reality. He comes to *trust*

The classical student does more than study reality. He comes to trust his own faculties to discern it. He does not tremble before contradiction. He sees in it the birth of better questions.

his own faculties to discern it. He does not tremble before contradiction. He sees in it the birth of better questions. Not having been conditioned to outsource perception to credentialed intermediaries, the classical thinker remains dangerously—perhaps subversively—willing to see for himself.

Consider astronomy, the subject of chapter 19 and the oldest of the sciences, which serves as an ideal example of a classical scientific education. Again, in modern classrooms, instruction typically starts with abstract models and complex theories from thick textbooks rather than with direct observation. Students are expected to absorb technical information and distant concepts without first developing a sense of wonder. They rarely look to the heavens with curiosity, or follow the paths of the planets, or notice the changing face of the moon. The awe once inspired by the stars is too often lost in a sea of data and diagrams.

The classical method begins with direct encounter—with the sky as it appears to the unaided eye. It is as if the long story of humanity is written overhead, where generations have watched the heavens with patient attention, treating each star as a sign to be read. The student enters this tradition by first standing beneath the open sky, noticing the regular arc of the sun, the slow rotation of the stars around a fixed point, and the shifting face of the moon. These are not just sights, but rhythms that imprint themselves over time. Only after this long acquaintance with the celestial order does the desire for explanation arise. The mind, having been steeped in the visible motions above, begins to ask what causes them. Wonder matures into inquiry. The student's path follows a natural unfolding—from attentive watching to thoughtful questioning. In this steady movement from experience to understanding, he retraces the steps taken by early astronomers, whose search for meaning was always shaped by the mystery and majesty of the heavens.

Thus, the classical approach holds that true understanding arises through an active encounter with the world, through direct experience joined with thoughtful reflection. By grounding learning in careful observation, it fosters what Martin Heidegger described as "the wondering gaze,"[18] a way of seeing that approaches the familiar with fresh eyes. This gaze does

18 Martin Heidegger. *What Is Called Thinking?* Translated by J. Glenn Gray. New York: Harper & Row, 1968. "The wondering gaze" is a paraphrase of Heidegger's concept of *Staunen* (wonder) and the meditative *Gelassenheit* (releasement) toward things that allow beings to reveal themselves as they are.

not pass over the ordinary but lingers, attentive to the hidden structure and beauty that often go unnoticed, like the precise geometry of a leaf's venation, or the quiet unfolding of a flower's symmetry as it turns toward the light. The student formed in this tradition learns to look with care, to think with patience, and to allow curiosity to guide his inquiry. Through this disciplined attentiveness, his vision becomes more than passive sight; it becomes a means of discovery, a way of drawing nearer to truth.

This vision takes shape through what the medieval universities called the quadrivium, a course of study in the mathematical arts that formed the foundation for understanding the order woven into the natural world. Through this tradition, the classical student comes to recognize that mathematical principles are not inventions imposed upon reality, but truths uncovered through careful observation and reflection. Mathematics becomes more than a means of calculation; it becomes a way of seeing. Geometry, for instance, opens the student's eyes to the hidden structures that shape both the smallest patterns in nature and the vast arrangements of the cosmos. Astronomy, likewise, invites a sense of awe at the regularity of the heavens, not as a matter of utility alone but as a reflection of deeper harmony. In this way, the study of number and proportion fosters a habit of mind attuned to the intelligibility and beauty of the world.

This discovery that the world reveals a meaningful structure open to human reason may be the deepest insight offered by classical science. It serves as the groundwork for all later scientific achievement. The classical approach holds that such insight arose not from speculation alone, but from long attention to the natural world, shaped by the belief that reality itself is ordered and knowable. It understands that genuine progress in science has come through a careful balance: neither dismissing theory nor neglecting observation, but allowing each to inform and deepen the other. Through this harmony of mind and sense, the path to understanding unfolds.

This discovery that the world reveals a meaningful structure open to human reason may be the deepest insight offered by classical science. It serves as the groundwork for all later scientific achievement.

Consider William Harvey, who uncovered the circulation of blood. He did not discard older ideas outright. He closely studied anatomical structures and experimented with how blood moved through living bodies. His discovery emerged from careful dissection, sustained observation, and a willingness to question inherited assumptions when the evidence required it. Or consider Charles Darwin, who spent years observing the natural world, gathering specimens, and reflecting on patterns of variation and adaptation before arriving at his theory of natural selection. His insight did not come from speculation alone, but from a mind shaped by both observation and deep reflection on the interconnections of life. Or Gregor Mendel, whose quiet work in a monastery garden revealed the basic laws of heredity. By patiently tracking the traits of pea plants over generations, he uncovered patterns that had remained hidden in plain sight. It is important to note that these thinkers advanced biological understanding through a sustained effort to perceive the underlying order within living systems with an effort that combined imagination and disciplined attentiveness.

This integration of observation, reasoning, creativity, and rigor reveals a deeper dimension of classical science, one that resists the simplifications often found in modern accounts. Today's portrayal of "the scientific method" as a fixed linear procedure—observe, hypothesize, experiment, conclude—offers a narrow and misleading picture of how science actually unfolds. In reality, scientific inquiry moves through a dynamic and often unpredictable process, shaped by the ongoing exchange between theory and evidence, the careful weighing of interpretations, and the imaginative efforts of individuals working within a broader intellectual community. When reduced to a mechanical routine, science loses its character as a disciplined pursuit of understanding, one that calls for discernment, reflection, and judgment at every step.

These intellectual virtues take root through sustained engagement with the natural world, guided by those who have cultivated a disciplined way of seeing. The student advances by imitating the habits of careful observers and thoughtful interpreters, learning how to follow the evidence (*not* "follow the science") where it leads and how to judge its meaning with care. In this way, scientific knowledge grows as a deeper mode of attention, an attunement to the world and its order.

Such formation may be the most subversive element of classical science education in a culture captivated by speed, efficiency, and control. While modern trends push students toward quick answers and marketable outcomes, the classical approach draws them into a slower, more interior transformation. It encourages wonder before it demands mastery, and it values understanding even when it yields no immediate result. In doing so, it preserves the dignity of science as a human endeavor shaped by discipline, curiosity, and the love of truth.

This emphasis on understanding for its own sake does not devalue practical applications but places them in proper relation to the more fundamental purpose of science: to know reality. It recognizes that the most transformative practical innovations have typically emerged from deeper understanding of natural phenomena pursued for the sake of knowledge itself. But let it be said: the classical approach does not reject technology. It only insists that technology serves human understanding rather than replacing it. It should allow for the enhancement of observation rather than substituting for it.

In the classical science classroom, technology plays a supporting role in the work of observation and thought. Instruments like the telescope and microscope do not stand in for the eye but extend its reach, allowing students to see more deeply into the structure of things. A telescope makes distant stars visible, not by replacing human attention, but by enriching what that attention can perceive. A microscope reveals hidden forms without removing the need for thoughtful interpretation. Even complex tools like computers serve best when they help uncover relationships too subtle or vast for unaided calculation. In each case, the instrument remains an aid to human inquiry, not a substitute for it. The heart of the scientific endeavor remains the cultivated habit of seeing, questioning, and understanding the world as it reveals itself to disciplined and attentive minds.

Let us reclaim the classical approach as a return to science's original unity of observation and understanding. Science not only serves practical purposes but also deepens human insight. It fulfills intellectual curiosity while revealing the beauty and complexity inherent in the natural world, from the smallest details to the vastest reaches. The aim of scientific education is not necessarily to create specialists, but to cultivate observers who think with discipline, reason with clarity, and discern truth from mere opinion. The best scientists and medical professionals will be those who possess a broad education, shaped by a classical approach to understanding the world and the scientific discoveries that emerge from it.

This reclamation does not dismiss modern knowledge. But it does seek to recover the foundational principles that make such knowledge meaningful. It does not oppose scientific progress, but calls for a renewal of the wonder that propels it. In this renewal, we rediscover the intellectual virtues that are essential for addressing contemporary challenges with wisdom. The classical approach to science is not an alternative to modern understanding, but the foundation that supports it. Without the virtues of disciplined observation, patient attention, and reasoning that integrates diverse insights, science becomes a mere collection of techniques, a tool of manipulation rather than a pursuit of wisdom, and a quest for power detached from the humility and reverence that define our best qualities.

Recommended Further Reading

1. *The Sense of Wonder* by Rachel Carson. Explores how cultivating wonder in nature forms the foundation for scientific understanding.
2. *The Power of Bad* by John Tierney. Critiques how modern science has become detached from its philosophical foundations.
3. *The World Beyond Your Head* by Matthew Crawford. Analyzes how direct encounter with reality cultivates attention against technological distraction.
4. *Scientism: The New Orthodoxy*, edited by Roger Scruton. Examines the cultural elevation of scientific authority above other forms of knowledge.
5. *Cosmos and Transcendence* by Wolfgang Smith. Challenges the reductionist view of nature in modern science and restores wonder.
6. *Darwin's Doubt* by Stephen Meyer. Examines how observational evidence challenges established scientific paradigms.
7. *The Lost World of Adam and Eve* by John Walton. Demonstrates how ancient scientific understanding contains wisdom modern approaches miss.

Chapter 19

The Subversive Art of Pursuing Beauty through Astronomy

How studying the heavens develops proper perspective on human existence

This chapter follows our exploration of the classical approach to science and turns to the most ancient branch of the observational sciences: astronomy. It is here, perhaps more than anywhere else, that the tension between modern and classical views of knowledge reveals itself. We have come to separate measuring from marveling. According to this modern way of thinking, the astronomer who studies the stars with tools and formulas is seen as entirely different from the poet who stands in quiet awe beneath them. Scientific knowledge of how the heavens move is treated as unrelated to the deeper questions those movements inspire. We've acted as though the ability to observe with precision has nothing to say to the part of us that seeks meaning. It's as if we've split the human mind in two, insisting that the side that measures must stay isolated from the side that reflects.

What makes this division so remarkable, aside from its philosophical incoherence, is its complete opposition to the lived experience of the greatest astronomical minds. The true astronomer—whether plotting the motion of the planets, peering through a telescope at distant moons, or contemplating the fabric of spacetime—has never sought knowledge of the heavens solely for its utility. Rather, the work is driven by a deeper awareness that the universe, in all its mathematical harmony, reveals a beauty so profound it borders on the sacred. Of course, many classicists would say that it is sacred. This sense of wonder is not a distraction from the scientific task but its very heart. It arises not from personal feeling but from an encounter with something real and intrinsic to the cosmos.

To pursue astronomy in the classical tradition is to enter into a dialogue with the heavens, raising one's gaze beyond the fleeting distractions of daily life and beholding the grand design stretched across the night sky. This pursuit becomes a kind of pilgrimage of the mind, one that seeks not only to observe but to reflect, to uncover meaning behind the lights that pierce the darkness. The classical astronomer approaches the cosmos with wonder, searching for harmony within complexity and discovering in each celestial motion a deeper resonance. In this vision, astronomy becomes an act of interpretation, a quest to reveal the hidden music woven into the fabric of the universe.

Building upon this vision of astronomy as a search for meaning and harmony, one finds that this impulse did not begin in the modern age but stretches deep into the past. For the ancients, the study of the stars was inseparable from the pursuit of wisdom. Across civilizations, from Mesopotamia to the Mediterranean, those who mapped the heavens believed they were engaging with the very structure of reality. Thinkers like Aristotle and Ptolemy, even within the constraints of a geocentric worldview, approached the cosmos with a desire to understand the intricate order they perceived above.

Aristotle saw the heavens as the realm of the unchanging and eternal, distinct from the mutable world below the moon. In his *Metaphysics* and *On the Heavens*, he described the celestial spheres as composed of a fifth element—aether—whose perfect circular motions reflected a divine rationality. As he wrote, "The heavens, being unchangeable and eternal, move according to a law and are not moved by chance" (*On the Heavens*, II.13). To Aristotle, the stars did not merely illuminate the night sky; they revealed a higher plane of existence, governed by laws of motion that pointed to the existence of an unmoved mover—a divine intelligence that sustains the cosmic order.

Ptolemy, writing centuries later, carried this vision forward in his *Almagest*, one of the most influential scientific texts of antiquity. Though his geocentric model would later be overturned, his mathematical sophistication and empirical rigor allowed him to predict planetary movements with remarkable accuracy. More importantly, Ptolemy did not see these calculations as mere technical exercises. In his later work, *The Harmonics*, he observed, "Certain musical sounds make us feel certain ways, and so music and our souls are harmonically related. Similarly, as the planets circle the heavens they stand in similar mathematical-musical proportions." He drew a profound connection between the mathematical ratios governing music and those governing the motions of the planets. For Ptolemy, the universe was a harmonious whole, a cosmic system in which mathematical precision revealed a kind of divine music.

When Kepler, Copernicus, and Galileo entered the scene, they extended this inheritance of knowledge. Their discoveries did not shatter the classical vision, as is oft alleged; rather, they illuminated it more fully, peeling back the veil of celestial mystery to reveal ever more of the vast and intricate eurythmy that had long invited human contemplation. Kepler, in particular, explicitly saw his laws of planetary motion as a fulfillment of the classical tradition. The music of the spheres had not vanished. It had simply become more precise. It became more richly understood.

Modern astronomy, when severed from its classical roots, often treats the universe as a lifeless expanse governed only by detached calculation. The vast distances between stars are reduced to abstract numbers, and the motions of planets are treated as little more than mechanical outcomes of force and mass. In such a view, the night sky loses its wonder and becomes a chart of data, stripped of its poetry. The classical astronomer resists a narrowing of vision. He approaches the heavens with reverence. The path of a planet speaks to him of a hidden order, as if each orbit were shaped by a mind beyond human comprehension. The sun's steady pull evokes more than physical law. It reflects a deeper unity, a principle that binds not just matter but meaning. Even the slow drift of the stars carries for him the weight of significance, pointing beyond themselves to a cosmos alive with purpose.

Consider the moment when a student comes to understand Kepler's third law: that the time a planet takes to orbit the sun is bound in a precise relationship to the size of its orbit. The law astonishes not only because it is true, but because it is graceful. Its power lies in the way it uncovers a hidden order within the motions of the heavens. What once appeared as irregular and wandering now takes on the form of deliberate motion, governed by a deep coherence. The planets no longer seem to drift aimlessly through space; they move with a purpose that can be expressed in a single, unifying principle. When the student sees this, something more than knowledge takes root. There is a moment of clarity, almost of joy, as the mind perceives that the universe does not merely function. It sings. The experience is as much aesthetic as it is intellectual, a glimpse of beauty through the language of mathematics, where structure and meaning are one.

This fusion of thought and wonder lies at the very core of classical astronomy. When one first glimpses Saturn's rings through a telescope, the response is no less than a moment of awe. Their symmetry stirs something deeper than curiosity; it evokes admiration. Upon learning that these rings consist of innumerable ice particles, each following its own precise path, the mind does more than absorb a scientific fact; it beholds an elegant resolution to the challenge of orbital stability. Similarly, when the spiral arms of a distant galaxy come into view, the impression left is not simply one of structure, but of form shaped by unseen laws that govern the whole. These experiences do not divide understanding from beauty but unite them. The knowledge gained is not complete without the sense of order it unveils, and the beauty perceived is not separate from the truth revealed. In this tradition, aesthetic perception is an essential part of what it means to truly know.

And what of the human place in this celestial order? This question, too, draws a clear distinction between the classical and the modern imagination. The classical mind refuses to accept that the immensity of the cosmos renders human life trivial. Beneath the arc of the heavens, it finds invitation. To observe the slow rise of Orion above the eastern horizon on a winter's night, or to mark the annual retreat of Arcturus toward the west, is to take part in a rhythm that predates and outlasts civilizations. These are not meaningless movements; they are part of a larger order in which the human intellect has a rightful role.

For the classical thinker, the ability of the human mind to comprehend this order is itself a sign of participation in it. Ptolemy wrote in the *Almagest* that "the goal of astronomy is to save the phenomena,"[19] not to erase wonder but to explain it in a way that deepens reverence. Aristotle held that contemplation of the heavens was the highest activity of the rational soul, and in this he saw evidence of human dignity. As he asserts in the *Nicomachean Ethics*, "For contemplation is both the highest form of activity . . . and also it is the most continuous, for we can reflect more continuously than we can carry on any form of action" (X.7). In this light, the stars do not diminish us; they call us upward. That we can chart the orbit of Mars, decode the shifting patterns of planetary retrograde, or grasp the subtle distortions of light caused by a distant black hole are not accidental abilities. These acts reveal a mind attuned both to its surroundings as well as to the deeper structure behind them. We are not simply creatures who endure within the cosmos. We are beings who seek to know it. Though our bodies are fragile and our years few, something within us reaches beyond those limits. The same order that governs the stars seems to resonate within the soul that longs to understand them. And while the stars remain far above, the desire to uncover their meaning lives close at hand. This longing, this search, belongs to us.

This act of "reaching beyond" reveals one of astronomy's most profound effects: it stretches the imagination beyond the limits of daily experience, unsettling the illusion that the present moment and the familiar world are all that matter. When a student comes to understand that the light entering the telescope began its journey long before the first cities rose or the earliest histories were written, time itself takes on new depth. The realization that this light has crossed vast, silent expanses before meeting the eye transforms a simple observation into a kind of communion with the ancient past. Likewise, the growing awareness of the immense gulfs between stars begins to reshape the mind. What once seemed like a sky full of scattered points now appears as a vast, ordered structure whose scale defies ordinary reckoning. The habitual sense that Earth stands at the center of things gives way to a broader vision, one that invites humility

19 Claudius Ptolemy. *Ptolemy's Almagest.* Translated by G. J. Toomer, Princeton University Press, 1998.

rather than self-importance. And yet, this expanded view does not leave humanity adrift in meaninglessness. On the contrary, it situates us within a grander narrative. By glimpsing the vastness of time and space, we come to see that our choices and inquiries are not isolated acts, but moments within a drama far larger than ourselves. In contemplating the cosmos, we are not reduced. We are elevated.

This perspective unsettles the narrow sense of time that pervades much of modern culture—a culture that often dismisses the inheritance of the past and treats the present as the culmination of all that came before. The mind shaped by astronomy, however, sees the present differently. It understands that this moment, for all its urgency, is brief when set against the scale of cosmic time. It grasps that our beliefs are not free-floating truths but are often shaped by the age in which we live.

Such an awareness fosters a humility born of proportion. We begin to see that our certainties, however well-reasoned, may one day be judged with the same puzzled amusement we sometimes reserve for ancient models of the universe. Yet this is not a license for doubt without direction. It is an invitation to think more carefully, to participate in the pursuit of truth with both conviction and modesty. For the recognition that we are limited does not diminish the reality of truth; it simply reminds us that our grasp of it must always be accompanied by humility and wonder.

Astronomical understanding also confronts the narrowness of vision that sees human concerns as the ultimate standard of value. This view often places Earth at the center not just of physical models, but of meaning itself, as though the worth of the cosmos could be measured by its relevance to human affairs. As Thomas Aquinas argued in his *Summa Theologiae*, the universe's vast order exists primarily for the glory of God, its diverse elements reflecting divine wisdom rather than merely serving human ends (I, Q. 65, Art. 2). By revealing the grandeur of the cosmos, astronomy decenters human pretensions, inviting contemplation of a divine purpose that transcends earthly measures of significance. From this recognition of the universe's God-given autonomy, the classical astronomer steps forward to engage its mysteries directly. He observes a vast order that unfolds independently of human desires, a structure governed by laws that neither require nor respond to our approval. And yet, this awareness does not diminish the human presence. It deepens it. To recognize that the stars shine whether or not anyone watches is not to feel excluded from their grandeur but to marvel all the more at our ability to understand them. Yet it is instructive to note that we alone, among all known creatures, can study the stars and grasp their harmony. In doing so, we come to see more clearly the remarkable capacity we possess: not to control or contain the universe, but to comprehend it.

Modern man, however, often mistakes this gift for license. The power to understand instead becomes the pretext to dominate, to bend the natural world to human will as though knowledge were merely a tool for mastery. This Promethean urge, cloaked in the language of progress, drives us not toward greater harmony with the universe but toward its exploitation. Consider the Manhattan Project, where scientific insight into atomic structure was mobilized to create weapons of unprecedented destructive power. Or the rise of algorithmic surveillance, where sophisticated knowledge of human behavior and data is used to control populations rather than to understand or liberate them. The modern approach is to measure the stars to mine their secrets; we study the laws of nature less to marvel at their elegance than to subvert their limits. This impulse is not born of reverence. It is an ambitious desire to *impose* rather than to *receive*. With this approach, we diminish ourselves. For in seeking to control what surpasses us, we forget what ennobles us. The classical astronomer did not look to the heavens to conquer them. He looked upward in awe and reverence to be instructed, to enter into a conversation with an order not of his own making. The modern mind, shaped by the machinery of utility and the appetite for manipulation, often refuses to see what cannot be used or altered. What once inspired wonder now becomes raw material for "innovation." And when the world is approached in this spirit, its deeper meanings begin to recede. The stars do not stop shining, but they cease to speak. Knowledge, once the servant of wisdom, is made into an instrument of power. In that reversal, the soul grows dim. It is not understanding that endangers us, but our unwillingness to be changed by it.

By contrast, the student who engages deeply with astronomical reality gradually acquires what philosopher Owen Barfield called "final participation,"[20] a conscious engagement with the cosmos that emerges not from ignorance, but from understanding. This "final participation" is not a passive awe, but an active co-creation of meaning. The universe astonishes not because its laws are unknown, but because those laws reveal an order that resonates with the mind's capacity to perceive it. The student recognizes that meaning and material causation intertwine, as a universe lawful enough to be known fosters a mind that shapes its significance. In this dynamic interplay, scientific insight and philosophical reflection unite. Such a disposition is the true aim of classical astronomy, cultivating a vision where understanding deepens the mind's participation in cosmic reality, illuminating its mystery.

To study astronomy in the classical tradition is to approach the cosmos with reverence rather than suspicion. The stars are not obstacles to be explained away but invitations to deeper understanding.

Astronomy, then, is an art of recognition, a poetic discipline that insists upon wonder. It is an ancient endeavor made new with every observation, a lifelong conversation with the heavens in which each generation refines the insights of the last. It is the study of time itself, the echoes of light across distances so vast they render human history a fleeting flicker. To study astronomy in the classical tradition is to approach the cosmos with reverence rather than suspicion. The stars are not obstacles to be explained away but invitations to deeper understanding. In the quiet precision of their movements, one senses a kind of music, structured yet mysterious. Dante's *Divine Comedy* captures this vision with poetic depth, guiding the reader through a universe where order and meaning are not imposed but discovered. In such a cosmos, nebulae glow as signs of creative intention. The steady path of each planet suggests more than calculation; it reveals a design that awakens both the intellect and the imagination. Here, the universe is not a void but a realm suffused with significance. It is a place where knowledge and wonder grow together.

---

20 Owen Barfield. *Saving the Appearances: A Study in Idolatry.* Wesleyan University Press, 1988.

Let us, then, approach astronomy as more than a technical pursuit. Let it be a discipline that frees the mind from the narrow confines of the immediate and the familiar. At its best, it trains the eye to observe with precision while inviting the soul to reflect with wonder. It reveals that the same heavens we chart with numbers can also move us toward wisdom. Through the study of celestial motion, students come to glimpse harmony discovered within the structure of the universe itself. As they grasp the scale and order of the cosmos, they learn how the heavens move and how thought can rise above the ordinary to touch something enduring.

Astronomy, rightly taught, awakens the human capacity to see with both clarity and reverence. Its value lies in the transformation it brings about in those who learn to ask deeper questions. The ability to measure distances beyond reach and trace events beyond memory reminds us that the power to understand the universe is itself a wonder worthy of contemplation.

Recommended Further Reading

1. *The Starry Messenger* (*Sidereus Nuncius*) by Galileo Galilei. The foundational work that revealed the beauty and order of celestial bodies through telescopic observation.
2. *Harmonies of the World* by Johannes Kepler. Explores how mathematical harmony underlies planetary motion, connecting cosmic order with aesthetic beauty.
3. *Cosmos* by Alexander von Humboldt. A masterwork that integrates scientific observation with philosophical reflection on cosmic wonder.
4. *Saving the Appearances* by Owen Barfield. Analyzes how human consciousness participates in creating meaning from astronomical observation.
5. *The Sleepwalkers* by Arthur Koestler. Chronicles how great astronomical discoveries emerged from both scientific rigor and intuitive wonder.
6. *The Sky: A User's Guide* by David Levy. Explores how direct astronomical observation cultivates both scientific understanding and wonder.
7. *God and the Astronomers* by Robert Jastrow. Examines how modern astronomy leads to profound philosophical and theological questions.

Chapter 20

The Subversive Art of Pursuing Beauty through Architecture

How classical design principles restore meaning to our built environment

I made mention in earlier chapters of a curious blindness in our age, a strange incapacity to see what stands plainly before us, as if we wandered past a blazing sun and called it shadow. Let us now consider our modern neglect of classical architecture, that splendid language of proportion and harmony which once shaped the soul of civilization itself. This is no mere shift in taste, but a deeper confusion, a notion that the order of our buildings springs from arbitrary whim rather than a glimpse of eternal truth. To call beauty in stone a mere decoration is to mistake a window for a wall. It is as if a man, standing in a library, forgot how to read, yet fancied himself wise. We have lost not just an art, but a way of seeing that binds truth to the world we build.

This forgetfulness that lingers despite the constant testimony of human experience is astonishing, because it upends a wisdom once as plain as daylight. The great tradition of Western building, the noble art that raised the Parthenon and the Gothic cathedral, did not treat architecture as a flight of fancy. The architect (once understood and translated as "chief craftsman") approached his craft as a discovery of truth, as if each column, arch, and vault revealed a hidden score of the universe's music. Every proportion, every line, every carefully measured space testified to an order already present in nature, a harmony waiting to be found rather than invented. Our ancestors shaped their cities to echo this cosmic rhythm, imbuing stone with meaning and lending the human spirit a sense of belonging. In the modern age, by contrast, we too often erect structures without reverence, producing spaces that neither elevate nor endure, that speak of utility alone and neglect the music that once guided human hands. This classical understanding of beauty as "truth made visible" stood at the heart of what we might call the traditional vision of architecture. Thinkers and builders from Vitruvius to Alberti, from Palladio to Jefferson, embraced this vision. They recognized that aesthetic principles were not human inventions. They were, rather, understood as discoveries of patterns inherent in reality itself. The architects of the past did not believe they were imposing order upon a formless world. Rather, they held that the world already possessed a deep and intelligible structure, and that their task was to uncover and echo that structure in stone. Vitruvius articulates this clearly in his *Ten Books of Architecture* (*De Architectura*), the oldest known treatise to catalog the fundamental principles of order, arrangement, symmetry, eurythmy, propriety, and economy. In doing so, he draws extensively on the wisdom of the Greeks, particularly as embodied in their temple architecture. The Parthenon in Athens, for example, exemplifies proportion and symmetry, with its careful column spacing and subtle optical corrections reflecting a deep understanding of visual harmony. The Temple of Apollo at Delphi demonstrates propriety and eurythmy, balancing ritual function with aesthetic grace. Through these and other structures, Vitruvius shows how Greek architects discovered, rather than invented, enduring principles that govern both beauty and utility in the built environment. To build with classical understanding was to answer a call already present in the nature of things. The proportions of a temple or the rhythm of a facade were not crafted as inventions of the mind. They were received as echoes of a deeper harmony. Architects worked not as creators of order, but as stewards of a truth they had no authority to rewrite. They possessed only the wisdom to reveal. Architecture, in this view, was not what titillated the senses or flattered contemporary taste. It revealed through visible form the underlying structures of reality, allowing the eye to perceive what the mind might otherwise miss: the ordered intelligence at the heart of existence.

To speak of classical architecture is to engage with a structured language, one as precise as mathematics, as expressive as poetry, and as purposeful as any system of communication devised to order human experience. The classical tradition, developed over millennia, is fundamentally about ordering the elements of the built environment to foster understanding and to shape human experience in a way that is both intelligible and ennobling. Rooted in the pursuit of harmony and intelligibility, classical architecture is governed by key principles that, much like the rules of language or mathematical axioms, form a framework through which architects translate material into meaning, shaping the structures that define our cultural and civic life.

Order, in the architectural sense, is the systematic arrangement of elements according to established rules. It is an expression of logic and hierarchy that renders the built environment legible. Just as syntax in language dictates the proper sequence of words to convey meaning, architectural order ensures that individual elements relate coherently to one another and to the whole. It is no aesthetic preference but an intellectual framework that transforms raw material into a meaningful composition. This principle is most clearly embodied in the classical orders—Doric, Ionic, and Corinthian—which function as a structured vocabulary, each with its own syntax of proportion, ornament, and spatial relationships. The application of order extends beyond individual columns and entablatures to the entire organization of buildings and urban spaces. From the articulation of facades to the sequencing of rooms and courtyards, order provides the logic that underpins classical architecture's ability to communicate clearly and with purpose.

Arrangement, in Vitruvian terms, concerns the thoughtful placement of architectural elements to achieve clarity, hierarchy, and functional harmony. It ensures that each component—columns, walls, doorways, and windows—occupies a deliberate position in relation to the whole, guiding the eye and the body through space with purpose. Well-considered arrangement also balances aesthetic and practical concerns, organizing circulation, light, and visual focus while reinforcing the building's intended message or function. In Greek temples, for instance, the positioning of the cella, pronaos, and peristyle created a progression from the public to the sacred, while in Roman forums, the sequencing of basilicas, porticos, and open courts orchestrated both civic activity and visual impact. Through careful arrangement, architecture communicates order, meaning, and experience simultaneously, ensuring that every element contributes to a coherent, legible whole.

Symmetry, much like balance in an argument or rhythm in verse, governs the equilibrium of architectural form. It ensures that architectural compositions resonate with a sense of stability and intention, reinforcing the innate human preference for order and predictability. Beyond mere visual regularity, symmetry influences movement and spatial perception. A symmetrical facade welcomes the observer with a sense of repose and stability, while an interior arranged according to symmetrical principles offers an intuitive sense of orientation and flow. Just as coherent language fosters understanding, symmetry in architecture fosters a spatial dialogue between form and inhabitant.

Proportion, which Vitruvius describes as the foundation of eurythmy, provides the mathematical underpinning of architectural harmony, ensuring that relationships between parts are meaningful and intelligible. It functions in architecture much as meter governs poetry or harmony governs music: an unseen but deeply felt order that shapes the experience of a space. Classical architects employed a variety of proportional systems to achieve balance and elegance. The golden ratio, approximately 1:1.618, recurs in nature, art, and architecture, imparting an ineffable sense of harmony to structures. Pythagorean musical ratios informed the dimensions of walls, columns, and openings, establishing consonance between parts much as intervals create balance in sound. Human bodily proportions, articulated by Vitruvius and immortalized in Leonardo da Vinci's *Vitruvian Man*, ensured that buildings were attuned to the scale and rhythm of human experience. These proportional relationships governed everything from the height and width of columns to the overall dimensions of rooms and facades, creating spaces in which every component relates meaningfully to the whole. In such a well-proportioned building, the coherence is immediately grasped, even when the precise rules remain implicit, fulfilling the Vitruvian ideal of eurythmy as visible harmony that unites human perception with architectural form. Eurthymy, sometimes translated as "harmony," is the synthesis of diverse elements into a unified whole, much like the interplay of syntax and diction creates literary eloquence. It is the resolution of competing forces—solid and void, structure and ornament, mass and light—into a composition that feels both inevitable and effortless. Achieving harmony demands more than intuition. It requires the disciplined application of proportional relationships and the careful sequencing of architectural elements. Harmony also emerges from a thoughtful balance between structure and ornament, where each detail reinforces the whole rather than competing with it. Just as a well-crafted sentence integrates clauses seamlessly, a harmonious building integrates disparate parts into a cohesive entity. Ornament must enhance rather than overwhelm, mass must be counterbalanced by open space, and complexity must be tempered by clarity. When executed successfully, harmony in architecture produces an experience akin to reading a masterfully written passage: a moment of recognition, of understanding, of aesthetic and intellectual satisfaction.

Ornament is architecture's rhetorical flourish, its means of articulating structure, function, and meaning. Far from mere decoration, ornament serves as a visual grammar that reinforces architectural logic. Just as rhetorical devices in language clarify and emphasize meaning, classical ornament enriches the built environment by making its structural principles legible and engaging. Ornament serves as a bridge between the rational and the expressive, transforming abstract principles into tangible beauty. It ensures that architecture, like language, remains not just functional but meaningful, engaging the intellect as well as the senses.

The language of classical architecture has long been an evolving system of communication, one that has endured because it is rooted in universal principles of human perception and cognition. Just as grammar structures language and mathematical laws structure the physical world, classical architecture structures space in a way that is intelligible, purposeful, and elevating. The classical tradition speaks across centuries, a silent witness to the human impulse to create order and beauty from the chaos of material existence. In the Doric, one senses a spirit that values strength without show. In the Ionic, there is a suggestion of cultivated grace, a kind of thoughtfulness made stone. The Corinthian, more intricate and lively, seems to rejoice in the sheer possibility of order shaped into beauty. These are not just means of construction. They are imaginations made visible—statements, almost, about what it means to carry the weight of the world and yet remain upright.

The principles of classical architecture are vital keys to understanding a deeper, almost forgotten order—an order of space, form, and proportion that once governed the way we built and lived. Classical architecture, like a language, speaks to us in the structure of columns and arches, the precision of geometries and ratios. It's a language that, when understood, grants access to a kind of intellectual clarity, an aesthetic grammar that mirrors the syntax of language or the logic of mathematical equations. Just as students of Latin decode the structures of sentence and syntax, so too must students of classical architecture decipher the formal rules that underlie the design of buildings, comprehending not only how to construct with stone but how to read the deeper, universal principles that shape our built environment.

Classical architecture, like a language, speaks to us in the structure of columns and arches, the precision of geometries and ratios. It's a language that, when understood, grants access to a kind of intellectual clarity, an aesthetic grammar that mirrors the syntax of language or the logic of mathematical equations.

The classical tradition, developed over millennia, is fundamentally about ordering the elements of the built environment to foster understanding and to shape human experience in a way that is both intelligible and ennobling. Rooted in the pursuit of harmony and intelligibility, classical architecture is governed by fundamental principles that form a framework through which architects translate material into meaning, shaping the structures that define our cultural and civic life.

Consider the analogy of language. Just as one might learn to conjugate verbs in Latin or memorize the irregularities of French grammar, so too must a student of classical architecture learn to "conjugate" the elements of design. The column, the entablature, and the pediment, for example, are tools that function as symbolic devices that make sense of the world's chaos, organizing the intangible energies of human desire and ambition into visible, permanent structures. These tools have a syntax: the Ionic column versus the Doric, the semicircular arch versus the elliptical, the balance of weight and space that grounds the design as surely as a sentence relies on subject and predicate. Like the rules of grammar, the elements of classical architecture must be understood as integral parts of a whole system. Break the rules, and you risk distorting meaning; follow them, and the result is clarity—clarity of vision, of form, of space. The same can be said of a beautiful quatrain or an orderly equation.

When classical students first encounter the Parthenon, they see more than an ancient ruin; they behold a kind of argument in stone. Its proportions, according to Vitruvius, reflect that mysterious harmony known as the golden ratio—a recurring numerical relationship that was observed by the ancient Greeks and acknowledged as a law of nature written into the grain of the world. The Greeks did not carve such a structure from whim or accident; they built according to a conviction that beauty was not a matter of taste but of truth, that a building might echo the balance of a well-ordered soul. In tracing the lines of the Parthenon, students begin to sense the deeper aim of Greek architecture: to reveal the underlying unity between the physical world and the moral order.

This insight, once glimpsed, begins to shape the way students move through history. In time, they arrive at the Renaissance, and with it, the rebirth of ancient ideals. Here again they find the golden ratio, a sign of something rediscovered and revered. When they study Bramante's Tempietto, for example, they are not simply analyzing a structure; they are witnessing a moment when architecture sought once more to align itself with enduring truth. The small domed sanctuary, rising with calm precision on its circular plan, speaks of more than geometry. It reflects a worldview, revived after centuries of neglect, in which reason and faith, nature and number, came again into harmony. To study the Tempietto is to study an age that believed form could speak—and that what it said mattered.

But their discovery does not remain in the realm of marble and drawing. As they turn from the pages of architectural treatises to the living patterns of nature, students begin to find the same proportions at work in the world around them. In the unassuming spirals of a seashell, in the unfolding of leaves toward the sun, even in the humble seed-head of a sunflower, there reappears that same mysterious ratio. Nature, it seems, is fluent in this mathematical language—and long before human beings gave it a name, she had already written it across her works.

In the study of these patterns, another thread begins to emerge. Students come to see how the golden ratio and the Fibonacci sequence move in tandem, how number and growth dance together in a kind of silent music. What was once a chapter in a math book now appears as a key—opening doors not only in science, but in art and philosophy. And in making these connections, they begin to see with different eyes. They come to understand that truth is not locked in any one discipline, but rises up where fields of knowledge meet and enrich one another.

In the study of classical architecture, we find a profound harmony between the world of art and the world of mathematics, between the poetic and the precise.

In the study of classical architecture, we find a profound harmony between the world of art and the world of mathematics, between the poetic and the precise. The Doric column is not just a stylized form of decoration but a logical manifestation of the geometric principles that govern our reality. The proportions of a building, derived from the Fibonacci sequence or the golden ratio, resonate with the same mathematical elegance that drives the natural world. When students learn to recognize these patterns, they learn not only to read architecture, they learn to read the world itself.

This is the heart of the classical approach: not the compartmentalization of subjects, but their communion. When students study ancient literature alongside Latin, or explore natural forms while considering the designs of Vitruvius, they are not leaping from one topic to another. They walk a unified path, drawn deeper into the mystery of a world that is coherent, beautiful, and purposeful. Instead of merely mastering material, they are encouraged to reflect on how that material reveals meaning. Through this, educators aim to cultivate in them more than academic skill—a sense of wonder and an openness to discerning harmony, whether in a cathedral or a pine cone.

They pursue an education that extends beyond the classroom, finding resonance between their studies and their lives. The golden ratio serves not only as a design principle but also as a symbol of a purposeful, nonrandom world. It reveals to them a universe marked by intention, where their creations and lives can reflect a higher order. In exploring it, they do not merely study history; they learn to dwell in a world that is both rational and radiant, a world where truth and beauty remain united, and where knowledge, rightly sought, becomes an act of reverence.

To use the golden ratio, then, is not to indulge a personal fancy, as though beauty were a matter of whim. It is to confess that reality has a structure, and that the work of the craftsman is, at its best, a participation in that structure. He does not speak a dialect of his own invention, but a tongue already inscribed into nature. His task is to listen and to translate—not to command, but to echo.

Classical architecture functions not just as an art, but as a language—one that, if taught with rigor and insight, offers its students a richer, more profound understanding of the world they inhabit. It is an education in how to read the world through structures. It is the deciphering of a syntax that governs not only the construction of walls but the arrangement of the universe. In this sense, classical architecture becomes a way of understanding the language of the world, and perhaps more significantly, a means to speak back to it. In this way, classical architecture can be seen as a language not unlike Latin. A student of Latin must first memorize vocabulary words, but then learns how these words interact within the larger framework of syntax and grammar. He learns how words function together to create meaning, how small shifts in structure can create entirely different outcomes, how the flow of a sentence depends not just on the words themselves but on their relationship to each other. So too the student of classical architecture learns that achieving harmony in architecture requires a careful and disciplined understanding of how each element relates to the whole. Palladio's Villa Rotonda demonstrates this through its perfect symmetry and the way the proportions of its porticos and dome create a subtle dialogue between interior and exterior spaces. The building's sense of balance emerges naturally, guiding the viewer's perception without drawing attention to individual components. In the Laurentian Library, for example, Michelangelo shapes movement and perspective so that the stairs, columns, and reading rooms work together to produce a continuous experience of order and rhythm. The spatial composition conveys intention and coherence, transforming practical necessities into an expression of intellectual and aesthetic principles. In both cases, the architecture communicates through the disciplined interplay of parts, teaching students to read and understand the language of classical design as a reflection of beauty and order.

Moreover, just as the study of Latin unlocks the history of thought and culture, so too does classical architecture reveal the history of human society and intellect. It is the embodiment of culture's intellectual evolution, from the geometric precision of the Greek temple to the soaring, harmonious designs of the Renaissance. It is an education in how different epochs have shaped the principles of beauty and order, how human beings have, over time, come to articulate their aspirations through material forms. The classical principles are living evidence of the intellectual movements that birthed them: an intellectual grammar whose cadence can be traced across centuries, from the lofty ideals of ancient Greece to the grand visions of Palladio, Wren, and Jefferson.

To introduce students to these principles is not so much to teach them how to design buildings, although they may one day go on to do that. It is to introduce them to a method of thinking, to a mode of inquiry that transcends architecture and permeates all human intellectual endeavor. The precision of a classical building's proportions, the interplay of light and shadow across its surfaces, mirrors the precision of a mathematical proof. Mathematics itself, the purest of languages, relies on a careful order of symbols and operations to communicate a fundamental truth. In much the same way, classical architecture relies on a harmonious balance of form, function, and aesthetic to communicate a certain truth about human existence. Just as a properly balanced equation reveals a truth about the nature of numbers, so too does a well-proportioned building reveal truths about the relationship between the human body, the surrounding environment, and the cosmos.

And so, for educators in classical schools, teaching the principles of classical architecture is an invitation to show students the world through a new lens, if the modernist vernacular term may be used, a lens where geometry and poetry coalesce, where form and function converse, and where the lessons of the past are not just remembered, but brought into a new understanding. In teaching students to see architecture not merely as a physical discipline but as a language, they open the door to a fuller, richer comprehension of the world they inhabit, one that is as structured, precise, and beautiful as the language of Latin, or the harmony of a perfect equation.

This literacy becomes increasingly countercultural—and therefore increasingly subversive—as our built environment becomes more dominated by commercial interests, technological determinism, and the cult of novelty. The student who understands the grammar of classical architecture possesses a critical tool for evaluating contemporary buildings, for discriminating between genuine innovation and mere novelty, between meaningful adaptation of tradition and empty historicism, between buildings that will nurture human flourishing and those that will diminish it. He has, in effect, a balderdash detector for the built environment, a means of distinguishing between architecture that serves genuine human needs and that which merely serves the ego of its creator or the profit of its developer.

The classical school that teaches architectural principles thus performs a profoundly countercultural service: preserving a vocabulary for beauty in an age of ugliness, cultivating discrimination in a culture of aesthetic relativism, and nurturing a sense of continuity in a world obsessed with rupture and revolution.

Recommended Further Reading

1. *The Ten Books on Architecture* by Vitruvius. The foundational classical text on architectural principles that shaped Western building traditions for centuries.
2. *The Classical Language of Architecture* by John Summerson. A masterful introduction to reading and understanding the grammar of classical design.
3. *The Four Books of Architecture* by Andrea Palladio. The Renaissance master's influential treatise on classical proportion and design principles.

4. *On the Art of Building in Ten Books* by Leon Battista Alberti. The Renaissance humanist's comprehensive treatise that systematized classical architectural principles and connected them to civic virtue and human flourishing.
5. *Elements and Theory of Architecture* by Julien Guadet. The influential text that codified classical design methodology and continues to influence traditional architecture education today.
6. *The Aesthetics of Architecture* by Roger Scruton. A philosophical exploration of how classical design principles reflect deeper truths about human nature.
7. *A History of Architecture on the Comparative Method* by Sir Banister Fletcher. The definitive reference work that systematically analyzes architectural traditions throughout history, with particular emphasis on the classical language of architecture and its global variations.

Part V

Subversive Acts of Digital Resistance

Chapter 21

The Subversive Art of Resisting Technological Determinism

Why human formation cannot be delegated to algorithms

In recent years, the integration of artificial intelligence into education has been heralded as both a revolutionary breakthrough and an inevitable progression. The heralds of this New Inevitability—and they are legion—announce with perfect confidence and impeccable credentials that the latest digital innovation will finally transform education forever. These prophets of techno-optimism speak with a peculiar blend of revolutionary zeal and corporate pragmatism, promising "disruption" in the language of quarterly reports and radical transformation through the medium of PowerPoint slides—or the latest equivalent. They assure us that while previous technological revolutions—be it the internet, the iPad, the smartboard, or the smartphone—may have fallen short of their educational promises, this one, most emphatically artificial intelligence will deliver us to a pedagogical promised land where learning is frictionless, personalized, and efficient.

Techno-optimism, at its core, is a kind of faith, often unexamined, that each algorithmic advance is a step toward utopia. Among the high priests of AI, it takes the form of an unshakable belief that machine intelligence will bring boundless efficiency, endless insight, and perhaps even a painless transcendence of our human limitations. Beneath this optimism hums a quiet eschatology: the hope that progress, encoded and recursive, will redeem us faster than we can ruin ourselves.

These proclamations reverberate with regularity through the echo chambers of institutional prestige and technological ambition. Whether on the TED stage, at high-profile tech summits, or in the musings of Silicon Valley titans like Marc Andreessen and Bill Gates, one hears the same confident refrain. Across the broader landscape of techno-optimist discourse, such declarations resurface with almost liturgical consistency, asserting that AI will—and must—reshape education as we know it.

What makes these declarations particularly noteworthy is not any novel insight but their perfect distillation of the assumptions that govern elite discourse about technology and education, assumptions so deeply embedded in the worldview of the professional-managerial class that they are no longer recognized as assumptions at all but rather as simple and obvious truths requiring at most a token gesture acknowledging potential complications. These assumptions, laid bare for those with eyes to see, constitute a kind of implicit theology of technological progress, a faith system complete with its own eschatology, soteriology, and moral imperatives.

There is a growing mythos in our cultural imagination that treats technological progress as a kind of destiny rather than a set of choices. This belief, maintained with remarkable certainty by people who pride themselves on rationality, holds that technological developments arrive not as human choices but as forces of nature, beyond questioning or democratic deliberation. This superstition manifests most vividly in discussions of artificial intelligence in education. The rhetoric shifts from possibility to inevitability with practiced smoothness. AI-driven learning isn't presented merely as an option worth considering but as an inexorable tide to which institutions must adapt or perish, more akin to a meteorological event rather than a series of deliberate human decisions about how and what students should learn.

The first and most fundamental of these articles of faith is what critics might call the Doctrine of Inevitable Adaptation. According to this belief, technological developments occur with the force of natural law, beyond human agency or choice, requiring only acceptance and adjustment rather than evaluation or deliberation. Techno-optimists express this dogma with perfect clarity when they assure their audiences that educational institutions "will adapt" to AI just as they adapted to previous technologies, that academic departments "will change" in response to AI's capacities, that the educational landscape will be transformed whether we like it or not. The only question, in this view, is not whether to embrace AI but how quickly and thoroughly to surrender to its inevitable advance.

What makes this technological determinism so remarkable isn't just its fatalism but its convenient inconsistency. Our educational technocrats oscillate effortlessly between presenting algorithms as natural phenomena (when implementation is questioned) and celebrating them as brilliant human achievements (when their capabilities are praised). Technology becomes cosmic inevitability in one breath and heroic innovation in the next. This rhetorical pendulum swings with suspicious precision. When concerns arise about privacy, equity, or the diminishment of human connection in learning, technology is framed as an unstoppable force. Resistance is futile. Adaptation is the only rational response. Yet in the next moment, these same innovations are presented as triumphs of human ingenuity deserving substantial rewards and acclaim.

The very same prophets who insist that technological advancement unfolds with the inevitability of gravity—beyond the reach of human will or democratic oversight—are often the same voices who tout their own ingenuity in designing, deploying, and monetizing these innovations. The algorithm is cast as an unstoppable natural force when critics raise questions, but as a triumph of human creativity when its achievements are being lauded. This convenient oscillation between determinism and voluntarism permits the techno-optimist to claim credit for progress while evading accountability for its consequences—a rhetorical sleight of hand that might be seen as innocuously ironic were it not so effective in foreclosing serious public deliberation about the future we are, in fact, choosing.

It's a worldview that manages to be simultaneously deterministic and self-congratulatory. Technology arrives like weather, yet somehow warrants stock options and keynote speeches for its creators. This intellectual sleight of hand wouldn't matter if it weren't so effective at shutting down the conversations about educational values and choices that we most urgently need.

The truth, of course, is that artificial intelligence in education did not arrive by accident. It came into being through deliberate decisions, shaped by those with particular aims and convictions. These technologies reflect the priorities of the institutions that produced them and the purposes for which they were designed. It is important to reiterate that any given technology's presence in education is not the result of some unstoppable momentum but of choices made at many levels, choices that could have gone in other directions. To acknowledge this is to recognize that we are not merely passengers on a technological current but participants in shaping its course. The path forward depends not on what machines can do, but on what we believe education is for and how we intend to form the next generation.

The truth, of course, is that artificial intelligence in education did not arrive by accident. It came into being through deliberate decisions, shaped by those with particular aims and convictions. These technologies reflect the priorities of the institutions that produced them and the purposes for which they were designed.

It is worth noting, too, that their motivation lies not in improving education or enriching the lives of students, but in capturing markets and maximizing returns.

The second article of the techno-optimist creed might be called the Principle of Utilitarian Disruption. This is the belief that technologies should be judged primarily by their ability to maximize efficiency, minimize effort, and eliminate inconvenience. Other goods—such as depth of understanding, the quality of human relationships, and the formation of character—receive, at best, cursory attention.

This utilitarian framework is most clearly expressed in the obsession with quantifiable outcomes and measurable efficiencies that dominates techno-optimist discourse. Artificial intelligence is celebrated because it can grade more papers, process more information, and generate more content, all with less expenditure of human effort. Nowhere is this more evident than in the rhetoric surrounding "cognitive offloading," which reduces education not as the cultivation of intellect and virtue, but as a logistical challenge to be optimized. Education is sadly mistaken for an exercise in data transmission and task automation, and learning is thus reduced to inputs and outputs, never mind the initiation of the young into the moral and intellectual inheritance of civilization. The question of whether these efficiencies serve or undermine deeper purposes is quickly brushed aside, drowned out by the unrelenting jargon of optimization, streamlining, and enhancement.

The prevailing enthusiasm for AI in elite educational discourse carries with it a particular vision of learning. In this view, education becomes a system for producing efficient minds, optimized for performance and measurable outcomes. Instruction is shaped around tasks that yield clear data, and students are trained to operate within frameworks that mirror the logic of machines. This approach fits comfortably within an economic system that prizes speed, adaptability, and output. The deeper aims of classical education, those that concern the shaping of character, the pursuit of truth, and the development of wisdom, tend to fade from view, not through explicit denial, but through quiet neglect. As schools become sites of technical refinement, the fuller dimensions of human formation are increasingly set aside.

The third and perhaps most insidious element of the techno-optimist faith is what critics identify as the Myth of Neutral Enhancement. This is the notion that technologies like AI represent mere tools that amplify human capabilities without altering their essential nature. This myth allows techno-optimists to present AI as simply "augmenting" education rather than replacing or reconceptualizing it.

What this view ignores is the profound way in which AI tools shape not merely what humans can do but what they want to do, not just how they work but what they consider worth doing. The student who turns to AI for essay writing may appear to gain efficiency, but the cost is deeper than missed practice. He begins to lose sight of argument as a process of discovery, mistaking it instead for a product that can be manufactured on demand. Writing no longer feels like the slow shaping of thought but like a task to be outsourced, and in the process his very sense of thinking starts to thin out. The professor who relies on AI to grade papers may also save time, yet the trade-off is significant. Evaluation becomes less an act of personal engagement and more a mechanical sorting, which diminishes the feedback students receive and erodes the relationship that makes teaching formative rather than transactional.

Consider the writing process, which draws students into a slow and often demanding engagement with language, thought, and discovery. Through this engagement, students come to understand that writing is not merely a way to convey what they already know. More importantly, the student comes to understand that writing is an important means through which knowledge itself is formed. The effort to shape an idea into words often clarifies that idea, revealing its limits, its implications, or even its instability. In this way, the difficulty of writing becomes essential to learning. Those who champion AI's role in writing, however, tend to focus on how it might reduce the time or difficulty involved. By producing text quickly or offering immediate feedback, the tools appear to streamline a burdensome process. But when students delegate the labor of articulation to a machine, something more than a task is shifted.

The integration of AI into education often proceeds under the assumption that existing goals remain intact, merely supported by new tools. Yet as these tools are taken up, they begin to influence how those goals are understood. What once seemed clear—what it means to learn, to understand, to grow intellectually—slowly takes on a different shape. The demands of the technology begin to guide how learning is framed, how it is structured, and what is ultimately pursued. As this process unfolds, subtle shifts occur. The human richness of education can begin to give way to more streamlined patterns of engagement. Depth becomes harder to sustain. The focus moves toward what can be more easily captured and managed. And through this gradual transformation, the heart of education may come to resemble the logic of the machine rather than the needs of the student.

This reshaping of purposes to fit technological affordances—what philosophers of technology call "reverse adaptation," whereby humans modify their goals to match what their technologies can readily provide—remains largely unacknowledged in the techno-optimist account. Instead, society is offered a vision of technologies that merely extend existing capacities, enhance current practices, and serve predefined ends, rather than one that acknowledges how profoundly tools reshape our understanding of ourselves and our activities, including education.

The fourth article of the techno-optimist creed might be termed Salvation Through Personalization, the belief that technologies like AI will finally deliver the long-sought Holy Grail of education perfectly tailored to each student's unique needs, interests, and capacities. Proponents gesture toward this ideal when they imagine students who "might feel more comfortable asking questions of an AI," suggesting that the machine offers a kind of pedagogical perfection: infinitely patient, endlessly responsive, and miraculously free from the flaws of human teachers.

But this vision collapses a crucial distinction: the difference between personalization and genuine relationship. Instruction finely tuned to individual preferences is not the same as an encounter with another thinking, feeling person who challenges, stretches, and calls the student to move beyond his current horizons. At its best, the student-teacher relationship is not a frictionless transactional exchange of information, but a transformative dialogue—often difficult, sometimes uncomfortable—that awakens new forms of understanding, self-awareness, and growth. The AI, however sophisticated, offers only a simulation of this encounter. It is effectively a digital mirror that reflects and reinforces what is already there, rather than the human presence that beckons toward what might yet be.

The final, and perhaps most foundational, tenet of the techno-optimist creed is what might be aptly termed the Dogma of Information Equivalence: the implicit belief that education is chiefly the transmission of information and the acquisition of discrete, utilitarian "skills," rather than the cultivation of judgment, the refinement of taste, the formation of character, and the pursuit of wisdom. This assumption underwrites the claim that AI is educationally "transformative" simply because it can access, process, and efficiently generate enormous volumes of information, as though learning were primarily an informational problem rather than a human and moral endeavor.

Nowhere is this reductionist vision more evident than in discussions of mathematics, where AI is presumed to render certain computational skills obsolete while shifting curricular emphasis to others. Yet what often goes unexamined is whether mathematics education is ultimately about computing answers, or whether it is, more profoundly, about developing habits of mind, modes of reasoning, and intellectual virtues that are bound up with the very processes AI proposes to bypass. If the aim of mathematical education is to shape disciplined thought, foster abstraction, and instill a deep sense of order and truth, then the kind of "cognitive offloading" so enthusiastically embraced by AI proponents does not enhance learning—it evades its essential purpose.

Similar questions arise across the curriculum. Does writing education aim primarily at producing grammatically correct prose expressing clear ideas—something AI can indeed help with—or at developing the capacity to discover what one thinks through the act of articulating it, to refine understanding through the struggle for expression, to find one's voice through the discipline of putting words on the page? Does history education aim primarily at acquiring accurate information about the past—something AI can certainly facilitate, though not always accurately—or at developing the capacity to evaluate competing interpretations, to recognize the difference between primary and secondary sources, to understand how narrative frameworks shape our perception of events? Does scientific education aim primarily at learning existing theories and experimental results—information readily available through AI—or at developing the habits of observation, hypothesis formation, experimental design, and interpreting evidence that characterize genuine scientific thinking?

In each case, the techno-optimist account assumes an informational model of education that aligns conveniently with what AI systems can provide, while ignoring or minimizing the formational dimensions of learning that may be inseparable from precisely the cognitive "labors" that AI promises to eliminate or reduce.

What emerges from these articles of techno-optimist faith is a vision of education remarkably aligned with the values and interests of the professional-managerial class, a vision that prioritizes efficiency over depth, and fails to recognize the importance of moral formation and the passing on of a cultural inheritance. It is a vision that treats education primarily as preparation for economic functionality rather than as formation for full humanity, that values what can be quantified over what must be qualitatively discerned, that prioritizes what serves market needs over what develops human capacities that may have no immediate economic utility.

This vision manifests not through crude instrumentalism—techno-optimists are too sophisticated for that—but through subtle emphasis, implicit framing, and the cumulative weight of assumptions left unexamined. They acknowledge potential concerns about AI in education, but these acknowledgments function more as inoculation against deeper critique than as serious engagement with the profound questions that AI raises about the nature and purpose of education itself. Their calls to be "highly mindful of the risks of cognitive offloading" serve not to question the informational model of education that makes such offloading seem appropriate but merely to suggest moderation in its implementation, a classic example of what philosopher Albert Borgmann calls "the device paradigm," wherein technological systems are accepted in principle while their potential excesses are rhetorically managed through appeals to responsible use.

The close relationship between technological enthusiasm and economic interest often passes without scrutiny in conversations about AI's educational potential. The boldest claims about AI's role in transforming learning rarely come from those immersed in the daily work of teaching and mentoring students. Instead, they are most often voiced by individuals whose roles place them at a distance from the classroom and whose professional goals align with models of education centered on efficiency and productivity. Their language of innovation and disruption carries with it more than technical evaluation—it reflects a worldview shaped by institutional priorities and ideological commitments.

The boldest claims about AI's role in transforming learning rarely come from those immersed in the daily work of teaching and mentoring students. Instead, they are most often voiced by individuals whose roles place them at a distance from the classroom and whose professional goals align with models of education centered on efficiency and productivity.

Within this framework, the enduring purposes of education gradually lose visibility. The patient work of shaping judgment, nurturing discernment, and guiding the growth of character becomes harder to articulate in systems governed by metrics and optimization. These dimensions of learning, though more difficult to quantify, remain essential to the educational endeavor. When AI systems are introduced as substitutes for pedagogical relationships, the risk is not only a change in method but a quiet redefinition of the end toward which education aims.

In contrast to the prevailing techno-optimist vision, classical education offers a genuinely countercultural alternative, one that conceives of education not as a system for processing information or adapting to technological change, but as a humanizing enterprise aimed at the formation of the whole person. Rather than viewing students as nodes in a network or inputs in an economic engine, classical education treats them as souls to be cultivated through engagement with enduring truths, serious inquiry, and the lived experience of a shared cultural inheritance. It does not reject technology outright but insists that its use must be subordinate to purposes rooted in the nature and dignity of the human person.

Where the advocates of AI begin with the question of utility—how best to integrate the latest tool—classical educators begin with a deeper question: what is the primary purpose of education? Before assessing the usefulness of any new device, classical education requires a clear understanding of its ultimate ends. These ends cannot be determined by market forces or technical capability alone. It sees education not as the passive absorption of content or the efficient acquisition of competencies, but as a long and often difficult apprenticeship in wisdom, virtue, and self-governance—a preparation not simply for work, but for living a meaningful life.

Classical education proceeds from a different starting point. It understands education as a formative endeavor, one that aims at shaping the whole person through sustained engagement with enduring ideas, meaningful texts, and serious intellectual effort. This vision is animated by a belief that learning is not simply a matter of acquiring techniques or responding to external pressures, but a matter of becoming.

Where the advocates of AI begin with the question of utility—how best to integrate the latest tool—classical educators begin with a deeper question: what is the primary purpose of education?

The classical approach to education rests on a particular understanding of the human person. It sees the student not as a machine to be optimized, but as a being shaped by relationships, habits, and ideals. Learning, from this perspective, engages the whole person—mind, heart, and character—through sustained effort and meaningful encounters with what is worth knowing and becoming. The tools brought into this process, including those offered by artificial intelligence, must be considered in light of this understanding. Their value depends not on what they can do, but on what kind of growth they make possible. At each point, the guiding question becomes whether a given tool strengthens or weakens the formative work at the heart of true education.

From the standpoint of classical education, the role of AI must be determined not by what technology makes possible or what markets demand, but by a clear understanding of what education is for. When used judiciously—perhaps to extend access to certain resources, to support practice in discrete tasks, or to free the teacher for more meaningful engagement—AI may offer limited assistance. But when it begins to displace the elements that make education formative rather than merely functional, its promise turns hollow. No algorithm, no matter how sophisticated, can replicate the depth of a real human encounter or the intellectual discipline forged through sustained effort when presented with a content-rich curriculum. When seamless efficiency supplants the hard-won struggle that builds intellectual character, the result is not enhancement but erosion.

Within this framework, technology may play a role, but that role remains secondary. Tools are welcomed when they serve genuine educational ends, but they are never allowed to define what those ends must be.

Attending to the deeper aims of education calls for a kind of discernment that looks beyond novelty or utility. It requires a thoughtful approach to new technologies—one that asks how they relate to the deeper task of forming human beings. This approach resists the temptation to let tools reshape the ends they are meant to serve. It holds fast to the idea that educational questions reach into the realm of meaning, purpose, and human good. The way forward depends on the clarity with which we understand what education is for and what kind of persons we hope to cultivate through it.

This formational understanding explains why the classroom remains the essential locus of education despite centuries of technological innovation allegedly threatening to replace it. From correspondence courses to educational radio, from television lectures to early computer-based instruction, from MOOCs to the latest AI applications, waves of technological enthusiasm have repeatedly proclaimed the imminent obsolescence of traditional educational forms. Yet the classroom persists not from institutional inertia or resistance to change but because education at its best involves precisely the kind of embodied, relational, integrative experiences that technological mediation struggles to provide: experiences of intellectual community, of dialogue and disagreement, of shared inquiry and discovery, of mutual recognition and challenge, of the subtle interplay between explicit instruction and implicit formation that occurs when human beings learn together under the guidance of those further along the path of understanding.

Some argue that the shortcomings of contemporary classroom teaching create a need for technological solutions that can compensate for what is lacking. Yet the real need lies in a renewal of sound educational practice. When teaching falls short, the answer is found in returning to methods that have long proven effective—approaches grounded in thoughtful pedagogy, careful instruction, and meaningful relationships between teachers and students. The path forward involves cultivating a culture of serious teaching and learning, where the teacher's presence, example, and guidance shape the student's intellectual and moral growth.

This persistence does not mean that classrooms should or will remain unchanged by technological developments, including AI. It means rather that the effective integration of technology into education requires understanding the distinctive value of embodied, relational learning rather than simply assuming that more technology always means better education. It means recognizing that the proper role of AI in learning emerges not from technological possibility or market demand but from substantive educational purposes that may sometimes be enhanced and sometimes undermined by technological mediation. And it means insisting that educational policy and practice be guided by these purposes rather than by the institutional imperatives or ideological commitments that often drive technological adoption in educational settings.

Unlike the techno-optimist narrative, which cloaks itself in inevitability and appeals to the logic of optimization, the classical vision rests on an altogether different foundation. It arises from a richer understanding of human nature and a firmer grasp of what education is ultimately meant to accomplish. Its concern is not with keeping pace with innovation, but with forming persons who are thoughtful, self-governing, and attuned to the demands of truth, beauty, and goodness. In this light, education is not a race toward ever-greater efficiency, but a moral and intellectual apprenticeship. It is at once a cultivation of judgment, an awakening of the soul, and a preparation for a life worth living.

In this light, the techno-optimist vision of education appears not as the balanced assessment of inevitable technological change that it presents itself to be. Rather, its particular conception of education is shaped by specific values, assumptions, and interests that align conveniently with those of the techno-capitalist order. The classical educator responds to techno-optimism with insistence on proper ordering—on the priority of human formation over technological possibilities. This response recognizes that the question is not whether education will change in response to technological developments—it surely will and always has—but whether those changes will be guided by substantive understanding of educational purposes or merely by the technological, economic, and ideological currents of the moment. Do we really want Bill Gates or Marc Andreessen to plot our course in education?

At its heart, the debate over AI in education turns not on the merits of the technology itself, but on fundamentally different visions of what education ought to be. One vision treats education as a means of keeping pace with a changing economy, where the goal is adaptation and the measure of success is efficiency. The other sees education as a deeply human endeavor, oriented toward the cultivation of judgment and moral character and understanding. The techno-optimist perspective, dominant in much public discourse, mirrors the assumptions of a market-driven culture in which acceleration and utility are mistaken for progress. By contrast, the classical vision insists that educational tools must be judged in light of enduring truths about human nature and the moral ends of learning. It asks not what technology can do, but what human beings are for—and how education can help them become what they are meant to be.

Artificial intelligence in education emerges from deliberate human decisions. It reflects the intentions of those who design and deploy it, shaped by the values and assumptions they bring to their work. Its presence in schools grows not from necessity but from choices made about the direction of learning. Understanding its role in education calls for thoughtful reflection on the nature and purpose of learning itself—reflection that draws on philosophical insight, moral seriousness, and educational experience. These are the capacities that guide wise decision-making in shaping the future of education.

It is also worth acknowledging this important truth: education has survived for millennia without the assistance of AI; it can continue to do so.

It is also worth acknowledging this important truth: education has survived for millennia without the assistance of AI; it can continue to do so.

Let us, then, approach AI in education not with the breathless enthusiasm of techno-prophets, but with the thoughtful discernment proper to educators concerned with genuine human formation. Let us ask how AI might serve or undermine the development of wisdom, virtue, judgment, and appreciation that constitute genuine educational aims. Let us evaluate technological tools not by their novelty but by their capacity to support substantive educational purposes that transcend mere information processing. And let us resist the false inevitability that techno-optimists present, recognizing that how we incorporate technologies like AI into education represents not passive adaptation to unstoppable change, but active choice shaped by our understanding of what education is and ought to be.

Recommended for Further Reading

1. *The Dumbest Generation* by Mark Bauerlein. Documents how digital technologies diminish rather than enhance intellectual development in students.
2. *Alone Together* by Sherry Turkle. Examines how technological mediation transforms human relationships and undermines authentic connection.

3. *The Glass Cage* by Nicholas Carr. Explores how automation, including educational technology, creates learned helplessness and skill atrophy.
4. *The Flickering Mind* by Todd Oppenheimer. Investigates the false promises of computer technology in education through decades of evidence.
5. *Technopoly* by Neil Postman. Examines how technology redefines cultural institutions including education when efficiency becomes the primary value.
6. *Shop Class as Soulcraft* by Matthew Crawford. Defends the cognitive value of manual work against technological abstraction and outsourcing.
7. *The Shallows* by Nicholas Carr. Documents how digital technologies reshape neural pathways and diminish capacity for deep thought and contemplation.

Chapter 22

The Subversive Art of Technological Discernment

Why wise use of tools requires wisdom beyond the tools themselves

Thirty years ago, a New York University professor argued that Americans were drifting, seemingly unaware, into a soft form of technological tyranny—not enforced by government decree, but eagerly adopted, purchased, and celebrated, much like the dystopia imagined in Aldous Huxley's *Brave New World*. Neil Postman's *Technopoly: The Surrender of Culture to Technology* didn't predict smartphones or social media, but it mapped the mental landscape that would make us desperately want them. Today, as we debate whether artificial intelligence will save or doom us, Postman's framework feels less like prophecy than like reading glasses, suddenly bringing into focus patterns that were always there, hiding in plain sight. What makes Postman's work so remarkable is not merely its Huxleyan prescience, though it certainly possesses that quality in abundance, but its peculiar position in our intellectual landscape—respected yet disregarded. *Technopoly*, a kind of sequel to his 1985 polemic *Amusing Ourselves to Death*, is a book that many educated people know they ought to have read without having actually read it. Alas, it is a text more cited than understood, more praised than heeded. It represents our collective capacity to recognize wisdom while systematically failing to act upon it, like a man who nods vigorously at his doctor's warning about his diet while reaching for another chocolate éclair.

Postman's work offers a central insight that remains both accessible and deeply illuminating: technologies function not just as tools at our disposal but as environments that subtly shape how we think, what we value, and how we relate to one another. When a society adopts a new technological system, it does more than increase its capabilities. It enters a new framework for understanding reality. With each new development, familiar habits and assumptions are gradually reoriented. Certain activities become more central, while others fade from view or lose significance. The deeper questions about technology, then, concern not just its functions or benefits, but the ways it reorganizes attention, reshapes priorities, and alters the conditions in which human life unfolds.

Postman's ecological understanding of technology reveals its role as a powerful influence in shaping human thought and social experience. Rather than functioning only as a means to fulfill established purposes, technology gradually influences how those very purposes are understood. Think of the internet, the iPad, the smartphone. The effects of these technologies are not confined to improved function or enhanced convenience. Instead, they quietly reframe our assumptions about what is desirable, what counts as success, and how time and value are measured. In this view, technology does not simply operate within human goals but contributes to the ongoing formation of those goals, becoming an active participant in shaping our understanding of what it means to live, to learn, and to act in the world.

Consider education. As explored in the previous chapter, the ancient art of soul-craft is increasingly being reconceived as a technical problem awaiting technological solution. The modern school, enthralled by this gospel of innovation, has become a servile arm of technological determinism, trading wisdom for data. The classroom, once the sacred domain of the teacher, is now a shrine to digitized "learning experiences" whose fundamental assumption is that the newest tool is the best tool and that "twenty-first-century skills" represent not merely adaptations to contemporary conditions but objective advances over the capacities and virtues cultivated in previous eras.

Technological enthusiasm often carries with it an unspoken assumption: that the tools now available serve to support and improve what education has always aimed to do. Yet beneath this optimism lies a quieter transformation. Digital tools do not merely assist in carrying out familiar tasks; they begin to recast the nature of those tasks, subtly altering the aims they once served. What appears as continuity in vocabulary often masks a shift in substance, as the practices associated with learning adapt to fit the logics of the digital environment. When students work within systems that guide their choices, structure their responses, and supply information in carefully designed fragments, the experience of learning begins to follow different contours. These shifts do not announce themselves with trumpet blasts, yet over time they reshape how students conceive of knowledge, how they relate to intellectual effort, and how they come to understand the work of learning itself.

The transformation of education into a process focused on data reflects the cultural condition Postman described as "Technopoly." In this condition, technology comes to define the framework through which human purposes are understood. Rather than serving broader goals, technological standards begin to shape those goals. Efficiency takes on an unquestioned status, information gains authority without the need for deeper reflection, and innovation becomes a virtue in itself, often pursued without clarity about what is being altered or to what end.

The rise of Technopoly in education becomes most evident in the way knowledge is increasingly treated as mere information, and the way data is mistaken for wisdom. This outlook aligns neatly with what digital technologies are best equipped to handle, but in doing so, it sets aside deeper forms of learning that resist digitization or automation. Classrooms equipped with the latest tools are often successful in distributing content, yet they rarely succeed in fostering judgment, taste, or deep understanding. Education is approached as a problem of delivery and measurement rather than as an effort to shape the whole human person—mind, heart, and character.

This view takes root most obviously in the language now used to describe education. Students are viewed primarily as receivers of information. They are passive consumers in a delivery system rather than embodied souls engaged in the slow, formative process of becoming. The rich tradition of education as the cultivation of wisdom and virtue is quietly displaced by sterile metaphors borrowed from business and technology:

"learning outcomes," "content delivery," "data-driven instruction." Teachers, once stewards of a living tradition, are now expected to "facilitate learning" and "manage engagement," as if they were technicians in a behavioral lab rather than mentors guiding the moral and intellectual development of the young. Schools are increasingly designed to optimize efficiency, standardization, and scalability. They are not imagined as communities of inquiry or character formation but as cold, modular systems for distributing disaggregated content.

Teachers, once stewards of a living tradition, are now expected to "facilitate learning" and "manage engagement," as if they were technicians in a behavioral lab rather than mentors guiding the moral and intellectual development of the young.

These shifts in language and structure are not neutral; they signal a fundamental change in how we conceive of education itself. What was once understood as a humane and dialogical enterprise is being refitted to serve the imperatives of a technocratic culture, one that prioritizes metrics over meaning. The new model fits the logic of our machines, not the nature of our humanity. It promises optimization but often yields alienation, replacing the shared search for truth with the efficient transmission of trivia. And in doing so, it quietly erodes the goods that education exists to cultivate: attention, wonder, character, memory, judgment, and the capacity to love what is true and good.

The classical model of education, by contrast, offers a vision rooted in enduring human needs and aspirations. It continues to uphold practices and purposes that remain vital even as they become less visible in contemporary discourse. Education, in this view, seeks to shape students in ways that prepare them to contribute thoughtfully and meaningfully to the shared life of culture and civilization. This shaping happens through long-term engagement with meaningful ideas and works, guided by those whose experience and understanding provide orientation. It relies on the slow development of habits and dispositions that are not easily measured but are essential to a life of depth and purpose.

The technological and classical approaches to education emerge from fundamentally different ways of understanding what education is and what it seeks to accomplish. One approach tends to frame education in terms of delivery systems, outcomes, and functional readiness for modern demands. The other sees it as a human endeavor oriented toward the growth of the person in depth and character. These differing views are not merely about pedagogical technique or classroom tools; they reflect opposing intuitions about what it means to live well and to be fully formed. The conversation that surrounds educational reform, then, is shaped less by debates over devices or programs and more by these underlying assumptions about purpose and meaning. What Postman helped us perceive is that such divergences are not accidental. They arise from a broader cultural disposition, one that treats technology as the primary lens through which to understand progress and another that remains attentive to the deeper effects of our tools on the human soul. This is not so much a debate about whether to use technology, but about how to remain faithful to those enduring insights that ought to shape our choices, even in an age of constant innovation.

The classical educator meets the pressures of a technocentric age with a quiet but firm resolve to keep first things first. Rather than allowing the excitement of new tools to dictate the shape of the classroom, the educator begins with a clear vision of the proper ends of education and lets that vision determine how, or whether, technology plays a role. This approach does not reject innovation but subjects it to deeper reflection, measuring its worth by its capacity to support genuine formation rather than distract from it. It draws upon the long memory of education's history—a history in which tools have always played a part—yet resists the temptation to let tools become the masters of their own use. In this posture, what matters is not whether a device is available or impressive, but whether it helps bring students more fully into the habits of attention, the depth of understanding, and the cultivated relationships that education, at its best, has always sought to foster.

At the core of Postman's concern lies a call to recover the habit of asking deep and prior questions about what education is and what it is for, questions that risk being silenced in an age too quick to equate innovation with progress. He warned not against tools themselves, but against a cultural mood in which the presence of a new device seems to settle the question of whether it ought to be used. Nowhere is this more evident than in the current enthusiasm for artificial intelligence in education. We are told, with great urgency, that AI is necessary—necessary to keep pace with global competitors, to personalize instruction, to automate feedback, to fill gaps left by teacher shortages, to prepare students for the so-called future of work, on and on and on. But beneath these appeals lies an unexamined assumption: that the educational enterprise must conform itself to the capabilities and logics of the newest technologies, rather than shaping those technologies according to the enduring aims of education.

Seldom acknowledged, yet deeply significant, is the role of interest and incentive behind the widespread push for AI in education. Those most actively advancing this movement often approach the classroom not as a place of formation, but as an opportunity for expansion—an arena where new technologies can gain foothold, generate profit, and secure influence. Their engagement with education tends to be shaped less by pedagogical commitment than by the strategic logic of the marketplace. As AI tools are introduced with the promise of transformation, the metrics used to justify their presence often reflect commercial priorities rather than educational ones. In this context, the emphasis shifts away from the growth of the student and toward the optimization of systems, where what matters most is not what kind of persons are being formed, but how efficiently and widely a product can be adopted.

We find ourselves in a world that moves faster than it thinks, where technologies are adopted because they exist, because competitors are using them, because investors expect growth—not because they have been shown to deepen learning or enrich the life of the mind. The simple act of pausing to ask whether a given tool serves or distorts the purposes of education begins to seem out of place, not because the questions lack merit, but because the surrounding culture has ceased to provide the conceptual and institutional space in which they can be seriously considered. This is the essence of Technopoly: not a world without questions, but a world in which the most important ones no longer seem worth asking.

The most insidious feature of our current educational landscape is the quiet but thorough surrender of cultural authority to the demands of technology. What Postman foresaw is now plainly visible: schools no longer defend the integrity of their formative mission but increasingly allow the tools themselves to dictate the ends they serve. This is not the benign adoption of helpful innovations, but a capitulation in which purposes are hollowed out and replaced by whatever is most compatible with the capabilities of the latest device or platform. The classroom becomes a showroom for gadgets, its pedagogical aims flattened into measurable outputs, its moral and intellectual traditions displaced by the logic of optimization and scalability. Again, this is no mere change in delivery method or instructional supplement. It is a reordering of reality—of what counts as learning, of what constitutes knowledge, of what it means to be educated. The digital apparatus does not support education; it redefines it according to its own values: speed, efficiency, novelty, automation. Under the regime of Technopoly, the school no longer resists this redefinition. It internalizes it, institutionalizes it, and reproduces it. It becomes an instrument not of cultural preservation or moral formation, but of technological indoctrination.

We find ourselves in a world that moves faster than it thinks, where technologies are adopted because they exist, because competitors are using them, because investors expect growth—not because they have been shown to deepen learning or enrich the life of the mind.

This condition finds haunting literary expression in Ray Bradbury's *Fahrenheit 451*, where the chatty Clarisse McClellan serves as a fragile but luminous symbol of what authentic education might look like—an education grounded in curiosity, wonder, conversation, and attentive perception of the world. Clarisse is not a rebel in the conventional sense, but she is dangerous to Bradbury's dystopian society because she still remembers what it means to be truly human. She walks, talks, observes the sky, tastes the rain, asks questions. And for this, she is regarded as abnormal, even pathological. Her schooling, as she describes it, offers no real learning—only distraction, conformity, and coercion. Students are bombarded with facts but deprived of meaning; they are conditioned to react, not reflect; to consume information, not contemplate truth.

This dystopian educational vision, once thought the stuff of speculative fiction, has crept alarmingly close to reality. Today's schools increasingly mirror the world Clarisse fled from. Rather than inviting students into the slow, sometimes painful labor of formation—of reading deeply, thinking carefully, engaging in discussions over big questions—they are asked to interface with screens, complete modules, generate outputs, and adapt to systems designed for tracking rather than teaching. The values that define digital technologies—speed, surface, segmentation—shape both the content and form of education, leaving little room for the habits of mind Clarisse embodies: attention, leisure, silence, memory.

And just as in Bradbury's imagined future, those who resist or even question this transformation are subtly pathologized. They are "behind the times," "anti-technology," "holding back innovation." The philosophical questions are not even asked, because the logic of Technopoly has already rendered them unintelligible. As in *Fahrenheit 451*, where books were not banned all at once but gradually abandoned, we risk losing not only the content of tradition but the capacity to care that it be preserved. Clarisse's marginalization is not the result of overt oppression. Rather, it is the quiet, cumulative effect of a culture that no longer sees the value of wonder, dialogue, or the past. In such a world, the school ceases to be a bulwark against forgetting. It becomes an accelerator of the Great Forgetting, a pipeline not to wisdom but to utility. In the name of progress, it extinguishes those human faculties that genuine education was meant to kindle.

Likewise, the modern school no longer functions as a sanctuary for thought or formation. It has become a staging ground for obedience, an institutional pipeline designed not to educate but to condition. In its unthinking embrace of every new device or platform, it hollows out the capacities that education was once meant to nourish. Reflection gives way to reaction; depth is replaced with speed; memory is subordinated to search. Students are trained to meet the demands of the digital machine but left unformed in the deeper faculties of mind and character. What the school now rewards is not intellectual independence or moral clarity, but a kind of practiced docility, an ease with the systems in place and an instinctive accommodation to their logic.

Rather than cultivating free and thoughtful individuals, it manufactures compliant users, fluent in interfaces but estranged from inquiry, familiar with networks but severed from heritage. The student, once imagined as an heir to civilization's accumulated wisdom, is recast as a consumer of content streams and a generator of outputs. There is no space left for silence or for difficulty—only for acceleration, integration, and performance within systems whose values remain unexamined. In surrendering itself to these mechanisms, the school betrays its oldest and most sacred duty: to draw the young into an inheritance of reason, virtue, and judgment that might equip them not only to navigate the world but to understand why it is worth navigating at all. In this light, what is so often celebrated as innovation reveals itself more truthfully as abdication. The school no longer stands apart from the forces that shape mass consciousness. It no longer questions, tempers, or resists the tides of technology and commerce. It becomes their most efficient agent: the institutional face of a culture that confuses progress with motion and advancement with surrender.

> *The student, once imagined as an heir to civilization's accumulated wisdom, is recast as a consumer of content streams and a generator of outputs. There is no space left for silence or for difficulty—only for acceleration, integration, and performance within systems whose values remain unexamined.*

This abdication is vividly imagined in Lois Lowry's *The Giver*, where the school is no longer a place of initiation into truth but a tool for erasing history, suppressing emotion, and regulating thought. The children of that society learn to conform, to obey, and above all, to forget. They are trained to comply, to follow procedures. What passes for education is in fact a process of containment: the elimination of difference, the flattening of experience, and the systematic prevention of memory. Only the Receiver of Memory is permitted to know the world as it truly is, to see beyond the sterile sameness into the depths of human joy and sorrow. And yet the need for such a figure testifies to the profound failure of the educational order: a society that must assign memory to a single custodian is one that has already abandoned its collective soul.

Our own trajectory, while less overt, bears troubling resemblance. For what the modern school now promotes under the banner of "twenty-first-century skills" or "digital readiness" is often nothing more than the systemic removal of every obstacle to technological immersion. With each app deployed, each screen introduced, each data system installed, the possibility of a genuinely human education slips further from view. We are no longer educating children to be free human beings; we are training them to be efficient functionaries in systems whose purposes they are never taught to question.

The true tragedy, however, is not that the machine has taken over the classroom, but that the school itself has welcomed it, embraced it, and evangelized on its behalf. It is no longer the monastery preserving the light of civilization in a darkening age; it is the showroom, brightly lit, hawking the instruments of our cultural eclipse.

The enduring relevance of Postman's warnings lies in their ruthless exposure of a culture enthralled by its own machinery. He forces us to see what we are otherwise conditioned to overlook: that technology is never neutral, never merely a set of tools awaiting responsible use, but a powerful cultural force that remakes the world in its image. It does not enter the classroom—or the human imagination—harmlessly. It rewrites the purposes of education, recasts the meaning of knowledge, and quietly substitutes the conditions of understanding with the illusions of access and speed. Postman does not ask us to tinker with our tools; he demands that we confront what those tools are doing to us. To ask whether a technology "works" is already to submit to its logic. The deeper questions—what kind of human activity it displaces, what kind of soul it cultivates, what kind of world it quietly builds—are the ones our institutions have forgotten how to ask. Or worse, no longer wish to ask.

As artificial intelligence embeds itself into the classroom, the language of promise—optimization, personalization, enhancement—masks a deeper concession. AI does not simply alter instructional technique; it recasts the conditions of education. Beneath the enthusiasm for speed and adaptability lies a fundamental failure to grasp what learning demands: not automation, but struggle. The student who relinquishes the labor of thinking to a machine does not become more efficient; he becomes something else entirely. He trades the slow, formational work of reasoning for the passive act of prompting and selecting. What is lost is not time but the internal transformation that only difficulty makes possible.

This shift is not additive; it is corrosive. It hollows out the educational process from within, replacing inquiry with interface. And yet, it is marketed not only as progress but as inevitable. Here, Postman's warning echoes with renewed urgency. The danger is not malfunction but misdirection—not that AI will fail to perform, but that it will perform perfectly while quietly severing education from its human purposes. The systems will deliver on every measurable metric, all while displacing the unmeasurable dimensions of wisdom, judgment, and self-knowledge.

In a culture eager to outsource its thinking, the school becomes complicit, not just by adopting these tools, but by surrendering the authority to ask what they are for. The classroom risks becoming a delivery mechanism for whatever the latest software promises. The student becomes a user. The teacher becomes a technician. And education itself becomes a simulation—efficient, seamless, and empty.

Postman did not write to defend the past. He wrote to demand that we remain human. His critique is not a call to reject every innovation, but to submit each to the judgment of values that precede and transcend it. Education is not the management of information or the training of skills; it is the cultivation of persons capable of living wisely within a shared inheritance. When the school forgets this, it does not modernize. It abdicates its calling.

Recommended Further Reading

1. *That Hideous Strength* by C. S. Lewis. Explores how scientific materialism and technocratic control systems attempt to eliminate the human soul and natural order, revealing the spiritual dimensions of technological totalitarianism.
2. *Brave New World* by Aldous Huxley. Depicts a dystopia where technological comfort creates willing submission to dehumanizing systems.
3. *Fahrenheit 451* by Ray Bradbury. Illustrates how education becomes a tool for conformity rather than formation when wonder and questioning are eliminated.
4. *The Giver* by Lois Lowry. Shows how educational systems can become mechanisms for erasing memory and suppressing human depth.

5. *The Technological Bluff* by Jacques Ellul. Reveals how technological discourse masks the loss of human agency and meaningful choice.
6. *Tools for Conviviality* by Ivan Illich. Distinguishes between technologies that enhance human capability and those that create dependency.
7. *You Are Not a Gadget* by Jaron Lanier. Argues that digital culture, dominated by algorithms and crowd-sourced thinking, risks flattening human individuality and creativity by reducing people to data and machines to be optimized.

Chapter 23

The Subversive Art of Analog Thinking

How non-digital approaches preserve uniquely human cognition

The quiet act of choosing slowness has become an act of rebellion. To pick up a pencil now signals backwardness rather than contemplation. To write by hand appears as stubborn refusal rather than deliberate practice. To think without digital mediation registers as aberrant behavior—a rejection of evolution itself. The prevailing orthodoxy no longer proposes technology as a tool; it demands submission to it as a creed. To be modern, to be taken seriously in educational circles, one must inhabit the digital order unquestioningly, not use it judiciously. Speed has become virtue, and the algorithmic spectacle has dazzled us into a capitulation we mistake for inevitability.

This is not progress. Beneath the sleek rhetoric of innovation lies a profound impoverishment: the systematic erasure of the analog mind—that slow, embodied intelligence forged through the discipline of reading, shaped by dialogue, and refined through the patient work of hands. This mind carries the memory of pen moving across paper, of thought taking physical form through the act of writing, of ideas emerging from silence rather than stimulus. Cultivated through stillness rather than speed, this way of thinking is being abandoned with quiet obedience and without grief. To resist this abandonment is to refuse the terms of what is being engineered in its place. It means insisting that education must form minds rather than upgrade them, that learning requires depth rather than data processing, and that wisdom emerges from contemplation rather than optimization. In reclaiming the analog, we stage a necessary revolt against the reduction of human consciousness to computational processes.

What makes this new orthodoxy particularly insidious is not its enthusiasm for technology—every era has had its machinery to praise—but its radical inversion of the proper relationship between human mind and tool. No longer do digital instruments extend the reach of human thought; now the mind is reconfigured to resemble the machine. Where once technology served distinctly human ends, now men and women are asked to conform themselves to the demands of computation. This shift reveals itself most clearly in language. Terms such as "upgrade" and "optimization" no longer function as metaphors for reflection but as directives for self-maintenance. Minds are imagined as code bases, subject to revision, testing, and deployment. Students are recast as users moving through digital systems, their growth measured in outputs and protocols. What once unfolded as learning is now processed as compliance, a series of inputs and feedback loops. Dialogue gives way to data streams, and the inner life of the student is reduced to dashboards that track but never understand.

Even the oldest forms of education have been rewritten in code. Chalkboards, lectures, and marginalia are displaced by platforms whose chief function is management rather than instruction. The learning management system assures efficiency, its glowing dashboards pretending to offer insight, red notifications taking the place of Socratic questioning. Essays arrive as files to be stamped and sorted by algorithm. Teachers, meanwhile, are enlisted as custodians of metrics, responsible less for awakening minds than for administering digital performance. The costs are measurable. Studies consistently show that students using digital devices in lectures—eyes flitting between slides, messages, and browser tabs—score lower in comprehension than those wielding pen and notebook. The constant stream of notifications creates what researchers call "attention residue," fragmenting consciousness into manageable, monetizable bits. This represents more than mere inconvenience; it is an epistemological catastrophe. After all, the ability to inhabit a single thought long enough to perceive its shape forms the foundation of intellectual endeavor.

Meanwhile, handwriting—the analog sacrament of education—faces quiet euthanasia, stroke by keystroke. Only a small percentage of schools still bother teaching cursive, having traded ink and loop for typing speeds and Chromebooks. Yet neuroscience reveals what scribes have always known: to write by hand is to embody thought. It is to anchor the ephemeral in the physical through neural pathways that typing cannot replicate. Memory, spatial mapping, and tactile cognition flourish through the marriage of graphite and paper in ways that screens cannot match.

Central to understanding the analog mind is recognizing something the digital economy systematically destroys: the essential role of boredom in human formation. Not the restless kind born of overstimulation, but the spacious kind that precedes insight—the pregnant pause that opens doors to imagination, reflection, and wisdom. The digital marketplace, built on capturing and monetizing attention, operates on the opposite assumption. Every app and interface is designed to eliminate gaps in stimulation. Scroll, swipe, click, repeat—the rhythm of online life compresses the line between stimulus and response until interiority, the slow private unfolding of thought, has no room to emerge. We have learned to fear silence, to fill every moment with input, to mistake the absence of entertainment for the absence of value.

Yet boredom—honest, unstructured boredom—creates the conditions necessary for distinctly human forms of knowing. In the space between activities, minds learn to wander. They begin to make unexpected connections and follow internal rhythms rather than external timers. Children allowed to experience genuine boredom discover something remarkable: thoughts arise naturally when not constantly summoned by notifications. Ideas emerge when the mind is not perpetually reactive. This is the analog mind.

Classical educators understand this intuitively. The great contemplative traditions—from Aristotelian philosophy to monastic practice—have always recognized periods of apparent "unproductivity" as essential to the highest forms of intellectual life. Augustine's *Confessions*, Aquinas's *Summa*, and Dante's *Comedy* all emerged from minds trained in sustained attention, capable of dwelling with questions long enough for profound answers to emerge. And this is precisely why the most subversive act in contemporary education may be the creation of space for boredom. A study hall with no devices. A library period with no assignment. Time to sit with a single book until something stirs within. These practices appear inefficient to administrators trained in optimization metrics, but they cultivate capacities no algorithm can replicate: the ability to be alone with one's thoughts, to pursue questions without immediate answers, to discover interests that arise from within rather than from external stimulation.

If boredom creates the conditions for thought, dialogue provides its natural expression.

If boredom creates the conditions for thought, dialogue provides its natural expression. Here, classical education offers perhaps its most powerful alternative to digital reductionism: the Socratic method, that ancient art of thinking together through speech. In small seminar rooms across classical schools, students gather without laptops, without projectors, without bullet points sliding across screens. The only technology visible might be light bulbs and radiators. Students sit in circles with physical copies of Plato or Tocqueville, speaking slowly, haltingly, sometimes brilliantly into expectant silence. This is not educational nostalgia; it is educational resistance.

The Socratic method refuses the easy flow of digital exchange. It demands presence: eye contact, silence, interruption, the unquantifiable drama of real-time thought unfolding between individuals. Unlike debate clubs or TED Talks, it prioritizes understanding over performance. Questions hang in the air longer than feels comfortable. Answers, when they come, arrive tentatively. Through hesitations and contradictions, something remarkable happens: shared worlds of meaning begin to form.

This ancient pedagogy thrives precisely where digital efficiency fails—in uncertainty, in the slow emergence of understanding, in the irreducible complexity of human conversation. It produces no tidy metrics and generates no data points. Yet it accomplishes something rarer and more valuable: rooms full of people who know how to think aloud in public without fear or fury, who can hold questions in common, who understand that truth emerges through patient attention to both text and neighbor.

Of course, what unites all genuine Socratic discussion is encounter with actual texts—not screens, not hyperlinks, but physical pages where ink meets paper. The materiality of books is not incidental to their educational power; it is foundational. To read on paper engages the mind differently than reading on screens, creating cognitive and even moral formations that digital text cannot replicate. The screen, for all its convenience, invites distraction as a feature rather than a bug. Tabs multiply, notifications ping, hyperlinks beckon toward endless tangents. Reading digitally becomes an act of constant triage, attention perpetually divided between the text at hand and the infinite alternatives a click away. The printed page, by contrast, demands monastic focus. It shuts the door to digital noise, creating boundaries that discipline attention toward depth rather than breadth.

When students annotate physical books—scribbling thoughts in margins, underlining passages, dog-earing pages—they transform reading from consumption to conversation. The book becomes a partner in thought, marked by the traces of encounter, transformed through engagement. This embodied interaction anchors abstract ideas in physical reality, making learning tangible.

Classical schools, by necessity and conviction, are universally pro-book—not merely pro-reading or pro-literacy, but pro-object, pro-shelf, pro-space. Walk into any great classical school library, and you find rooms lined with spines where centuries rest in quiet conversation. Homer leans into Herodotus, Dante brushes shoulders with Aquinas. These are not just names. They are voices—waiting. The presence alone of these volumes reminds students and faculty alike that they are not isolated intellects consuming information but participants in a civilizational inheritance. A shelf of books says: "You belong to something." And that something is weighty, slow, and worth the weight. To build such a library is to make an anthropological statement. It is to assert that the human person is not a processor but a soul capable of attention, memory, and reflection. The digital age, for all its accelerations, has no equivalent to the way a book slows the mind down just enough to let it deepen. The act of reading a physical book is never just informational; it is also ethical and aesthetic. It trains habits of stillness and stamina. It sharpens the senses. It calls forth presence. To build libraries—not just subscriptions or databases but sanctuaries of binding and paper—is to stake a claim for human interiority.

For students, a rich library becomes an analog intellectual habitat. It is where the spark of curiosity meets the patience of study. Where young minds are shaped by prose that doesn't pander, by arguments that unfold slowly, by poetry that refuses to yield its full meaning in a single scan. It is a place where they learn to pursue the good, the true, and the beautiful—yes, through books that demand rereading, and reward it.

For faculty, the library is no less vital. It is the site of professional renewal, of deeper preparation. A teacher who returns regularly to Augustine or Burke is not just reviewing content, but refining judgment. When teachers have access to the great nonfiction works—biography, history, science, philosophy—they are better able to guide students through the complexity of the world without collapsing it into slogans or simplicity.

No, the book is not dead. But it does need defending. It needs defending with space—literal space—for quiet, for shelves, for pages that turn. Every classical school library is a small, stubborn outpost of sanity. A brick-and-mortar declaration that there is still room for memory, for meaning, for minds made strong not by speed but by depth. To furnish such a library is an act of educational fidelity. It is a gift to students and teachers alike. And it is, above all, a commitment to forming human beings capable not just of answering questions, but of asking them. Of sitting with them. Of reading—and rereading—the books that do not expire.

Of course, a library offers more than access to knowledge; it offers permission to linger. To be surrounded by books is to be invited into slowness and silence, it is to be able to experience the unhurried rhythms that serious thought requires. It is in these spaces, away from the hum of devices and the pressures of constant stimulation, that the mind learns to wonder. And it is here that another boredom quietly reasserts itself, opening the door to imagination, reflection, even wisdom.

The renewal of analog education, however, requires more than books and boredom, more than Socratic dialogue and handwritten essays. It demands spaces where mind and hand unite in the ancient dance of making: workshops where students encounter the irreducible reality of materials that resist manipulation, tools that require mastery, projects that unfold according to their own logic rather than digital convenience.

After all, there is something quietly subversive in wood shavings. Curled on the floor of a workshop, they seem like remnants of another era—fragments of a world that moved more slowly, more deliberately. Look closer, and those shavings begin to feel revolutionary. They speak of time spent learning with the hands, of the callus earned from a chisel or a violin bow. When most of our work disappears into the cloud, analog craftsmanship is beginning to reassert itself—not as a nostalgic option, but as necessity.

Woodworking, calligraphy, hand-drawn maps, and even live music all belong to a tradition that once defined the notion of skill. For generations, the apprentice learned by watching, by failing, by trying again. Mistakes were not deleted with a keystroke; they were sanded down, stitched over, or practiced through. Today, that kind of learning seems increasingly rare. We live in a representational culture, one obsessed with simulation. Artificial intelligence can now conjure paintings in the style of Vermeer or compose symphonies at the touch of a button. The ease of the digital world belies something essential: its disconnection from the real.

The real, of course, is difficult. It resists speed. It leaves splinters and demands repetition. It hurts your back and humbles your ego. In short, it builds character—an increasingly unfashionable word, but one that may prove indispensable as we try to raise a generation not just of users but of makers.

The Waldorf schools, long dismissed as whimsical or vaguely cultish with their emphasis on handwork, storytelling, and delayed screen exposure, now seem oddly prescient. Originally founded in 1919 by the Austrian philosopher Rudolf Steiner, Waldorf education prizes the integration of intellectual, artistic, and practical disciplines. That means kindergartners learn to knit before they learn to code, and middle schoolers may spend more time with a hand plane than a Chromebook.

For a long time, this approach was easy to mock. In an era of test scores and STEM panic, it looked like a rejection of progress. Yet the fact is, Waldorf students, more than their peers, can cook without recipes, sew buttons, solder circuits, sharpen blades. They can navigate using analog tools and manage long-term projects without digital reminders. More interestingly, they demonstrate what researchers called "resilience fluency"—a capacity to remain composed and resourceful in unpredictable environments. In other words, they were competent in the face of inconvenience.

It is tempting to see this as a quirky outcome of educational ideology. But craft returns us to a more ancient rhythm. It reintroduces slowness, error, and physical feedback. A bowed cello string does not allow shortcuts. A dovetail joint cannot be photoshopped. None of this is to say that we must all return to the lathe. It does suggest that our obsession with the virtual may have come at a cost. We are losing the feel of things. We touch glass all day but rarely wood, wool, or paper. As digital tools promise more power with less effort, we risk forgetting how effort shapes us and that effort is formative. It requires that we not only try, but try again. That we fail in ways that are instructive. One cannot fake a sonnet or bluff a carved bowl. These crafts require humility—the humility of the novice, the apprentice, the beginner who doesn't yet know how but is willing to learn.

In educational circles, there is growing recognition that this kind of humility may be more important than any particular content area. Employers, too, are beginning to look not just for technical skills, but for habits of mind—perseverance, attention to detail, the ability to learn from feedback. It turns out that sanding a tabletop teaches all three.

All of this points to a crucial strength of classical schools: their commitment to an integrative liberal arts education naturally lends itself to the inclusion of hands-on crafts and embodied learning—not as electives or "extras," but as essential to the intellectual and moral formation of students. Here, geometry is not confined to diagrams on a whiteboard, but comes alive through the construction of models. Literature is not only analyzed but internalized, as students copy great passages with pen and ink. Science unfolds through the texture and tang of real dissections. These practices are not gimmicks. They are reminders that learning is incarnational. That truth has weight, texture, and form. The real world is not something to scroll through, but something to grasp.

This same principle extends to the training of the body. A robust, intentional physical education program—one rooted in the classical ideal of harmonious development—offers a vital analog counterweight to the disembodied tendencies of the digital age. Drawing on the philosophy of Iliad Athletics, we might say that physical education is not ancillary to the intellectual life, but foundational to it. The gymnasium, like the classroom, is a place of formation. Here, students are not simply burning calories or learning rules of a game. They are being shaped in habits of attention, courage, perseverance, humility, and grit. Movement becomes more than exercise; it becomes a philosophical act. We ought to remember that to train the body is to awaken the soul, to cultivate virtues that cannot be downloaded, simulated, or hacked. Through daily physical challenge—running, lifting, climbing, wrestling—students learn the limits and potential of their own bodies. They learn that strength is not given but earned. That pain can be instructive. That fatigue is often the threshold to growth. Most importantly, they begin to see that their bodies are not accessories to their minds but instruments of their humanity.

This vision of education, where even the body is enlisted in the shaping of character, points to a deeper, unified anthropology at the heart of classical schooling. It is the conviction that the human person is not a bundle of separate parts to be trained in isolation, but a single, integrated whole: body, mind, and soul.

Classical physical education affirms what the ancients understood: true education does not cultivate disembodied intellects but forms whole persons. The arena teaches lessons no less profound than the classroom. In the strain of training, the student learns discipline; in the endurance of exertion, fortitude; in the mastery of desire, temperance. These habits of body and spirit prepare him to wrestle with a demanding text, to speak with clarity, and to stand firm when tested by adversity. Physical training, then, is more than exercise. It becomes a kind of embodied pedagogy, a visible enactment of the classical pursuit of the good, the true, and the beautiful—a truth written not only in words but in motion, struggle, and sweat. This vision of education, where even the body is enlisted in the shaping of character, points to a deeper, unified anthropology at the heart of classical schooling. It is the conviction that the human person is not a bundle of separate parts to be trained in isolation, but a single, integrated whole: body, mind, and soul. Just as the arena forms virtue through motion, so too the classroom, the workshop, the studio, and the library are arenas of formation. Each discipline, each encounter with difficulty and beauty, offers a different mode of becoming fully human. Together, they resist the flattening effects of digital reductionism by rooting students in something more elemental, more enduring: the lived reality of human experience.

In reclaiming the analog, classical education reasserts the primacy of the human person—our capacity to think, feel, and create in ways no machine can replicate. The classical approach to education stands as a living alternative to this digital reductionism. It is a deliberate cultivation of distinctively human capacities increasingly threatened by the imperatives of algorithmic thinking. It recognizes that education serves not merely the development of marketable skills but the formation of persons capable of wisdom, virtue, and meaningful participation in "real life."

Recommended Further Reading

1. *The Hand: How Its Use Shapes the Brain, Language, and Human Culture* by Frank Wilson. Reveals the neurological connections between manual work and cognitive development.
2. *The Slow Professor: Challenging the Culture of Speed in the Academy* by Maggie Berg and Barbara K. Seeber. Advocates for contemplative approaches to learning against digital acceleration.
3. *How to Do Nothing: Resisting the Attention Economy* by Jenny Odell. Defends boredom and unstructured time as essential to creativity and critical thinking.
4. *The Revenge of Analog: Real Things and Why They Matter* by David Sax. Documents the resurgence of analog practices as resistance to digital overwhelm.
5. *Deep Work: Rules for Focused Success in a Distracted World* by Cal Newport. Explores how sustained concentration on cognitively demanding tasks creates unique value in the modern economy.
6. *Irresistible: The Rise of Addictive Technology and the Business of Keeping Us Hooked* by Adam Alter. Exposes how digital platforms are designed to capture and fragment human attention.
7. *Bored and Brilliant: How Spacing Out Can Unlock Your Most Productive and Creative Self* by Manoush Zomorodi. Explores how unstructured mental time fosters creativity and insight.

Chapter 24

The Subversive Art of Permanence

Why lasting communication challenges the ephemeral nature of social media

There exists a curious invention of our digital age, a contraption so perfectly aligned with our moral confusions that it might have sprung from some allegorical tale meant to illustrate the peculiar vices of modernity. This invention—this parable made software—bears the playful name Snapchat, a name suggesting childish diversion while concealing a more profound significance. For in its seemingly innocent design lies a perfect embodiment of our ethical discontents: an application deliberately engineered to make human communication vanish into the digital ether, leaving behind no record for what has been said or shown or promised or threatened. And therefore, no accountability.

Snapchat's defining feature, of course, is the automatic deletion of messages after viewing, and this encapsulates a distinctly modern fantasy: communication without consequence. It is the technological manifestation of a moral universe where nothing remains to bear witness to our words and deeds. It creates a universe calibrated to undermine the development of ethical consciousness in precisely those years when such development is most crucial.

This is not, it should be noted, an accidental feature of the platform. It is its foundational purpose. According to the origin story of this digital contrivance, the entire enterprise began with a conversation about sexting, with one of the founders expressing a desire for photographs that would later disappear. This genesis in facilitating secretive intimate exchanges foreshadowed the platform's broader impact on youth communication and moral development. What was conceived as a tool for evading consequence has become a dominant medium through which adolescents develop their understanding of communication, relationship, and moral responsibility.

The consequences of this design choice radiate far beyond the original intentions, shaping the moral landscape of adolescence in ways both subtle and profound. Consider first the psychological impact of communication without record. Snapchat's design alters the mental calculus of ethical decision-making. When messages disappear by default and the natural consequences of ill-considered images are technologically circumvented, the developing moral consciousness is deprived of one of its most essential teachers: the opportunity to reflect on one's actions through their persistent effects. The adolescent who sends a cruel message that immediately vanishes is robbed of the chance to return to those words later in order to reconsider them and, one may hope, recognize their impact through their continued existence. The teenager who shares an inappropriate image that automatically deletes, however, is shielded from the natural consequences that might otherwise prompt sober reflection and moral growth.

This technological circumvention of consequence undermines the traditional path of moral development, which will typically unfold through accumulated experience, reflection, and the gradual shaping of a coherent ethical framework. In fact, the disappearing message may be best understood as the antithesis of genuine moral development. Rather than supporting the growth of conscience, it actively disrupts it by erasing experience as soon as it occurs, thereby severing the link between actions and their consequences. It is as if we had created a tool precisely calibrated to undermine the formation of moral memory. Snapchat can be best understood as a kind of conscience-resistant technology introduced at the moment when lasting impressions matter most.

Yet Snapchat's impact on moral development goes beyond disrupting individual reflection; it also affects the social processes essential to ethical growth. Morality is not confined to the level of the individual. It emerges through shared experiences, including action, response, dialogue, and reconciliation within human relationships. By design, Snapchat creates an environment detached from these normal patterns of interaction, shielding users from the social feedback and accountability that help form a mature ethical understanding.

In traditional settings, harmful communication often carries natural consequences. These take many forms, for example, a friend's visible pain, the concern of others, or a conversation with a trusted adult. These moments be can punitive in many cases; more importantly, they serve as formative experiences, helping adolescents understand the impact of their actions, the norms that sustain community life, and the possibility of making amends. Snapchat, by contrast, is designed to sidestep these formative encounters. Its features insulate users from the kind of social feedback that is essential for ethical growth, creating a space where actions often escape both memory and consequence.

This circumvention manifests most clearly in the platform's approach to evidence and accountability. The screenshot notification feature, ostensibly designed to protect privacy, serves in practice to establish a new and peculiar norm: that preserving a record of communication represents an act of aggression rather than a natural aspect of meaningful exchange. Under this inverted logic, the person who maintains evidence of harmful behavior becomes the transgressor, while the original sender of problematic content claims the status of victim. This remarkable inversion transforms accountability itself into a form of violation, teaching adolescents that the normal expectation in communication should be an immunity from having to stand behind one's words or images.

This lesson reaches well beyond the digital world, shaping how adolescents come to understand responsibility in all areas of life. A student who grows used to consequence-free communication online may begin to expect the same in face-to-face interactions, believing that words can simply vanish, that actions leave nothing behind, and that one need not be accountable to his own past. Such a mindset runs counter to the formation of integrity, which depends on a sense of continuity over time, an awareness that one's choices matter and that character is built through the lasting connections between past and present.

Equally concerning is how Snapchat's design transforms human relationships into gamified competitions through features like "streaks," which reward users for maintaining daily communication chains with friends. This system, which reduces friendship to a numerical score and transforms genuine connection into a competitive obligation, represents another dimension of the platform's moral distortion. Students report waking early or staying up late to maintain these artificial metrics, demonstrating how thoroughly the platform's game mechanics can override authentic relational impulses. The messages exchanged to maintain streaks are often contentless. In other words, they are empty communications sent not to express meaning but merely to prevent the breaking of the chain. Here we see another inversion: whereas traditionally the message served the relationship, now the relationship serves the message, existing primarily as the justification for continued engagement with the platform itself.

This gamification extends to the platform's sophisticated array of augmented reality filters, which allow users to present dramatically modified versions of their appearance. While seemingly playful, these features contribute to a disturbing dissociation from authentic self-presentation, creating a generation increasingly uncomfortable with their natural appearance and constantly seeking validation through artificially enhanced images. This dynamic particularly affects young women and girls, who report increasing levels of body dysmorphia and anxiety related to their unfiltered appearance. The platform thus simultaneously encourages self-objectification through modified images while creating permanent insecurity about unmodified reality. Of course, this is a perfect mechanism for ensuring continued dependence on the technologies, like Snapchat, that generate the insecurity in the first place.

Perhaps most insidious is how Snapchat's design actively undermines the development of moral reasoning capabilities. Traditional social interactions, whether digital or physical, create opportunities for reflection and growth through their persistence. When young people can look back on past conversations or actions, they can analyze their behavior. They can potentially understand its impact on others and consequently develop more sophisticated ethical frameworks. Snapchat's ephemeral design—here one moment, gone the next—promotes instead a kind of moral amnesia, where actions exist only in the moment and cannot be examined or learned from later. This prevents the accumulation of ethical understanding that occurs through reflection on past actions, their consequences, and how they might have been handled differently.

The platform's "Discover" section exemplifies how commercial interests have been promoted to the detriment of moral development. This feature bombards young users with a constant stream of sensationalistic content, celebrity gossip, and clickbait, crowding out more substantive material that might contribute to civic education or ethical growth. The rapid-fire nature of these disappearing stories trains young minds to process information superficially rather than engaging in critical analysis or deeper reflection, creating consumers of sensation rather than discerning evaluators of content.

Location-sharing features create additional vectors for problematic behavior while normalizing constant surveillance. The app's mapping function, showing users' real-time locations to their friends, has been implicated in numerous incidents of stalking and harassment. Young users feel social pressure to share their whereabouts or risk exclusion, yet this transparency can be exploited by malicious actors. Particularly concerning is how this feature can enable real-world harassment, especially among younger users who may not fully understand the risks of location sharing or feel empowered to refuse it.

Parents and educators report unprecedented challenges in guiding young people through social situations when evidence of concerning behavior vanishes instantly.[21] Traditional parenting strategies, which rely on being able to discuss and process specific incidents, become ineffective when the content in question disappears. This creates parallel social worlds where young people operate without meaningful oversight or guidance, developing their own questionable moral (or amoral) frameworks in an environment optimized for impulsivity rather than reflection.

The cumulative effect of these design choices extends beyond individual behavior to threaten the foundations of civic virtue. Democratic societies depend on citizens capable of thoughtful deliberation, ethical

21 J. D. Shapka and H. M. Onditi. (2023). "Parental Monitoring of Early Adolescent Social Technology Use: Relationships with Psychosocial and Social Media Outcomes." *Journal of Child and Family Studies* 32(6): 1680–92.

reasoning, and genuine human connection. Yet Snapchat's architecture actively works against these capabilities, creating instead a generation accustomed to consequence-free communication, superficial relationships, and the constant performance of artificial personas. It undermines the development of patience and long-term thinking, crucial qualities for civic engagement and moral development, conditioning users to expect immediate responses and temporary consequences, struggling to engage with the slower, more deliberative processes necessary for democratic participation and ethical decision-making.

Democratic societies depend on citizens capable of thoughtful deliberation, ethical reasoning, and genuine human connection.

This is not to suggest that technology is inherently harmful or that all forms of digital communication inevitably erode moral development. The problem usually lies not with technology itself, but with particular design choices—choices driven by commercial interests and engagement metrics rather than by concern for human flourishing. These choices bypass the natural developmental processes by which ethical understanding is traditionally formed. Yes, of course, technology could be shaped differently. With more deliberate design, digital platforms might reinforce rather than weaken the habits and relationships that support moral growth. But perhaps there are even better solutions that involve weaning the young off such morally debilitative technologies and replacing them with a more traditionally personal approach.

Classical education offers a compelling model for this more deliberate and humane approach. It places technology within a broader educational vision that prioritizes the cultivation of virtue, the pursuit of wisdom, and the development of deep, meaningful relationships. Within this framework, students participate in structured, face-to-face conversations that nurture attentiveness, empathy, and moral reasoning, free from the distortions of filters or the erasure of disappearing messages. Recognition for genuine achievement does not hinge on streaks or follower counts. It rests instead on character, especially on contributions made to the common good. Teachers and mentors lead by example, modeling lives of purpose, integrity, and lasting connection. By doing so, they demonstrate that real fulfillment can be found in the steady pursuit of what is true, good, and beautiful. While this vision is not unique to classical education, it is classical education that has most faithfully preserved and advanced it in recent years.

The ultimate question is not whether young people will engage with technology—they already do—but whether they will be prepared to meet that world with discernment and strength of character. This preparation does not happen in front of a screen. It happens in the classroom, in real conversation, in the steady work of forming habits of mind and heart. Classical education creates just such an environment. It cultivates the moral clarity that digital culture often obscures by directing students away from the fleeting allure of trends and toward what endures, where integrity is modeled and relationships are formed in the presence of real human regard. In other words, classical education restores a sense of what matters, and in doing so, gives students the inner resources they need to act wisely, both online and off.

This formation begins with the curriculum itself, which invites students into conversation with the greatest minds and noblest lives of the past. In history, they study individuals who shaped the moral and political order through courage, sacrifice, and love of truth—figures like Socrates, Cicero, Joan of Arc, Frederick Douglass, and Sojourner Truth. These are not abstract lessons. When approached with care, such stories become mirrors and models, challenging students to ask difficult questions: What kind of person do I want to be? What do I owe to others? How do I act with integrity when it costs me something?

The same holds true in the literature classroom, where students meet heroes whose journeys toward virtue unfold through struggle, marked at times by failure and at others by hard-won success. Homer's Odysseus, Shakespeare's Henry V, Austen's Anne Elliot, and Hugo's Jean Valjean each illuminate some aspect of the human condition. Each invites students to consider the shape of a life well-lived. These characters linger in the imagination. They become companions and counselors, giving moral weight to the decisions students must make in their own lives.

Yet this education is not limited to texts and classrooms. It is embodied in the daily presence of teachers who serve as mentors and moral exemplars. Students watch their teachers—how they respond to conflict, how they speak of those with whom they disagree, how they balance justice with mercy, and so on. In time, those observations become models to imitate. The example of an adult who lives with integrity has more formative power than a hundred lectures on character. The best classical schools recognize this and deliberately cultivate a faculty culture rooted in high standards, humility, and mutual respect.

These values extend into the life of the school itself. House systems, for example, offer far more than team spirit or friendly rivalry. When thoughtfully designed, they foster a culture of noble aspiration in which recognition is tied not to popularity or superficial performance but to the quiet cultivation of virtue. A student who pauses after class to help a peer with a difficult passage in Latin, who stands firm in defending what is right even when it is unpopular, or who perseveres through the long discipline of athletic training, embodies the kind of excellence that such a system seeks to honor. Students discover that honor differs from attention, and that their peers admire not only their lofty achievements but the character those achievements reveal. They learn that reputation built on virtue lasts longer and satisfies more deeply than fame built on performance or popularity.

Classical schools also cultivate what we might call "the long view"—an appreciation for enduring excellence over momentary sensation. Students study Latin for the mental discipline and cultural literacy it provides. They memorize poetry to carry beauty and wisdom within them throughout their lives. They engage in formal debate to develop the capacity for reasoned discourse that democratic citizenship requires. This emphasis on permanence and depth directly counters the superficiality and impermanence that characterize digital culture. Where social media promotes constant novelty and instant gratification, classical education cultivates patience and appreciation for what endures. Where digital platforms fragment attention across multiple simultaneous inputs, classical pedagogy develops the capacity for sustained focus and deep engagement.

The physical and social environment of classical schools also contributes to moral formation in ways that contrast sharply with the digital realm. Classical schools aim to create a space where students are known, valued, and encouraged to become more fully themselves—not as fragmented digital personas, but as whole human beings. Teachers greet students by name, offer counsel in quiet moments, notice when someone is struggling. In this atmosphere of attentive care, students learn to trust, to risk, to grow. Moral formation flourishes in such soil because it is supported by real relationships—relationships that can challenge, inspire, and ultimately guide students toward the kind of maturity that digital life too often undermines.

Rather than avoiding technology, classical education prepares students to engage it wisely.

Classical education recognizes that virtue develops through daily practice rather than occasional inspiration. Students participate in regular routines that cultivate good habits, beginning each day with a pledge or prayer and carrying that spirit into their interactions with others. They treat all members of the community with courtesy, take responsibility for shared spaces, support younger students, and approach their academic work with diligence and integrity. In this way, virtue becomes woven into the fabric of daily life rather than remaining an abstract ideal.

These practices may seem small, yet they lay the foundation for larger virtues. Listening attentively in seminar fosters the patience required for deeper relationships. Completing assignments with care, even when unobserved, cultivates the integrity necessary for principled leadership. Showing courtesy to custodial staff or kitchen workers nurtures the humility essential to genuine service. Such formation cannot be rushed or shortcut; it grows slowly through repetition and the patient attention that digital culture so often undermines. Classical education provides this attention through structures that value depth over breadth, quality over quantity, and character over performance. Rather than avoiding technology, classical education prepares students to engage it wisely. Students who have developed strong capacities for moral reasoning, sustained attention, and authentic relationship are better equipped to navigate digital spaces without being consumed by them. They approach social media with questions rather than assumptions: What purpose does this serve? How does this affect my relationships? What kind of person am I becoming through this engagement?

This preparation proves especially valuable as students mature and face increasingly complex technological choices offered by emerging digital technologies. The student who has learned to value substance over sensation is less likely to be manipulated by algorithmic design intended to maximize engagement regardless of human cost. The student who has experienced the satisfaction of deep friendship is less likely to accept the shallow connections that digital platforms offer as substitutes.

Classical education also provides students with alternative sources of meaning and identity, grounding them in experiences that make them less dependent on digital validation. Encountering heroes in literature and history offers models of excellence that extend beyond the fleeting metrics of social media. The joy of mastering difficult material fosters a confidence that does not rely on external approval. Contributing to a genuine community cultivates a sense of purpose that cannot be replicated through online performance. In all these ways, classical education offers more than a critique of digital culture. It offers positive formation for human flourishing. By grounding students in the richness of human tradition and the demands of virtue, it equips them to enter the online world with a clearer sense of self, deeper capacity for judgment, and stronger desire to use technology in service of what is good.

This formation creates what we might call "moral clarity," the ability to see through surface appearances to underlying realities, to distinguish between what seems immediately appealing and what proves ultimately satisfying. It helps students to choose the difficult good over the easy pleasure. Such clarity becomes especially important in digital environments designed to obscure these distinctions.

Students educated in classical schools will still use social media, but they will do so as people shaped by something deeper—by habits of attention, reverence, and moral responsibility. Students who have been exposed to a classical education will be less susceptible to the moral amnesia that Snapchat promotes because they will have developed strong moral memories through encounter with lasting excellence. They will be less vulnerable

Students educated in classical schools will still use social media, but they will do so as people shaped by something deeper—by habits of attention, reverence, and moral responsibility.

to the superficial relationships that social media offers because they will have experienced the depth and satisfaction of genuine friendship.

Classical education thus restores a sense of what matters, and in doing so, gives students the inner resources they need to act wisely, both online and off. It provides not escape from modernity but preparation for engaging it with wisdom, virtue, and hope.

Recommended Further Reading

1. *Glow Kids* by Nicholas Kardaras. Exposes how digital platforms create addictive behaviors that undermine moral and social development.
2. "The Virtue of Attention" (essay) by Gregory M. Reichberg. Explores how sustained attention forms the foundation for moral reasoning and character development.
3. *The Social Dilemma* (documentary film) by Jeff Orlowski. Documents how platform design deliberately undermines human well-being and moral development.
4. *The Coddling of the American Mind* by Greg Lukianoff and Jonathan Haidt. Examines how overprotective digital environments prevent the development of emotional and moral resilience.
5. *iGen* by Jean Twenge. Analyzes how digital natives develop differently from previous generations in concerning ways.
6. *Character Matters* by Thomas Lickona. Provides practical approaches to moral formation that contrast with digital culture's influence.
7. *The Distracted Mind: Ancient Brains in a High-Tech World* by Larry Rosen and Kerry Gazzaley. Examines how our ancient cognitive systems struggle to cope with modern digital environments and multitasking demands.

Chapter 25

The Subversive Art of Intellectual Solitude

How learning to be alone with ideas develops immunity to crowd thinking

There is a curious terror that has seized the modern mind when confronted with the prospect of being alone with its own thoughts. This peculiar phobia manifests itself most acutely in educational settings, where silence has become an emergency to be remedied rather than a condition to be cultivated. The contemporary classroom buzzes with collaborative learning, group projects, peer feedback sessions, and interactive discussions designed to ensure that no student ever suffers the apparent calamity of sustained solitary reflection.

This horror of intellectual solitude represents one of the most profound reversals in educational philosophy. Where once the greatest thinkers were celebrated for their capacity to withdraw from the crowd and think original thoughts, we now measure educational success by the speed with which students can access collective opinion and the skill with which they can synthesize the views of others. The student who prefers to read alone rather than discuss in groups, who chooses contemplation over collaboration, who seeks understanding of difficult ideas by doing hard and slow intellectual labor rather than through immediate consultation with peers increasingly appears not as a model of intellectual independence but as a problem to be solved.

Yet this terror of solitude reveals a profound misunderstanding of how genuine thinking actually occurs. Original thought emerges not from the constant stimulation of external voices but from the patient discipline of sitting alone with challenging ideas until something new is born. The mind that never experiences silence, that never dwells in the uncomfortable space between question and answer, that never endures the productive boredom of sustained reflection, remains perpetually dependent upon others for its opinions, preferences, and judgments.

Classical education has always recognized intellectual solitude as essential to human formation. The tradition understands that certain forms of learning can only occur in the silence of individual encounter with great ideas. When Augustine sat alone in his garden with the competing claims of faith and philosophy, when Aquinas spent hours in solitary contemplation before writing a single word of his *Summa*, when Pascal recorded his fragmentary thoughts in the privacy of his own reflection, they were not avoiding human community but preparing to contribute something genuinely valuable to it.

The digital age has made such solitude increasingly difficult to achieve and even more difficult to sustain. Our devices have been engineered with a sophistication that would have impressed medieval theologians for their capacity to make solitary reflection nearly impossible. Every moment of potential quiet is interrupted by notifications designed to capture attention. Every period of sustained thought is fragmented by alerts engineered to create dependency. Every attempt at deep reading is sabotaged by hyperlinks that promise more interesting content just a click away.

The result is a generation of students who have never learned to be alone with their thoughts for more than a few minutes at a time. They cannot read a book without simultaneously checking social media, cannot write an essay without consulting multiple online sources, cannot form an opinion without immediately seeking validation through likes, shares, and comments. Their minds have become permanently externalized, dependent upon constant input from digital networks rather than capable of sustained internal reflection.

This externalization of thought represents more than mere distraction. It constitutes a fundamental reorganization of consciousness itself. The mind that has never experienced sustained solitude develops different neural pathways than one trained in contemplative reflection. It becomes skilled at rapid information processing and multitasking but loses the capacity for deep thinking that requires sustained attention to a single problem or text.

The classical student, by contrast, learns early the discipline of solitary engagement with difficult ideas. She spends hours alone with challenging texts, perusing concepts that resist easy comprehension, dwelling in the discomfort of not knowing until genuine understanding emerges. This training in intellectual solitude develops mental muscles that prove essential throughout life: the capacity to think independently, the ability to sit with complexity without immediately seeking resolution, the strength to hold unpopular opinions when evidence demands it.

Such solitary discipline becomes particularly crucial when encountering the great books that form the backbone of classical education. These texts cannot be read quickly or superficially. They demand the kind of sustained attention that only solitude can provide. When a student engages alone with Plato's *Republic* or Augustine's *Confessions* or Dante's *Divine Comedy*, he enters into a direct conversation with minds separated from him by centuries but addressing questions that remain as urgent today as when they were first posed.

This solitary encounter with great texts produces forms of understanding unavailable through collaborative learning approaches. The student who has reflected alone upon Hamlet's soliloquies develops an appreciation for the complexity of human motivation that no group discussion can replicate. The reader who has contemplated in silence the mathematical proofs of Euclid gains an understanding of logical necessity that collaborative problem-solving cannot provide. The young person who has reflected in private upon the moral dilemmas presented in Greek tragedy develops ethical sensitivity that peer consultation cannot match.

Unfortunately, the educational establishment has largely abandoned this understanding in favor of approaches that privilege collaboration over contemplation. Modern pedagogical theory treats solitary learning as a relic of authoritarian education, preferring methods that emphasize social construction of knowledge and peer-to-peer learning. While these approaches offer certain benefits, their exclusive application impoverishes students by depriving them of opportunities to develop the intellectual independence that only solitude can cultivate.

The classical school creates deliberate spaces for such solitary engagement. Students spend significant time alone with books, not because the school cannot afford enough computers for collaborative learning but because it recognizes that certain forms of understanding emerge only through individual engagement with challenging ideas. The library becomes a sanctuary of silence where students can encounter texts without the mediation of peer opinion or instructor guidance.

This emphasis on solitary reading cultivates what might be called intellectual courage—the habit of forming judgments through careful attention to evidence rather than deference to popular opinion.

This emphasis on solitary reading cultivates what might be called intellectual courage—the habit of forming judgments through careful attention to evidence rather than deference to popular opinion. A student who has learned to think alone acquires a resilience against the groupthink that dominates much contemporary discourse. She learns to weigh arguments by their substance, to recognize truth even when it cuts against prevailing sentiment, and to hold fast to her convictions in the face of social pressure.

Such intellectual independence becomes especially valuable in our current media environment, where opinion formation increasingly occurs through echo chambers and algorithmic filtering. The person who has never learned to think alone remains vulnerable to manipulation by voices that confirm existing prejudices or by platforms designed to maximize engagement rather than promote understanding. The student trained in solitary reflection, by contrast, possesses internal resources for evaluating claims and forming judgments that do not depend upon external validation.

The historical record provides abundant evidence of breakthrough insights emerging from periods of intellectual isolation. Newton's revolutionary work in mathematics and physics developed during his enforced solitude at Woolsthorpe Manor during the plague years. Darwin's theory of evolution took shape during decades of private reflection and correspondence rather than through collaborative research. Einstein's most profound insights emerged through thought experiments conducted in the privacy of his own mind rather than through group brainstorming sessions.

These examples illustrate a crucial principle often overlooked in contemporary education: original thinking requires periods of intellectual solitude. The mind that is constantly stimulated by external input never develops the capacity for the kind of sustained internal reflection that produces genuinely new ideas. Innovation emerges from the patient cultivation of understanding in the silence of individual reflection.

Original thinking requires periods of intellectual solitude. The mind that is constantly stimulated by external input never develops the capacity for the kind of sustained internal reflection that produces genuinely new ideas.

The classical curriculum provides numerous opportunities for such solitary cultivation. Students spend hours alone with mathematical proofs, working through logical steps without peer collaboration or instructor intervention. They engage in private reading of challenging texts, developing their own interpretations before consulting commentaries or discussing with classmates. They practice writing that emerges from their own reflection rather than from research into what others have written about their topics.

This training in intellectual solitude also strengthens emotional resilience. A student who learns to be at ease with challenging ideas on her own becomes less reliant on external validation for her sense of worth. She gains the freedom to pursue lines of inquiry that may lack peer approval, the stamina to remain engaged with difficult subjects without constant encouragement, and the steadiness to endure confusion and uncertainty that would unsettle those unaccustomed to the discipline of solitary thought.

The discipline of solitude also cultivates what the contemplative tradition calls "attention." Unlike the scattered, reactive attention that characterizes digital engagement, contemplative attention involves the sustained focus of mental energy upon a single object of inquiry. This focused attention allows for depth of understanding impossible to achieve through the rapid switching between topics that characterizes online learning.

When students learn to read alone without digital devices, they develop the capacity for what psychologists call "flow states." These are periods of sustained engagement where the boundary between reader and text temporarily dissolves. These experiences of deep reading create lasting memories and profound understanding that superficial engagement cannot match. The student who has experienced such deep reading carries within herself a standard for intellectual engagement that resists the shallowness of digital consumption.

The practice of intellectual solitude also develops humility. The student who has struggled alone with complex problems learns to appreciate the genuine difficulty of understanding complex ideas. She recognizes the difference between quick opinions and carefully formed judgments, between confident assertions and genuine knowledge. This humility serves as an antidote to the intellectual arrogance that often accompanies easy access to information.

Classical education provides practical structures for cultivating such solitude. Silent reading periods become sacred times when students encounter texts without mediation. Study halls must be deliberately shaped as spaces of intellectual engagement—occasions for thought, reading, and reflection—rather than lapsing into idleness, distraction, or sleep. Independent research projects invite students to pursue questions that arise from their own curiosity rather than from prescribed curricula.

The physical environment also supports intellectual solitude. Classical schools often design their campuses with spaces that invite reflection and quiet study. Libraries function not merely as repositories of books but as sanctuaries of silence, where the very architecture encourages concentration and reverence for learning. Individual study carrels provide the privacy needed for deep engagement, while reading rooms establish a common culture of stillness in which students can encounter great books without distraction. Even the arrangement of furniture, the use of natural light, and the presence of beauty in architectural detail can reinforce the atmosphere of contemplation. In such environments, students sense that the school esteems intellectual solitude as a good in itself, and they learn to associate silence and stillness with the pursuit of truth.

Teachers in classical schools also personally model intellectual solitude. They read deeply in their subjects, pursue questions that interest them personally, and share with students the fruits of their own contemplative engagement with difficult ideas. They understand that they cannot give to students what they do not themselves possess: the capacity for sustained reflection and the appreciation for the insights that emerge only through patient, solitary thinking.

The digital platforms that dominate contemporary culture have been engineered to make such solitude psychologically difficult. Social media applications use variable-ratio reinforcement schedules—these are the same psychological mechanism that makes gambling addictive—to create dependency upon external validation. "Users" become accustomed to receiving regular doses of attention in the form of likes, comments, and shares. When this external stimulation is removed, withdrawal symptoms emerge that make solitude feel punitive rather than productive.

The student who has never experienced genuine intellectual solitude remains vulnerable to this manipulation throughout life. She becomes dependent upon others for validation of her ideas, uncertain of her judgments without external confirmation, unable to pursue unpopular lines of inquiry that might lead to important insights. Her intellectual life becomes permanently externalized, shaped by algorithmic feeds rather than by her own careful reflection.

Classical education provides the opportunity for immunity to such manipulation by training students in the discipline of solitary thinking before they encounter the powerful psychological pressures of social media. The student who has learned to find satisfaction in reflecting in solitude upon challenging ideas develops internal resources that resist the artificial rewards engineered by digital platforms. She can pursue understanding for its own sake rather than for the social validation it might provide.

The cultivation of intellectual solitude also develops aesthetic appreciation. The student who has learned to sit quietly with beautiful texts, musical compositions, or mathematical proofs develops sensitivity to excellence that cannot be achieved through hurried consumption. She learns to distinguish between entertainment and art, between information and wisdom, between clever content and profound insight.

This aesthetic education becomes particularly important in an environment where entertainment and education increasingly converge. Digital platforms use entertainment techniques to capture attention, creating content that feels educational while actually promoting passive consumption rather than active learning. The student trained in intellectual solitude can recognize the difference between genuine learning and engaging content, between understanding and mere exposure.

The practice of solitude also cultivates spiritual depth. Whether or not students embrace particular religious traditions, the discipline of quiet reflection develops capacities for transcendence that purely social learning cannot provide. Students learn to recognize dimensions of experience that cannot be captured in words, to appreciate mysteries that resist easy explanation, to find meaning in experiences that transcend immediate utility.

This spiritual dimension of solitary learning connects students to the long tradition of contemplative education that has characterized classical learning from its ancient origins. They join the ranks of scholars, monks, philosophers, and scientists who have found in solitude not loneliness but communion with the deepest realities of existence.

The recovery of intellectual solitude requires institutional commitment to creating spaces and times where such reflection can occur. Schools must resist the pressure to fill every moment with stimulation, every silence with activity, every pause with input. They must trust that students can benefit from periods of productive boredom, from encounters with difficult texts that resist easy comprehension, from questions that have no immediate answers.

Teachers must also recover confidence in their authority to assign solitary work despite student resistance. Many contemporary educators, having absorbed the collaborative learning paradigm, feel apologetic about requiring students to work alone. They must remember that learning to think independently is not selfish individualism but preparation for genuine contribution to human community.

Parents too must resist the cultural pressure to ensure that their children never experience boredom or intellectual isolation. They must understand that the capacity for solitude is not a luxury but a necessity for intellectual development. The child who never learns to be alone with her thoughts grows into an adult who cannot think independently about the challenges she will face.

The ultimate goal of cultivating intellectual solitude is not withdrawal from human community but preparation for more meaningful participation in it. The person who has learned to think carefully in private becomes capable of contributing genuinely original insights to public conversation.

Intellectual solitude thus serves not as escape from social responsibility but as preparation for it. The great teachers, leaders, and innovators throughout history have been those who combined deep solitary reflection with generous public service. They could contribute to others precisely because they had first learned to commune with the best that has been thought and said in the solitude of their own minds.

In our hyperconnected age, the decision to think alone stands as a radical act of independence. It resists the constant pressure to outsource thought to trending opinions, curated feeds, and external algorithms that subtly dictate what deserves attention.

In our hyperconnected age, the decision to think alone stands as a radical act of independence. It resists the constant pressure to outsource thought to trending opinions, curated feeds, and external algorithms that subtly dictate what deserves attention. To choose solitude in thought is to affirm that judgment is not a collective echo but a personal responsibility. It signals a commitment to cultivating the inner resources necessary for discernment, clarity, and genuine understanding. More than a withdrawal from noise, it is an assertion that the human mind, when granted silence and space, remains capable of insight that is both original and enduring. Such independence of thought is not only an intellectual discipline but also a moral stance, for it proclaims that truth is worth seeking even when it is unfashionable, and wisdom worth cultivating even when it requires patience and struggle. The classical school stands as a guardian of this ancient discipline, preserving space for the kind of solitary reflection that our digital culture threatens to eliminate. In doing so, it prepares students not merely for academic success but for intellectual freedom, not merely for information processing but for wisdom, not merely for connectivity but for the kind of deep thinking that emerges only in the fertile silence of the contemplative mind.

Recommended Further Reading

1. *Solitude: A Return to the Self* by Anthony Storr. Explores how periods of solitude have been essential to creativity and psychological development throughout human history.
2. *The Lonely City: Adventures in the Art of Being Alone* by Olivia Laing. Examines the difference between loneliness and solitude through the lives of artists who created their greatest works in isolation.
3. *Silence: The Power of Quiet in a World Full of Noise* by Thich Nhat Hanh. Demonstrates how cultivating silence and solitude develops deeper awareness and understanding.
4. *Deep Work: Rules for Focused Success in a Distracted World* by Cal Newport. Argues that the ability to focus deeply on cognitively demanding tasks has become increasingly rare and valuable.
5. *Walden* by Henry David Thoreau. The classic meditation on simple living and solitary reflection as means to deeper understanding of self and nature.
6. *How to Be Alone* by Sara Maitland. A practical and philosophical exploration of solitude as a valuable discipline rather than a problem to be solved.
7. *The Inner Life: Selections from the Imitation of Christ* by Thomas à Kempis. A foundational text on contemplative practice that shows how solitary reflection leads to wisdom and spiritual maturity.

Part VI

Subversive Acts of Reclamation

Chapter 26

The Subversive Art of Teaching as Philosophy

How the teacher's role transcends mere facilitation

In modern educational discourse, a curious insult is tossed about with such casual certainty that its deeper philosophical confusion goes unnoticed. The phrase "sage on the stage" gets deployed with ritual disdain, as if it were the perfect label for an ancient pedagogical villain. Meanwhile, the supposedly enlightened alternative—the "guide on the side"—receives breathless celebration as liberation from tyrannical hierarchy. This linguistic inversion reveals something more troubling than professional fashion. It exposes a profound misunderstanding of the philosophical relationship at the heart of genuine education.

The true teacher has never been a mere performer of knowledge or reciter of encyclopedic information who renders students passive recipients of disconnected facts. The true teacher has always been a philosopher in the original and literal sense: a lover of wisdom who invites students into that same love. He embodies intellectual virtue alongside intellectual achievement. This understanding completely subverts the reductionist caricature implied in the "sage on the stage" dismissal.

The philosopher-teacher is a seeker whose own inquiry continues even as he guides others. He embodies ongoing intellectual development, always learning alongside those he teaches. His guidance emerges from lived experience and hard-won wisdom. He delivers no final pronouncements from on high but offers direction rooted in his own passage through difficult terrain.

The humility he models flows naturally from recognizing the vastness of what remains unknown, the provisional nature of current understanding, the endless pursuit that constitutes genuine intellectual development. This humility grounds his authority in something more substantial than institutional position or technical expertise. The philosopher-teacher's authority emerges from demonstrated wisdom and service to student intellectual development. He knows which questions matter and understands how to pursue them effectively. His authority invites students into inquiry instead of imposing conclusions. He guides discovery instead of dictating outcomes. Most importantly, he models the intellectual virtues that constitute genuine education: clarity of thought, precision in expression, honesty about limitations, and perseverance through difficulty.

We have mistakenly learned to equate authority with authoritarianism. We assume that hierarchical relationships must be oppressive. We imagine that genuine equality requires the abolition of distinction instead of its proper acknowledgment and orientation toward the common good.

The modern denigration of philosophical teaching reflects a deeper confusion about the nature of authority itself. This confusion pervades contemporary culture well beyond educational contexts. We have mistakenly learned to equate authority with authoritarianism. We assume that hierarchical relationships must be oppressive. We imagine that genuine equality requires the abolition of distinction instead of its proper acknowledgment and orientation toward the common good. This confusion produces the strange notion that teacher authority inherently diminishes student agency. It assumes that teacher wisdom necessarily suppresses student voice. It suggests that teacher guidance inevitably restricts student freedom. The reality is quite different: properly exercised authority creates a collaborative endeavor that enables growth which would otherwise be impossible.

Authority isn't enlightenment's villain; it's its backbone. A master doesn't hand an apprentice tools and expect the Parthenon; he teaches, corrects, leads. The classical understanding recognizes that genuine authority, properly exercised, enables freedom. This freedom transcends the superficial license to do whatever one momentarily desires. It represents the deeper freedom that comes from developing the capacities, virtues, and understanding necessary for genuine self-determination and flourishing. The master carpenter empowers the apprentice to achieve what would otherwise remain impossible by correcting technique. The experienced guide expands the territory that can be safely traversed by warning of dangerous paths. The philosopher-teacher opens intellectual horizons that would otherwise remain closed by challenging faulty reasoning. Each exercises authority in service of expansion rather than restriction.

This stands in sharp contrast to the "guide on the side" model that has become dogma in many schools—an approach that emphasizes "facilitation" over teacher-led instruction, prioritizes student-directed learning over teacher-guided inquiry, and values process over content. This model implicitly denies the asymmetry of knowledge experience, and wisdom that makes genuine teaching possible. It imagines education as primarily a matter of drawing out what already exists within the student. Yet the reality involves something far more transformative: a relationship through which the student becomes capable of understanding that would be impossible without guidance.

Consider the absurdity of applying this facilitation model in other contexts where mastery transfers from one generation to the next. A violin teacher who refused to demonstrate proper technique but merely encouraged students to "discover his own relationship with the instrument" would be guilty of malpractice. A master chef who declined to explain the principles of flavor development but simply created "opportunities for culinary exploration" would be abdicating responsibility. A surgical educator who rejected direct instruction in favor of "facilitating each student's unique approach to the scalpel" would be committing professional negligence.

We would immediately recognize the abandonment of students to the frustration of reinventing wheels that have already been perfected through centuries of collective effort. We would see the failure to transmit hard-won wisdom that cannot be rediscovered in each generation. Yet in general education—in the teaching of literature, history, mathematics, science, philosophy, and the arts—we have somehow come to accept this same type of abdication as "progressive," to celebrate this abandonment as "empowering," and to praise this failure as "student-centered."

Behind this approach lies a misplaced confidence in the powers of untutored nature. This complacency sees guidance as interference and formation as a kind of repression. In this view, development is believed to arise most authentically when nothing stands in its way. Classical education takes a different approach. It begins from the understanding that what is most worth knowing is not obvious or easily attained, and that students grow through thoughtful instruction of the enduring achievements of civilization.

The classical teacher holds fast to the responsibility of authority as a form of responsible stewardship. He exercises it with care and humility, always in pursuit of what is true and worth knowing. In doing so, he offers his students something far more valuable than the illusion of self-reliance. The classical teacher offers the gift of meaningful formation. Knowledge, especially in its higher forms, does not unfold by accident. It becomes accessible through the presence of those who have already labored to understand and are willing to guide others with patience and purpose.

This kind of teaching remains at the heart of philosophical education. The Socratic method, often misunderstood as little more than open-ended questioning, takes on a deeper role when practiced with intention. Its purpose is not to entertain speculation but to direct thought with precision and insight. The teacher shapes the conversation with quiet discipline, creating the conditions under which serious thinking can take root. His questions are not improvised or arbitrary; they reflect long reflection and a settled sense of what deserves attention. Through this method, the teacher does more than transfer knowledge. He offers a way of attending to the world, one marked by intellectual clarity and moral seriousness—qualities formed through years of study and a deep regard for the student's potential.

Genuine teaching unfolds through purposeful engagement. The teacher does more than share information or facilitate activity; he shapes the student's outlook and habits of mind in ways that unfold gradually through trust and sustained effort. His presence draws students beyond their current habits of thought, introducing them to ways of seeing that deepen their understanding of the world and of themselves. Over time, this influence sharpens their perception, guiding them toward a more thoughtful grasp of reality. Such development depends on a teacher who recognizes what the student has not yet grasped and who patiently leads him toward it—not by coercion, but by drawing forth the desire to know and to love what is worth knowing and loving.

> *Genuine teaching unfolds through purposeful engagement. The teacher does more than share information or facilitate activity; he shapes the student's outlook and habits of mind in ways that unfold gradually through trust and sustained effort. His presence draws students beyond their current habits of thought, introducing them to ways of seeing that deepen their understanding of the world and of themselves. Over time, this influence sharpens their perception, guiding them toward a more thoughtful grasp of reality.*

A diminished view of teaching often begins with a shallow account of knowledge. When understanding is mistaken for the mere possession of facts, the work of the teacher is reduced to managing the flow of information. Within this framework, education becomes a technical task, centered on systems of delivery rather than on the formation of judgment. But knowledge is not inert content to be passed along; it is something to be grasped, weighed, and internalized. The teacher, then, becomes essential not because of what he knows alone, but because of how he enables students to see more deeply, helping them recognize what matters and how it connects to a larger whole.

At its heart, education involves the shaping of intellect and character through the presence of those who live what they teach. The mind grows through intentional encounters with people whose habits of thought and attention give form to the learning process. In such a setting, facts find their meaning, and knowledge becomes something more than accumulation. The teacher who lives in pursuit of wisdom offers more than instruction; he offers himself as a model of how one might think, reflect, and live well. Over time, this sustained presence allows students to form new habits of mind and fosters new ways of seeing and responding to the world. The work is neither mechanical nor can it be reduced to a system. It unfolds in the space between persons, where influence is slow but lasting, and where what is cultivated is not only knowledge but a way of being.

To see the teacher once more as a philosopher is to recover a fuller understanding of authority—one rooted in the steady presence of wisdom directed toward the good of the student. This form of authority grows from a life shaped by thoughtful inquiry and deep conviction. It is sustained through commitment to the student's development, carried out with care and deliberation. The teacher's greater knowledge and experience serve not to dominate but to support, offering the structure within which a student gradually takes on the habits of thought that lead to greater independence. As the student grows, the teacher's guidance becomes less visible but no less essential, having shaped the conditions under which freedom becomes meaningful.

The philosopher-teacher leads with a kind of presence that arises from long familiarity with the landscape of thought. His own experience shapes the way forward, as a pattern of movement that invites students into deeper engagement with the world. Through this presence, the teacher makes visible what would otherwise remain hidden. He draws attention to the significance of what might be overlooked, and he brings the student into a shared pursuit marked by discipline and attentiveness. As the student learns to dwell within this pattern, new capacities begin to take shape. They emerge, however, only through sustained exposure to a life ordered by reflection and purpose.

In the literature classroom, this means sustained attention to a work like *Hamlet*. The teacher knows what such a play can awaken. His familiarity with Shakespeare's rich language and perennial themes becomes a wellspring of insight. Under his guidance, students may see in Hamlet's first soliloquy ("O, that this too too solid flesh would melt . . .") the raw conflict between despair and duty, a moment many readers skim past without realizing its depth of theological and philosophical resonance. He can help them hear the rhythm and irony of Polonius's advice to Laertes—"To thine own self be true"—and recognize how Shakespeare undercuts this apparently noble counsel by placing it in the mouth of a verbose schemer. In the same way, the classical teacher can slow students down at the graveyard scene, where Hamlet meditates over Yorick's skull, and draw out its confrontation with mortality, decay, and the leveling power of death that no mere summary can capture. Through such guidance, the play becomes not just a story of revenge but a meditation on moral choice, human weakness, and the search for truth in a world clouded by appearances. Without this kind of interpretive leadership, students may grasp plot points or offer personal reactions, but they are less likely to see how Hamlet's delay reflects a philosophical struggle about justice, or how Claudius's "O, my offence is rank" speech dramatizes the torment of conscience in unforgettable poetry.

The philosopher-teacher's approach applies equally to other subjects. In history, for example, he guides students toward understanding not just what happened, but why events unfolded as they did. He trains them to evaluate primary sources—such as Lincoln's Second Inaugural or a soldier's diary from the trenches—learning to weigh bias and credibility. He points out recurring patterns, like the rise and fall of empires or the tension between liberty and order, while also attending to the unique circumstances that shape particular moments. Most importantly, he opens students' eyes to the complexity of human motivation and institutional development: how fear, ambition, faith, and ideals can all converge in a single decision, and how institutions evolve in response to both principle and pressure. In this way, history moves beyond a list of names and dates to become a discipline of judgment, empathy, and understanding.

In mathematics, he helps students grasp not only procedures but the deeper structures of thought they reveal. For example, he can show how the Pythagorean theorem illustrates the beauty of deductive reasoning, how Euclid's proofs in *The Elements* display the elegance of logical progression from first principles, or how the symmetry of algebraic equations mirrors order in nature. He trains students to see that solving a quadratic equation is not merely about obtaining the correct answer but about discerning patterns and connections across mathematical domains. Through such guidance, students come to appreciate mathematical reasoning as a discipline of the mind—an exercise in clarity, precision, and creativity

In science, he initiates students into the methods of inquiry by guiding them beyond mere memorization of facts to the habits of observation, hypothesis, and experiment. He shows how Galileo's inclined plane experiments reveal the laws of motion, or how Darwin's careful observations of finches in the Galápagos supported his theory of natural selection. He helps students see the dynamic relationship between theory and evidence, whether in Newton's unifying law of gravitation or in the modern confirmation of Einstein's relativity through the bending of starlight. Most importantly, he cultivates an appreciation for the explanatory power of scientific understanding—how a single principle like conservation of energy illuminates phenomena as diverse as a pendulum's swing, a star's life cycle, and the metabolism of living cells. In this way, science becomes a disciplined search for truth in the natural world. Each subject requires specific forms of expertise, particular ways of thinking, and distinctive criteria for evaluation that students cannot discover through unguided exploration.

At the heart of philosophical teaching lies the cultivation of judgment, a capacity essential to all meaningful education. It is through judgment that students learn to perceive significance, to weigh ideas with care, and to sense the difference between the trivial and the profound. This discernment arises not by chance but through the long encounter with thoughtful minds, the slow refinement of attention, and the steady influence of those whose judgment has already been shaped by experience and reflection. The "facilitative model," an approach to teaching that withholds evaluative guidance, leaves students adrift in a sea of undifferentiated opinion. Without the steady hand of judgment to illuminate the path, they may speak freely, even passionately, yet remain unable to perceive the contours of sound reasoning or the marks of genuine insight.

The development of judgment in students unfolds through the steady influence of a teacher who not only thinks well but lives out the habits of intellectual virtue. In his classroom, students encounter a way of thinking that reveals what careful reasoning looks like, what it means to strive for clarity, and how one responds to error not with embarrassment but with renewed effort. Over time, as students come to trust both the teacher's expertise and his commitment to their growth, they begin to internalize higher standards for their own thinking. The teacher's deep knowledge, his moral seriousness, and his sustained presence form the conditions in which discernment can take root and flourish.

The philosopher-teacher recognizes that education unfolds within a civilizational context—it is not merely a means of self-advancement or workforce readiness, but a participation in something larger than the individual. Through the teacher's guidance, students come to see themselves as heirs to a great inheritance of thought, art, and inquiry. This tradition lives not as static content but as a living conversation, one that forms the imagination and shapes the soul. Such formation requires a teacher who sees the meaning in what is taught and senses the gravity of transmitting that meaning to others.

The prevailing model of teaching in many educational settings now rests on an approach that foregrounds efficiency, measurement, and procedural consistency. In this view, the effectiveness of teaching is gauged by its alignment with quantifiable results, with emphasis placed on methods that lend themselves to replication and evaluation. The role of the teacher becomes increasingly defined by the application of predetermined techniques—approaches selected less for their depth of insight than for their compatibility with systems of assessment. What is lost in such a framework is the recognition that teaching arises from the teacher's own encounter with what is worth knowing and from the capacity to draw others into that encounter with care and deliberation.

At the center of real teaching is more than the application of well-rehearsed methods. Its strength flows from a deeper sense of purpose, from the teacher's grasp of what education seeks to nurture in the human person. The teacher who cultivates in students a capacity for reflection does so through who he is and what he understands teaching to be. His presence in the classroom carries a weight shaped by years of his own careful reflection and a lived relationship with the material he teaches.

The recovery of the teacher as philosopher represents a substantive reconception of what teaching is and what it aims to accomplish. This reconception challenges both the authoritarian model of the teacher as mere transmitter of approved content and the facilitative model of the teacher as neutral guide to student-directed exploration. It offers instead a vision of teaching as philosophical practice, as the exercise of wisdom in service to student development, as the embodiment of intellectual and moral virtues that invite students into traditions of inquiry, understanding, and appreciation that they could not access alone.

The development of genuine intellectual independence unfolds through a relationship grounded in real authority—an authority rooted not in position but in the teacher's depth of knowledge and clarity of understanding. This kind of authority does not diminish the student's freedom; it makes that freedom possible by illuminating paths the student would not find alone. The presence of a guide who has already internalized the habits of mind and cultural inheritance that shape meaningful inquiry allows the student to engage more fully, more rigorously, and with greater confidence. Over time, the student begins to absorb what the teacher embodies—ways of seeing, reasoning, and evaluating that slowly become his own. Independence, in this vision, is not the absence of guidance but its fruit.

Recovering the teacher as philosopher transcends mere professional growth or instructional innovation. It calls for a profound reengagement with education's true aim: the cultivation of individuals capable of discernment, judgment, and wisdom. This renewal depends on teachers who grasp the philosophical essence of their vocation, embody the intellectual and moral virtues they aspire to nurture, and embrace the responsibility to lead students thoughtfully, exercising wisdom in pursuit of truth.

In this recovery of the teacher as philosopher lies educational renewal—a hopeful vision for teaching amid a culture increasingly shaped by technocratic reduction, market demands, and the abdication of adult responsibility for forming the young. The philosopher-teacher bears witness to the enduring truth that education is meant to cultivate wisdom, virtue, and meaningful engagement with the intellectual and cultural heritage that enriches human life. This witness serves as a vital cultural reminder that true human flourishing depends on developing discernment, judgment, and wisdom—capacities that only an education rooted in philosophy can fully nurture.

Recommended Further Reading

1. *Classical Education: The Movement Sweeping America* by Gene Edward Veith and Andrew Kern. Examines how classical teachers function as mentors and guides in the great conversation of Western civilization.

2. "Recovering the Lost Tools of Learning" (essay) by Dorothy Sayers. The foundational essay that defines the classical teacher's responsibility to develop students' capacity for learning itself.
3. *The Liberal Arts Tradition* by Kevin Clark and Ravi Jain. Explores the classical teacher's role as cultivator of wisdom and virtue through the liberal arts.
4. *The Seven Laws of Teaching* by John Milton Gregory. Though older, provides timeless principles for how classical teachers should understand their authority and responsibility.
5. *The Restoration of Christian Culture* by John Senior. Explores how classical teachers transmit cultural inheritance through personal example and love of learning.
6. *Tried & True: A Primer on Sound Pedagogy* by Daniel B. Coupland. Demonstrates through practical examples how classical teachers exercise wisdom and authority to develop student understanding.
7. *The Risk of Education: Discovering Our Ultimate Destiny* by Luigi Giussani. Explores how authentic teaching involves personal witness and the communication of living tradition through relationship.

Chapter 27

The Subversive Art of Clear Language

Why precise communication resists educational jargon

The language we use does more than describe reality; it shapes how we see it, how we interpret it, how we act within it. This fundamental truth, recognized by philosophers from Aristotle to Wittgenstein, becomes especially urgent in the realm of education, where words carry the power to form or deform entire generations of minds. When language serves truth, it illuminates reality and enables clear thinking. When it serves other masters—ideology, fashion, bureaucratic convenience—it obscures reality and corrupts thought itself.

Modern education has cultivated a strange and tangled garden of language. We no longer have the plain, sturdy words that have long sustained human understanding, but instead a dense growth of terms bred for the illusion of meaning. This linguistic overgrowth, thick with jargon and bureaucratic phrasing, has overtaken what was once fertile ground for clarity of thought. More than a matter of style or convenience, this proliferation of empty terminology functions as a kind of anti-language, designed for ambiguity or obscurity.

What makes this educational lexicon so pernicious is not its ugliness—it is indeed profoundly ugly, lacking both the precision of scientific terminology and the beauty of poetic expression—but its perfect embodiment of the intellectual and moral confusions that plague modern pedagogy and, more broadly, much of contemporary culture itself. The language of education has become a near-perfect mirror of education itself: detached from reality, obsessed with novelty, enamored of abstraction, and fundamentally dishonest about its own purposes and methods. Educational jargon is a language that has forgotten what language is for. Language's purpose is not to signal sophistication or manipulate perception but to communicate truth as clearly and precisely as possible.

The language of education has become a near-perfect mirror of education itself: detached from reality, obsessed with novelty, enamored of abstraction, and fundamentally dishonest about its own purposes and methods.

Against this degradation stands what we might call the "plain language challenge"—a simple but radical test for educational terminology. Any legitimate educational concept should pass three criteria: Can this term be explained clearly to the average parent or citizen? Does it refer to something specific and observable? Does it clarify or obscure what actually happens in teaching and learning? Terms that fail this test deserve suspicion as jargon rather than genuine vocabulary. Those that pass earn their place by illuminating rather than concealing, by enabling accurate communication rather than impressive-sounding vagueness.

Take, for example, that most lauded phrase in contemporary educational discourse: "data-driven instruction." Now a fixture in mission statements, echoed in faculty meetings, and splashed across classroom walls, this seemingly innocuous term offers a revealing glimpse into the scientistic mindset that dominates modern schooling. It evokes a vision of teaching governed by numerical precision. Objective metrics replace human judgment. Teachers become technicians—monitoring dashboards, adjusting inputs, and optimizing outcomes as if education were a system to be calibrated rather than a human endeavor to be cultivated.

What this clinical language conceals is the messy, fundamentally human reality of the classroom. It cannot account for the student whose test scores collapse after a parent's job loss. It misses the quiet flash of insight that no rubric can capture. It ignores the complex interplay of motivation, background knowledge, personal relationships, and circumstance that shapes every act of learning. In its place, it substitutes a mechanical model—stimulus and response, input and output, intervention and outcome. This is more than an oversimplification. It is a distortion so deep it threatens to hollow out educational practice itself.

A teacher trained to think in terms of "data-driven instruction" begins, often unconsciously, to see students not as whole persons undergoing intellectual and moral formation, but as datasets—variables to be tracked, managed, and optimized. His attention shifts from what is meaningful and formative to what is merely measurable. It discards the rich particularity of persons in favor of the clean abstractions of metrics. The teacher loses sight of the unpredictable, organic nature of real learning.

But what if we spoke honestly instead? Rather than "data-driven instruction," we might describe "teaching informed by careful observation and assessment." This language acknowledges the value of evidence while recognizing the irreducibly human dimensions of learning. It suggests that good teachers gather information about their students' progress, but it doesn't reduce the art of teaching to mechanical data processing. The phrase passes our plain language challenge: parents understand it, it refers to observable practices, and it clarifies rather than obscures what actually happens in thoughtful classrooms.

Consider another of modern education's more beguiling euphemisms: "twenty-first-century skills." This chronological badge of supposed progress is routinely affixed to a narrow set of favored competencies—collaboration, communication, creativity, and critical thinking—that are held up as the essential virtues of contemporary education. Yet beneath this honorific lies a striking form of temporal arrogance. The phrase suggests, however subtly, that the first twenty centuries of formal education were somehow benighted, their aims primitive, their methods obsolete. One would think that only in our present moment have we finally uncovered the true ends of learning. As though Socrates never taught his students to think critically. As though Newton failed to collaborate with the scientific minds of his day. As though Shakespeare lacked creativity, or failed to communicate.

This "presentist" conceit reveals itself most clearly in the curious assumption that these so-called twenty-first-century skills are somehow newly relevant, uniquely suited to our time. But nothing about these skills is new. The ability to reason well, to work with others, to speak and write with clarity, to imagine new possibilities have always been essential to human flourishing. They were as necessary in Periclean Athens, in medieval Paris, in Victorian London, as they are today. What is new is the tendency to isolate these capacities from the deep intellectual traditions that gave them shape and substance.

Indeed, the slogan achieves its most absurd effect when it casts these skills in opposition to the traditional disciplines—history, literature, philosophy, mathematics—as though one could meaningfully "think critically" apart from a body of knowledge to think about, or "communicate effectively" without something worth saying. One cannot collaborate in a vacuum. Creativity cannot flourish in the absence of form, structure, or inherited insight. These so-called skills are not educational alternatives to traditional knowledge; they are its fruits.

The phrase "twenty-first-century skills" simply performs a clever sleight of hand. It renames ancient aims in modern vocabulary, and in doing so, disguises continuity as innovation. It flatters our chronological vanity, seducing us into thinking we have surpassed the past, when in truth we are living from its storehouse. It replaces the humility of inheritance with the hubris of novelty—and that is no foundation for genuine education.

Here again, honest language serves us better. Instead of "twenty-first-century skills," we could refer to "enduring intellectual and moral capabilities" or simply name the specific capacities we mean: reasoning, communication, collaboration, creativity. When educators speak of helping students develop "critical thinking skills," they might instead describe "teaching students to reason carefully, evaluate evidence thoughtfully, and form sound judgments." Such language is both more specific and more honest about what such development requires. It acknowledges that these capabilities have always mattered while focusing attention on how to cultivate them effectively.

Then there is the ubiquitous phrase "student-centered learning," a tidy expression that simultaneously flatters our democratic instincts and conceals deep philosophical confusion. Now treated as educational dogma in many circles, this term is often wielded as a rebuke to supposed past models of instruction. Traditional education, we are told, placed the teacher at the center of the learning process. Only now have we heroically shifted the focus to where it properly belongs: the student. The implicit accusation is that older pedagogies—classical pedagogies—were somehow "teacher-centered," concerned more with the performance of the instructor than the growth of the learner.

This is a false dichotomy. It is like accusing traditional medicine of being "doctor-centered" rather than "patient-centered," as if the physician's primary concern were self-glorification rather than the work of healing. The analogy is apt because it exposes the confusion at the heart of the slogan. No competent doctor ever believed the patient existed to affirm the physician's sense of purpose. Likewise, no serious educator—classical, modern, or otherwise—has ever believed that students existed for the teacher's edification. The goal has always been the development of the student.

Classical education has always been centered on the student in the truest sense: it aims at the formation of the learner's intellect, character, and judgment. The real question is not whether education is student-centered, but how that aim is best achieved. The modern use of the phrase "student-centered learning" often signals a preference for pedagogical methods that downplay or even dismiss the teacher's authority, expertise, and role as a formative presence. It implies that learning must be driven by the student's choices, interests, or activities rather than guided by the wisdom, knowledge, and moral example of the teacher.

George Orwell, in his prescient 1946 essay "Politics and the English Language," warned that the corruption of language leads inevitably to the corruption of thought. He observed that "the great enemy of clear language is insincerity," and nowhere is that more evident than in contemporary educational discourse, where jargon often masks ideological conformity as pedagogical wisdom. The phrase "student-centered learning" exemplifies this corruption perfectly. It disguises a serious disagreement over educational methods as if it were a disagreement over aims. It reframes a debate about how best to teach as if one side were interested in students and the other in themselves. This is not merely misleading; it's corrosive. It undermines the teacher's legitimate role as intellectual and moral guide. It replaces an ordered vision of formation with a consumerist vision of preference and autonomy.

What is needed is not a retreat from student-centeredness, but a recovery of its classical meaning: education in which the student is at the center not because he drives the process, but because he is the subject of formation. And that formation depends, unavoidably, on the presence of a teacher who knows what is worth knowing, loves what is worth loving, and can lead others into that same inheritance.

Clear language helps us escape this false dichotomy. Instead of "student-centered learning," we might describe "education aimed at genuine intellectual and moral development in a teacher-led classroom." This language captures the proper focus without the implicit dismissal of teaching authority. It acknowledges that good education serves the student's growth while recognizing that such growth requires skillful guidance from those who have traveled the path before.

This rhetorical maneuver, the suggestion that educational innovation represents not a departure from traditional purposes but their authentic fulfillment, appears with remarkable consistency across the landscape of educational jargon. "Social-emotional learning" implies that traditional education neglected the non-cognitive dimensions of human development, despite the fact that great literature, philosophy, and history have always addressed emotion, character, and relationship. "Authentic assessment" suggests that traditional evaluation lacked genuineness, as if the careful judgment of student work by knowledgeable teachers represented some kind of fraud rather than the most authentic assessment possible.

When discussing "authentic assessment," teachers could speak more honestly of "evaluating student work through the informed judgment of those who understand both the subject matter and the student." This description captures what assessment should be without the implied criticism of traditional evaluation methods. It passes our plain language challenge by being both comprehensible and specific about what actually occurs when experienced teachers carefully consider student work.

In each case, the new terminology does not merely rename traditional educational concerns but subtly redefines them. It shifts "emotion" from the moral and philosophical domain to the psychological. It transforms "assessment" from a matter of judgment to a question of task design.

And in each case, the new term carries an implicit critique of tradition, suggesting that earlier approaches neglected what they in fact addressed differently.

This pattern of inflated terminology reaches its apex in the curious case of "digital literacy"—a phrase brandished with a kind of self-congratulatory assurance, as if its mere invocation constituted a forward-looking and enlightened approach to education. It is often deployed to justify the widespread integration of screens, devices, and digital platforms (now including AI) into the classroom, under the pretense that such tools are not only helpful but essential for preparing students for life in the twenty-first century.

In practice, what passes for digital literacy is often little more than operational familiarity with software—basic navigational competence in user-friendly environments designed precisely to minimize the need for thought. Students are taught to log in, upload, drag, drop, type into boxes, and click submit. These are not signs of intellectual maturity; they are the educational equivalents of learning to push the right buttons on a vending machine.

Yet upon inspection, the term "digital literacy" proves far less substantial than its impressive name suggests. Once, literacy referred to the capacity to read deeply and write cogently, the foundational skills of intellectual engagement and cultural transmission. Now, these venerable arts have been rebranded in technological garb, as though the ability to manage a shared Google Doc or click through a multiple-choice interface were on par with composing an argument in lucid prose or following the logical rigor of a Euclidean proof.

In practice, what passes for digital literacy is often little more than operational familiarity with software—basic navigational competence in user-friendly environments designed precisely to minimize the need for thought. Students are taught to log in, upload, drag, drop, type into boxes, and click submit. These are not signs of intellectual maturity; they are the educational equivalents of learning to push the right buttons on a vending machine. The use of the term "digital literacy" is an act of linguistic inflation, analogous to describing the ability to operate a car as "automobile literacy." No one would mistake the mechanical competence of driving with an understanding of engineering, transportation history, or civic infrastructure. Yet in the educational context, such conflations are routinely made—and rewarded.

This terminological legerdemain has real consequences. By elevating technical facility over intellectual substance, we risk confusing fluency with wisdom. We begin to imagine that preparing students for the digital world means simply accustoming them to its tools, rather than equipping them with the intellectual and moral virtues necessary to discern its uses, resist its excesses, and preserve their humanity within it.

What is needed is not a fetish for the digital, nor a fear of it, but a clear-eyed distinction between means and ends. Digital tools may assist in learning, but they are not themselves the substance of education. When we speak honestly, we might describe students developing "competence with digital tools in service of learning" rather than achieving "digital literacy." This phrasing maintains the proper hierarchy: technology serves learning, not the reverse. To equate basic digital operations with literacy is to reduce the art of learning to a set of procedural maneuvers, precisely the kind of reduction that impoverishes minds rather than expands them.

What ultimately unites these various terms, beyond their linguistic awkwardness and conceptual vagueness, is their function not as tools for genuine communication, but as badges of ideological allegiance. Their primary purpose is not to clarify thought but to signal belonging. When the educational bureaucrat or consultant lards his speech with the latest approved buzzwords—"student-centered," "data-driven," "twenty-first-century skills," "digital literacy"—he does not reveal a deep grasp of educational philosophy or pedagogical method. He announces instead his membership in a particular tribe, his adherence to the prevailing orthodoxy.

In this way, educational language has degenerated into a system of shibboleths. Much like the ancient test-word that revealed one's tribal origin, today's EduSpeak functions as a litmus test for ideological alignment. To speak the language fluently is to demonstrate compliance with the reigning doctrines of educational fashion. To question its vocabulary is to risk expulsion from polite professional circles, or worse, to be branded as retrograde, resistant to "innovation," or out of step with "best practices."

This shift in linguistic function reveals a fundamental reorientation of educational priorities. Education has, in many circles, moved from the pursuit of truth through disciplined inquiry to the performance of conformity through acceptable phrasing. The goal is no longer to uncover meaning but to mirror institutional rhetoric. The consequences of this transformation are profound. Language that once served as a medium of inquiry and illumination has become a tool of obfuscation and pretense. Where clarity and precision are essential to the cultivation of thought, the rise of hollow terminology encourages a kind of surface-level consensus, rewarding fluency in jargon and the repetition of sanctioned slogans.

The danger posed by degraded educational language is not merely stylistic; it is philosophical. When discourse abandons the duty to name things truthfully, it ceases to serve learning and instead manufactures perception, conceals failure, and manipulates reality. This is no exaggeration. When words are severed from meaning, the moral structure of education begins to collapse. Institutions once devoted to truth and character quietly shift their allegiance—from truth to trend.

Our plain language challenge offers a practical tool for resistance. When we encounter educational terminology, we should ask: Does this language help me understand something important about teaching and learning? Can I explain this concept to someone outside the educational establishment without resorting to more jargon? Does this term refer to something I can actually observe in a classroom? If the answer to any of these questions is no, we are likely encountering jargon rather than genuine vocabulary.

Consider how this challenge applies to common educational phrases. "Learning outcomes" fails the test. It means nothing different from "what students should know and be able to do," so why the pretentious substitute? "Best practices" often fails as well. Does it refer to methods proven effective through careful study, or to currently fashionable approaches? "Stakeholders" clearly fails. Are we acknowledging the legitimate interests of parents and community, or reducing education to a business transaction?

The classical educator practices linguistic discipline not from pedantic concern with terminology but from recognition that language shapes thought. Words matter because they influence how we perceive reality, how we understand our purposes, and how we conduct our practice. The teacher who thinks in terms of "learning objectives" may focus differently than one who considers "what is worth knowing." The administrator who speaks of "human resources" relates differently to teachers than one who thinks of "colleagues" or "faculty."

In an educational landscape increasingly dominated by abstraction and euphemism, the deliberate use of clear, honest language has become a quietly radical act—a matter of intellectual integrity. To speak plainly in the face of institutional jargon is to resist the bureaucratic impulse to obscure failure and soften truth. It requires the courage to describe reality as it is, not as we wish it to appear.

This commitment to linguistic clarity means naming educational struggles directly. A student who cannot read fluently is not an "emergent literacy learner," but a student who has difficulty reading. Homework is not a "differentiated reinforcement activity," but work—often challenging, sometimes resisted—done at home to practice or extend what was taught in the classroom. Such phrases may seem innocuous, even well-meaning, but they blur the contours of reality. Euphemism trades precision for politeness, and in doing so, undermines understanding. When we insist on words that mean what they say, we recover the ability to think clearly about what is happening in our schools—and only then can we begin to act wisely.

The discipline of clear language also requires acknowledging what we do not know and cannot precisely measure. Instead of claiming to assess "grit" or "growth mindset," classical educators might describe observing "students' persistence when facing difficulties" or "willingness to embrace challenges." Rather than measuring "twenty-first-century skills," they might evaluate "students' ability to work effectively with others" or "skill in communicating ideas clearly." This precision serves not only accuracy but humility, recognizing the limits of what can be captured in language and measurement.

Some will object that specialized terminology serves legitimate purposes, that educators need precise vocabulary to discuss complex realities, that certain concepts require technical language. This objection has merit but misses the crucial distinction between terminology that clarifies and jargon that obscures. Legitimate educational vocabulary—like "phonemic awareness," "mathematical reasoning," or "historical thinking"—refers to specific, observable phenomena that benefit from precise naming. Such terms earn their place by illuminating rather than concealing, by enabling more accurate communication rather than impressive-sounding vagueness.

These legitimate terms pass our plain language challenge easily. "Phonemic awareness" can be explained clearly to parents as "the ability to hear and manipulate the individual sounds in spoken words." "Mathematical reasoning" refers to "the capacity to think logically about numbers, patterns, and relationships." "Historical thinking" describes "the ability to analyze evidence, understand causation, and think about change over time." Each term points to something specific that teachers can observe and parents can understand. The contrast with empty jargon is stark. Try explaining "student agency" or "transformational leadership" or "culturally responsive pedagogy" without using more educational buzzwords. The exercise reveals how these terms function more as tribal markers than as meaningful descriptions of educational reality.

The turn to classical education demands more than a change in curriculum; it requires a recovery of language itself. We cannot reclaim an educational tradition grounded in truth, virtue, and reason while continuing to speak in the vague euphemisms and bureaucratic abstractions of contemporary pedagogy. Classical education begins with clarity, not only of thought, but of speech. It names things as they are. It teaches how to speak truthfully.

This linguistic recovery is not peripheral to the classical project. The premises of classical education rest on the belief that language is not merely expressive but revelatory, that words can illuminate reality and should not obscure it. Where modern education often manipulates language to simulate progress, classical education calls for language that seeks truth without adornment or evasion. The commitment to clear language reflects a deeper commitment to intellectual honesty, moral integrity, and respect for the reality we seek to understand and transmit.

Classical educators recognize that the corruption of educational language both reflects and accelerates the corruption of educational purpose. When we speak of "human capital" instead of students, we begin to see education as an economic investment rather than the formation of human beings. When we discuss "delivery systems" instead of teaching, we reduce the art of education to mere information transfer. When we focus on "achievement gaps" instead of the particular needs of particular students, we lose sight of the individual persons we are called to serve.

The classical tradition offers a different model. It insists that education is fundamentally about the formation of human beings—their intellects, their characters, their capacity for wisdom and virtue. This formation requires relationships between teachers and students, engagement with worthy content, and the gradual development of good habits of mind and heart. These realities can be described clearly and honestly without resort to jargon or euphemism. In classical schools, teachers do not "facilitate learning experiences" or "implement instructional strategies." They teach. They introduce students to great books, challenging problems, and worthy questions. They correct errors, encourage effort, and model intellectual virtue. They form relationships that enable growth. They exercise judgment based on knowledge and experience. All of this can be described in plain language that honors both the complexity and the dignity of the educational enterprise.

The recovery of clear language in classical education extends to how we discuss educational purposes and outcomes. We do not aim to produce "global citizens" or "lifelong learners" or "critical consumers of information." We seek to form human beings capable of wisdom, virtue, and meaningful participation in the inherited conversation of civilization. We want students who can read deeply, write clearly, think logically, speak persuasively, and live well. We hope to cultivate minds that love truth, hearts that recognize beauty, and wills that choose good. This clarity of language reflects clarity of purpose. When we know what we are trying to accomplish, we can speak about it directly. When we are uncertain about our aims, we take refuge in buzzwords and abstractions. The prevalence of jargon in contemporary education thus reveals not sophistication but uncertainty about fundamental questions of purpose, method, and meaning.

Classical education's commitment to clear language serves as both symptom and cause of its broader intellectual health. Schools that speak plainly about their purposes tend to pursue those purposes effectively.

Teachers who can explain their methods in ordinary language typically understand what they are doing and why. Students who encounter honest language learn to think and speak with greater precision themselves. The degradation of educational discourse has mirrored the degradation of educational purpose. If we wish to think with the clarity of Aristotle and write with the lucidity of Cicero, we cannot continue speaking in the incoherent idioms of the administrative memo. To embrace classical education is to reject the cant of the moment and to restore the dignity of words rightly used.

The prevalence of jargon in contemporary education thus reveals not sophistication but uncertainty about fundamental questions of purpose, method, and meaning.

This restoration begins with individual teachers and schools committed to linguistic honesty. It spreads through communities of educators who refuse to speak in euphemisms and demand clarity from their colleagues and institutions. It grows as parents and citizens insist on understanding what actually happens in schools, rejecting impressive-sounding terminology that conceals more than it reveals. Only by recovering honest speech can we hope to restore honest learning. And in that recovery lies not just a stylistic improvement, but the possibility of reawakening education itself—no longer as a performance of compliance, but as a pursuit of wisdom. The classical educator who speaks plainly about the work of teaching and learning becomes a guardian of both language and thought, preserving the possibility that words might still serve truth, that education might still form human beings, and that schools might still be places where young minds encounter the best that has been thought and said.

In the end, the subversive art of clear language is subversive precisely because it serves truth rather than fashion, reality rather than perception, understanding rather than impression. In a world increasingly dominated by sophisticated forms of dishonesty, the simple commitment to say what we mean and mean what we say becomes a radical act—one that classical education both requires and enables.

Recommended Further Reading

1. "Politics and the English Language" by George Orwell. The foundational essay exposing how corrupted language enables corrupted thinking in political and institutional contexts.
2. *The Language Police* by Diane Ravitch. Documents how euphemistic language in education conceals ideological manipulation of curriculum and instruction.
3. *Doublespeak* by William Lutz. Analyzes how institutional jargon deliberately obscures meaning and manipulates perception across various fields.
4. *The Sense of Style* by Steven Pinker. Explores how precise language serves understanding rather than obfuscation in academic and professional contexts.
5. *Weasel Words* by Paul Wasserman and Don Hausrath. Catalogs how euphemistic language corrupts discourse in education, government, and business.
6. *The Jargon of the Schools* by Richard Mitchell. Critiques how educational institutions use pretentious language to mask intellectual emptiness and institutional failure.
7. *The Tyranny of Words* by Stuart Chase. Exposes how abstract language and undefined terms manipulate thought and prevent clear reasoning.

Chapter 28

The Subversive Art of Socratic Dialogue

How guided questioning develops independent thinking

The Socratic dialogue poses a paradox for the modern educator: a method so radical it appears regressive, so forward-looking it feels ancient, so transformative it still bears the name of a man executed over two thousand years ago. Among the tools of classical education, few are more powerful—or more misunderstood. This is not the free-form student chatter found in many contemporary classrooms, but a disciplined art of guided inquiry that refines both thought and character. This was the method Socrates practiced in the Athenian agora. It is the pedagogy that formed the minds of Augustine and Aquinas. And it is the means by which twenty-first-century students can join what Mortimer Adler called "the Great Conversation"—that ongoing dialogue in which the greatest thinkers of history continue to confront life's most enduring questions. In an age saturated with information and shallow opinion, this ancient art offers something truly revolutionary: a return to genuine understanding, cultivated through careful questioning, rigorous reasoning, and thoughtful engagement with the texts that have shaped our civilization.

What makes this dialogue so remarkable is its perfect embodiment of a fundamental educational principle: learning at its best is not information transfer but guided participation in the enduring questions that have occupied the greatest minds throughout human history. The Socratic dialogue transforms the classroom from a venue for the delivery of facts into a temporary symposium where students and teacher gather around texts of extraordinary depth to examine, question, analyze, and ultimately understand the ideas that have shaped human understanding across centuries.

Yet contemporary education has largely misunderstood this ancient art. Modern pedagogy reduces Socratic dialogue to "student-centered discussion" or "collaborative learning" that abandons intellectual authority in favor of egalitarian opinion-sharing. Such misappropriation misses the essential truth: Socratic dialogue represents not the abdication of teacher authority but its most sophisticated exercise. The Socratic teacher guides inquiry with such subtle skill that students experience direction without domination, correction without diminishment, formation without coercion.

The Socratic dialogue, rightly conceived, is not a free-for-all of opinions or a classroom exercise in unstructured sharing. It is a disciplined pursuit of truth, led by a teacher whose authority rests not on power but on preparation. Such a teacher does not approach the text as a neutral moderator but as a thoughtful guide. He has read and studied the material, reflected on its meaning, and brought it into conversation with the cultural and philosophical inheritance of the West. This depth of engagement is not optional; it is what gives the dialogue its seriousness and shape. Without it, the inquiry risks collapsing into aimless chatter, where impressions take the place of insights and where questions float untethered from the search for answers.

Consider how this authority manifests in practice when examining Plato's allegory of the cave, the story in which prisoners mistake shadows on a wall for reality until one is freed and gradually comes to see the world as it truly is. The unprepared teacher might simply ask, "What do you think this means?" This open-ended question seems to invite participation but actually abandons intellectual responsibility. It leaves students to grope toward understanding without guidance. The skilled Socratic teacher, by contrast, might ask: "What does the sun represent in this allegory, and how does it relate to the concept of the Good discussed earlier in the dialogue? What is the significance of the prisoners being bound since childhood? How does the ascent from the cave relate to the divided line presented in the previous section?"

These questions do not dictate interpretation but guide it. They do not impose meaning but illuminate pathways toward it. They represent not the surrender of authority but its precise exercise. They direct attention to significant aspects of the text, highlight conceptual relationships that might otherwise go unnoticed, and guide students toward insights they could not easily reach alone.

As students begin to respond, the teacher's authority takes a subtler form—what Mortimer Adler called "the art of questioning." Through this art, the dialogue deepens. A student might offer that the cave represents ignorance. The teacher, rather than affirming or correcting, draws the student further in: "Is all ignorance alike, or is there a difference between not knowing and being prevented from knowing? Why are the shadows in Plato's cave man-made? Why does he tell us the prisoners have been there since childhood?" These are not rhetorical traps, nor mere prompts. They are invitations to think more precisely, to return to the text with fresh eyes, and to begin again the hard work of interpretation.

Such questioning appears fluid, even spontaneous, but it rests on careful preparation. The teacher must have internalized the text so completely that he can move within its world with ease. He adjusts to the turns of discussion without sacrificing clarity or purpose. His authority lies not in having the final word, but in knowing how to keep the conversation pointed toward what matters most. In this way, the Socratic classroom becomes something rare: a space where freedom and discipline coexist, where inquiry is rigorous but never rigid, and where meaning is not delivered but discovered.

This sophisticated exercise of authority depends upon thorough preparation. The teacher must know not only what the text says but what it means—not just its surface content but its deeper structure, not merely its explicit arguments but its implicit assumptions and unspoken implications. Consider the preparation required for a Paideia seminar on Plato's Republic. The teacher begins with careful selection of passages that will reward sustained examination. He chooses sections dense enough to support extended dialogue yet accessible enough to engage student minds. He identifies key concepts that students must grasp: the nature of justice, the relationship between soul and state, the critique of democracy, the theory of forms. He anticipates potential misunderstandings: students might conflate Plato's ideal state with totalitarianism or mistake his critique of poetry for aesthetic philistinism.

Most importantly, the classical teacher prepares questions designed to guide discovery rather than test recall. Primary questions open conceptual space: "What does Socrates mean when he says that justice in the soul resembles justice in the state?" Follow-up questions deepen understanding: "How does this analogy work? What are its limitations? What does it assume about human nature?" Clarifying questions ensure precision: "When Plato speaks of the 'guardians,' does he mean the same thing as when he discusses the 'philosopher-kings'?"

This preparation extends beyond individual texts to encompass the broader tradition of interpretation and commentary. The teacher familiar with Republic scholarship can guide students away from common misreadings while remaining open to genuine insights that emerge from careful textual engagement. He knows which interpretive pathways lead to fruitful understanding and which end in confusion or superficiality.

Such preparation cannot be improvised or delegated to study guides. It requires the teacher's own wrestling with difficult ideas, his own journey through the text's complexities, his own formation through engagement with great works. The teacher who has not himself experienced the intellectual transformation that comes from serious engagement with Plato cannot guide others through that same transformation. Authority in Socratic dialogue emerges not from institutional position but from intellectual achievement—from having traveled the pathways of understanding and being able to guide others along them.

The heart of Socratic dialogue lies in the teacher's ability to ask questions that do not seek predetermined answers but genuinely open conceptual space for deeper understanding. This art develops through practice and reflection, through careful attention to how questions function in actual dialogue, through sensitivity to the rhythm and flow

The heart of Socratic dialogue lies in the teacher's ability to ask questions that do not seek predetermined answers but genuinely open conceptual space for deeper understanding.

of genuine inquiry. Effective Socratic questions operate at multiple levels simultaneously. They focus attention on specific textual details while pointing toward broader conceptual issues. They challenge student assumptions while maintaining an atmosphere of intellectual safety. They push for precision while allowing room for genuine discovery. They guide without controlling, direct without dictating, correct without crushing.

A sequence from a seminar on Hamlet's famous soliloquy "To be or not to be" illustrates this artful questioning. The classical teacher might begin with a focusing question: "What exactly is Hamlet contemplating in this speech?" As students suggest suicide, the teacher might probe further: "Is he really considering killing himself, or something else? What does he mean by 'to be'?" When students explore the nature of existence and action, follow-up questions deepen the inquiry: "Why does Hamlet describe death as 'sleep'? What problems does this metaphor create for his argument? How does his uncertainty about the afterlife affect his reasoning?"

Notice how each question builds upon previous responses while opening new avenues for exploration. The teacher neither accepts student answers uncritically nor dismisses them arbitrarily. Instead, he uses responses as launching points for deeper inquiry, guiding the conversation toward increasingly sophisticated understanding of the text's complexities.

The skilled practitioner also knows when to allow productive confusion to work itself out through discussion. He recognizes when to introduce clarifying information and when to highlight contradictions that demand resolution. He can sense when students are approaching genuine insight and knows how to nurture that process without short-circuiting it through premature explanation. This sensitivity comes only through experience—through many seminars, many texts, many moments of watching understanding dawn in student minds. Once you witness this technique effectively in action, there's nothing to do but marvel at its quiet, subversive brilliance: how, by withholding answers and trusting the process, the teacher leads students not just to knowledge, but to the thrill of discovery itself.

The deepest purpose of Socratic dialogue, however, extends beyond comprehension of particular texts to the formation of intellectual character. Through sustained engagement with great works under skilled guidance, students develop what John Senior called poetic knowledge—the integration of intellectual comprehension with imaginative engagement. This formation produces specific intellectual virtues essential to genuine classical education. Intellectual humility emerges as students recognize that understanding is progressive rather than immediate. Complex texts yield their meaning gradually through sustained engagement rather than instantly through superficial reading. Students come to understand that learning is not something done to them or forced upon them, but an authentic experience they themselves engage in. They are not constrained by the idea of "reading for comprehension" in order to regurgitate content. Rather, they experience firsthand the joy and struggle of discovery. They learn to say "I don't understand" without shame, to sit with difficult passages without premature closure, and to revise initial interpretations when textual evidence demands it.

Alongside humility, students begin to cultivate intellectual precision. They grow more attuned to the weight of words and the contours of meaning, recognizing that much of philosophical and literary depth lies in the details. Whether unpacking Aristotle's theory of causation or grappling with Mill's conception of liberty, they learn that clarity often emerges only after slow, careful work. Or consider Frederick Douglass's *Narrative*, which provides a compelling example of how Socratic dialogue develops this precision. A student might initially focus on the brutality of slavery toward the enslaved. But as the conversation deepens, a skilled teacher may draw attention to Douglass's striking observation that slavery corrupts the slaveholder as well. "What does Douglass mean when he says that Sophia Auld, once a kind woman, was transformed into a tyrant by the institution of slavery? Is her moral decay merely a loss of empathy, or something deeper—a systematic deformation of the soul by the logic of ownership?" Parsing this distinction requires students to clarify terms like "corruption," "power," and "human dignity," and to explore the psychological and spiritual costs of domination. In this way, Socratic dialogue sharpens their sensitivity to conceptual nuance and trains them to approach language not as ornament but as a tool for truth.

Perhaps most importantly, intellectual honesty emerges as students learn to follow evidence where it leads. They acknowledge difficulties in their own positions and resist the temptation to oversimplify complex issues for the sake of comfort or convenience. They discover that genuine understanding often requires abandoning cherished assumptions, that intellectual growth demands a kind of courage that our culture rarely cultivates. The student who has participated in well-conducted Socratic dialogues on Plato's allegory does not merely know what the cave represents. He has imaginatively experienced the relationship between appearance and reality, and has perhaps even considered the ethical implications of returning to help those still in darkness. This integration of intellectual, imaginative, and ethical dimensions produces not merely information acquisition but formation of mind and character.

These intellectual virtues serve a larger purpose: initiating students into what Mortimer Adler called "the Great Conversation"—the ongoing dialogue between great minds across centuries about the fundamental questions of human existence. This conversation includes not merely the explicit exchanges between thinkers who influenced each other directly, but the implicit dialogue that occurs when any serious reader encounters the enduring questions that great works continue to raise.

When students read Aristotle's *Nicomachean Ethics* alongside Mill's *On Liberty*, they participate in a conversation about the nature of human flourishing that spans twenty-three centuries. When they examine Lincoln's "Second Inaugural Address" in light of Augustine's *City of God*, they engage with questions about providence, suffering, and justice that have occupied human minds since antiquity. When they explore Jane Austen's portrayal of marriage in relation to Plato's analysis of love in the Phaedrus, they enter discussions about human relationships that transcend any particular historical moment.

This entrance into the Great Conversation represents genuine liberation. It offers not the superficial freedom to express uninformed opinions but the deeper freedom that comes from possessing intellectual resources adequate to life's most pressing questions. The student who has never encountered Aristotle's analysis of friendship, who has never considered Augustine's account of time, who has never unpacked Aquinas's arguments for natural law, possesses a much more limited perspective than one who has engaged with these thinkers under knowledgeable guidance.

The Great Books tradition recognizes that certain works possess such intellectual depth, such conceptual richness, such enduring significance that they serve as ideal vehicles for this initiation. Whether Plato's *Republic*, Dante's *Divine Comedy*, Cervantes's *Don Quixote*, or Lincoln's Gettysburg Address, these works address fundamental questions of human experience with such profound insight that they continue to provoke, challenge, and illuminate centuries after their composition. They constitute a living conversation about perennial human concerns—a conversation that each generation enters anew.

How then might schools create conditions for authentic Socratic dialogue within contemporary constraints? The challenge is real but not insurmountable. Successful implementation requires several elements working in harmony.

First, teachers need sustained preparation in both the content of great works and the art of Socratic questioning. This cannot be accomplished through brief workshops or cursory training. It requires deep immersion in texts, practice in dialogue techniques, and ongoing reflection on what makes seminars succeed or fail. Many schools have found that summer institutes, mentoring relationships with experienced practitioners, and regular professional development focused on specific texts produce better results than generic pedagogical training. The bottom line is that teachers must themselves be educated well in the liberal arts and they must be willing to prepare themselves to enter into Socratic dialogue with a roomful of students.

Second, schools must allocate sufficient time for meaningful dialogue. Authentic Socratic seminars cannot be compressed into twenty-minute discussions or fragmented across multiple brief sessions. They require extended periods—ideally sixty to ninety minutes—that allow ideas to develop naturally through sustained conversation. This may mean restructuring schedules, combining class periods, or reimagining how instructional time is used.

Third, assessment must align with the goals of Socratic dialogue. Traditional testing measures recall and recognition rather than understanding and wisdom. Schools committed to Socratic methods often develop alternative assessment approaches: student reflection papers on seminar discussions, portfolios of written responses to great works, capstone projects that demonstrate ability to enter the Great Conversation through original thinking about enduring questions. These approaches offer incredible educational opportunities.

Most importantly, schools must commit to the long-term formation that Socratic dialogue represents. The fruits of genuine dialogue—wisdom, understanding, intellectual virtue—develop slowly through sustained engagement with worthy texts under skilled guidance.

The fruits of genuine dialogue—wisdom, understanding, intellectual virtue—develop slowly through sustained engagement with worthy texts under skilled guidance.

Schools must resist the pressure to abandon these methods when standardized test scores don't immediately reflect their value.

The Socratic dialogue is not merely a pedagogical technique but a relationship between minds mediated through texts of extraordinary depth and significance. The great practitioners—whether Adler guiding discussions of Aristotle, Senior exploring Dante with students, or contemporary classical educators leading seminars on Shakespeare, Austen, or Douglass—demonstrate not the absence of authority but its most refined manifestation.

This relationship between textual authority, teacher guidance, and student discovery stands at the heart of classical education's approach to intellectual formation. It recognizes that certain works possess such depth that they serve as ideal vehicles for developing not merely knowledge but intellectual virtue. The teacher's role in this process requires extraordinary preparation, sophisticated judgment, and genuine love for both texts and students. He must know great works intimately enough to guide others through their complexities. He must possess the questioning art that opens conceptual space without abandoning intellectual responsibility. He must understand how minds develop and what kinds of formation truly serve human flourishing.

When these elements combine successfully, something remarkable occurs. Students discover that they can think about the most profound questions human beings have ever asked. They realize that their minds are capable of engaging with ideas that have challenged the greatest thinkers in history. They experience the joy of genuine understanding, the satisfaction of intellectual achievement, the confidence that comes from possessing adequate tools for life's deepest challenges.

This transformation extends far beyond academic achievement to encompass the formation of persons capable of meaningful participation in the inherited conversation of civilization. Students formed through authentic Socratic dialogue become not merely informed individuals but thoughtful participants in the ongoing dialogue about what is true, good, and beautiful. They come to realize this is a conversation that began long before them, will continue long after them, but to which they can now contribute with understanding developed through disciplined engagement with humanity's greatest works.

In this commitment lies hope not merely for educational improvement but for cultural renewal—for the formation of young people who have not merely acquired information about the past but have engaged with its enduring wisdom, who have not simply learned about great ideas but have wrestled with their implications, who have not just studied civilization's achievements but have participated in the intellectual tradition that produced them. These students become guardians and contributors to the Great Conversation, ensuring that humanity's deepest insights continue to live, grow, and illuminate the path forward for generations yet to come.

Recommended Further Reading

1. *The Paideia Proposal* by Mortimer Adler. Outlines how Socratic seminars should function as the centerpiece of democratic education through guided questioning.
2. *How to Read a Book* by Mortimer Adler and Charles Van Doren. Demonstrates the levels of reading that prepare students for meaningful participation in Socratic dialogue.
3. *The Great Ideas* by Mortimer Adler. Shows how Socratic questioning explores the fundamental concepts that unite the Great Conversation.

4. *The Restoration of Christian Culture* by John Senior. Explores how Socratic dialogue cultivates "poetic knowledge" through imaginative engagement with great texts.
5. *Ten Philosophical Mistakes* by Mortimer Adler. Demonstrates how Socratic questioning can expose and correct fundamental errors in thinking.
6. *The Art of Teaching: The Meaning and Method of the Socratic Method* by Jay Parini. Explores how skilled questioning develops both intellectual understanding and character formation.
7. *Great Books: My Adventures with Homer, Rousseau, Woolf, and Other Indestructible Writers of the Western World* by David Denby. Chronicles how adult engagement with great texts through discussion transforms understanding.

Chapter 29

The Subversive Art of Liberal Arts Learning

Why classical education best prepares students for modern challenges

The conventional wisdom governing modern education has it exactly backward. While high schools rush to create specialized technology programs and parents demand that their children learn coding before calculus, the most successful innovators in Silicon Valley consistently trace their breakthroughs not to technical training but to their grounding in classical disciplines. This rather persistent misconception—that preparation for careers in technology requires an education similarly technological—has achieved the status of obvious truth without ever having been proved, or even seriously examined. Guidance counselors and tech evangelists proclaim with perfect confidence that one must learn to code before learning to read, master algorithms before mastering Aristotle, dabble in digital design before daring to approach Dante. Yet the evidence suggests precisely the opposite: that a classical liberal arts education, with its emphasis on ancient languages, philosophy, rhetoric, and mathematics, provides not merely adequate but ideal preparation for technological careers, including computer science and programming.

This misconception is all the more remarkable because it inverts demonstrable reality. Consider Steve Jobs, whose aesthetic revolution at Apple emerged directly from his calligraphy course at Reed College—a connection he made explicit in his 2005 Stanford commencement address, explaining how the study of typography's subtle relationships informed the visual principles that distinguished Apple products in a crowded marketplace. Or examine the background of Reid Hoffman, whose philosophical studies at Stanford and Oxford shaped his understanding of social networks that became LinkedIn's foundation. Susan Wojcicki's history and literature studies at Harvard cultivated the narrative thinking that guided YouTube's evolution from video platform to cultural phenomenon. These are not coincidental biographical details but foundational intellectual experiences that directly enabled technological innovation.

The irony, of course, is that this pattern represents not a new discovery but an ancient wisdom, temporarily forgotten in our rush toward specialization. The great technological innovators of history were polymaths whose creativity emerged from intellectual breadth rather than narrow focus. Leonardo da Vinci's engineering marvels grew from his anatomical studies; his architectural innovations from mathematical principles; his mechanical designs from artistic vision. Benjamin Franklin's electrical discoveries flowed from his classical education in rhetoric and moral philosophy, which taught him to see patterns across seemingly unrelated phenomena.

This historical pattern extends into the digital age's very foundations. Alan Turing's breakthrough insights into computation emerged from Sherborne School's rigorous classical curriculum, where he learned to think systematically about abstract relationships—the same mental discipline he later applied to theoretical machines. Grace Hopper's invention of the first compiler reflected her Vassar liberal arts training, which taught her to translate between different symbolic systems, whether moving from Latin to English or from human language to machine code. Tim Berners-Lee attributes his conception of the World Wide Web not to programming expertise but to his Oxford training in logical reasoning, which enabled him to envision information's universal connectedness.

What unites these figures is their refusal to compartmentalize knowledge into isolated academic domains. Rather than languishing in disciplinary silos, they moved fluidly between intellectual territories, allowing insights from one field to illuminate problems in another. This intellectual agility mirrors the essential nature of technological innovation, which thrives on unexpected connections between disparate ideas. The classical student who studies geometric principles immediately after parsing Latin syntax develops precisely this capacity for pattern recognition across domains—the ability to see structural similarities between a rhetorical argument and a computer algorithm, between poetic meter and data architecture.

Consider how classical training manifests in specific technological competencies. The student who masters Latin declensions develops an intuitive understanding of systematic relationships that transfers directly to programming syntax. Both Latin and code require attention to precise structural relationships where small changes in form produce significant changes in meaning. When debugging a program, the classically trained mind applies the same methodical analysis used to parse complex sentences: identifying the logical structure, isolating problematic elements, and testing systematic modifications until the intended meaning emerges clearly.

Similarly, training in formal logic provides the mental architecture essential for algorithmic thinking. A student who can construct and evaluate syllogisms has already mastered the conditional reasoning that underlies programming loops and decision trees. The ability to trace through a complex Platonic dialogue—following its premises, identifying hidden assumptions, and evaluating conclusions—develops the same analytical persistence required to design elegant algorithms or architect scalable systems.

Rhetoric, often dismissed as merely ornamental, proves especially valuable for user interface design. Classical rhetorical training teaches students to guide an audience's attention naturally from point to point, anticipating resistance and providing appropriate support for each logical step. This skill translates directly to interface design, where the goal is to guide users intuitively through complex interactions without confusion or frustration. The programmer who understands how Cicero structured his arguments to lead listeners toward inevitable conclusions brings that same persuasive architecture to software design.

Yet classical education's most crucial contribution may be its cultivation of creative imagination. Programming, in its essence, is an act of creation—each algorithm a composition in logic, each system a structured reality brought into being through disciplined thought. But genuine creativity requires more than technical facility; it demands the ability to envision what does not yet exist, to see beyond current limitations toward new possibilities.

Here the classical tradition proves unexpectedly modern. The myths of Homer train students to think in complex narrative architectures, managing multiple plot threads and character motivations simultaneously—precisely the skill needed for system design where multiple processes must coordinate seamlessly. Plato's dialogues develop the ability to hold contradictory ideas in productive tension while working toward resolution—essential for debugging complex code where multiple factors interact unpredictably. Sophocles's tragedies explore the unintended consequences of human actions, cultivating the foresight necessary to anticipate how technological systems might behave in unforeseen circumstances.

This imaginative training becomes increasingly vital as technology confronts profound ethical complexities. The architect of artificial intelligence must grapple with questions that transcend technical implementation: What constitutes intelligence? How should automated systems make moral judgments? What are the social implications of algorithmic decision-making? These philosophical challenges require precisely the kind of conceptual sophistication that classical education systematically develops.

Recent corporate recognition of this need validates classical education's contemporary relevance. Google's AI research teams increasingly recruit philosophy graduates whose training in ethical reasoning complements technical expertise. Apple's design principles explicitly invoke classical concepts of proportion and harmony, drawing on aesthetic theories developed by ancient Greek mathematicians. Amazon's leadership principles derive directly from Stoic philosophy, applying ancient wisdom about character and decision-making to modern business challenges.

As artificial intelligence begins to automate routine programming tasks, the premium on distinctly human capacities increases dramatically. The future belongs not to those who can implement existing solutions most efficiently but to those who can imagine fundamentally new approaches to persistent problems. Machine learning algorithms can now generate code, but they cannot question the assumptions underlying a project, envision alternative architectures, or integrate insights from seemingly unrelated fields.

Consider the challenges emerging in quantum computing, where classical physics intuitions fail and programmers must develop entirely new ways of thinking about information and causality. The quantum programmer cannot rely on familiar logical structures but must learn to work with superposition, entanglement, and probabilistic outcomes that seem to violate common sense. Success in this domain requires precisely the intellectual flexibility that classical education cultivates—the ability to set aside familiar assumptions and work creatively within new conceptual frameworks.

> *The future belongs not to those who can implement existing solutions most efficiently but to those who can imagine fundamentally new approaches to persistent problems.*

Similarly, the development of brain-computer interfaces demands programmers who understand not just electrical signals but consciousness, perception, and human identity. Creating systems that integrate with human cognition requires insights from neuroscience, psychology, philosophy of mind, and ethics. The narrowly trained technician lacks the conceptual resources to navigate such interdisciplinary challenges, while the classically educated programmer brings precisely the intellectual breadth necessary for genuine innovation.

Biotechnology presents even more complex challenges where programming intersects with genetics, evolutionary biology, and medical ethics. Designing systems that modify living organisms requires understanding life itself—questions that have occupied philosophers for millennia. The programmer working on gene therapy algorithms must consider not just computational efficiency but the nature of disease, health, and human flourishing. These are fundamentally philosophical questions that demand the kind of integrated thinking classical education has always sought to develop.

The classical curriculum's emphasis on enduring principles rather than current techniques provides crucial adaptability in rapidly changing technological landscapes. The student who understands the logical foundations of computation adapts readily to new programming languages because he grasps the underlying structures that all such languages must express. The mind trained to recognize patterns across diverse domains quickly grasps the potential of emerging technologies because it sees beyond surface differences to fundamental relationships.

This adaptability emerges from classical education's focus on principles rather than procedures, on understanding rather than mere application. When a new technology appears, the classically trained mind asks not just "How does this work?" but "What deeper patterns does this exemplify?" and "How does this connect to what I already understand?" This questioning approach proves far more valuable than memorizing current tools, which become obsolete as technology evolves.

We might look to the Renaissance engineer as our model: a figure who combined artistic sensibility with scientific rigor and mechanical ingenuity. Whether designing cathedrals or conceptualizing flying machines, this mind—epitomized by Leonardo but not confined to him—saw no contradiction between imaginative vision and technical precision. Such integration was possible because Renaissance education refused to separate intellectual domains, instead cultivating minds capable of moving fluidly between art and science, theory and practice, speculation and implementation.

The modern world urgently needs this Renaissance versatility. The most pressing technological challenges we face—whether in artificial intelligence, bioengineering, or sustainable energy—demand more than technical competence. They require judgment that is both informed and wise, creativity that is both inventive and grounded in human understanding, innovation that serves not just efficiency but genuine human flourishing.

This integrated intelligence represents classical education's distinctive contribution to technological preparation. It shapes minds capable not just of solving problems but of questioning the assumptions behind them, not just of implementing solutions but of envisioning fundamentally new approaches, not just of optimizing existing systems but of reimagining what technology might become. Such capabilities cannot emerge from narrow technical training alone but require the intellectual breadth, conceptual sophistication, and imaginative courage that classical education has always sought to cultivate.

Classical education thus offers not an alternative to technological competence but its most solid foundation. It provides not obsolete knowledge but timeless wisdom about how humans think, learn, and create—wisdom as relevant to programming as to poetry, as applicable to system design as to syllogistic reasoning. In an age when technology shapes every aspect of human experience, we need technologists who understand not just how to build systems but why they should be built, not just what is possible but what is desirable, not just how to optimize efficiency but how to serve authentic human purposes.

The apparent paradox of ancient wisdom preparing students for cutting-edge innovation dissolves when we recognize that human nature, human reasoning, and human creativity transcend particular historical moments. The fundamental questions that technology raises—about knowledge, reality, ethics, and human flourishing—are the same questions that have occupied the greatest minds for millennia. Classical education equips students to engage these enduring questions with both intellectual rigor and imaginative vision, preparing them not for yesterday's challenges but for tomorrow's unknowable possibilities.

We should set aside the misguided notion that the humanities and technology exist in opposition, as if classical education and technical training were competing rather than complementary pursuits. The most enduring preparation for work in the technological realm does not arise from narrowing the scope of education but from broadening it—by uniting distinct traditions of thought into a coherent whole. It is not by discarding the classical that we advance, but by returning to it with renewed purpose. For in reclaiming this intellectual heritage, we do more than restore a curriculum; we reassert a deeper vision of what it means to be human. This is the vision that equips us not only to build the tools of the future but to wield them wisely—with imagination, insight, and an understanding of the enduring questions that outlast any age of innovation.

Recommended Further Reading

1. *The Innovators: How a Group of Hackers, Geniuses, and Geeks Created the Digital Revolution* by Walter Isaacson. Documents how technological breakthroughs emerge from broad intellectual foundations rather than narrow technical training.

2. *Gödel, Escher, Bach: An Eternal Golden Braid* by Douglas Hofstadter. Demonstrates how classical training in logic, mathematics, and art enables breakthrough thinking in computation and artificial intelligence.
3. *The Second Machine Age* by Erik Brynjolfsson and Andrew McAfee. Explores how liberal arts skills become more valuable as machines automate routine technical tasks.
4. *The Fuzzy and the Techie: Why the Liberal Arts Will Rule the Digital World* by Scott Hartley. Shows how liberal arts graduates drive technological innovation through creative problem-solving and human insight.
5. *You Are Not a Gadget: A Manifesto* by Jaron Lanier. Argues that humanistic understanding is crucial for creating technology that serves rather than diminishes human flourishing.
6. *Program or Be Programmed: Ten Commands for a Digital Age* by Douglas Rushkoff. Demonstrates how liberal arts training in critical thinking enables mastery rather than submission to digital systems.
7. *The Nature of Technology: What It Is and How It Evolves* by W. Brian Arthur. Explores how technological innovation emerges from combining existing elements—precisely the skill classical education develops.

Chapter 30

The Subversive Art of Pursuing Wisdom

How the ultimate goal of education remains human flourishing

To speak of wisdom today is, to many, a quaint or even antiquated endeavor. The notion that education ought to be oriented toward wisdom—let alone that such a pursuit is subversive—may strike the reader as odd or overly romantic. But classical education has never sought to conform to the prevailing ideologies of its day. It is not interested in producing compliant workers or credentialed consumers. Rather, it seeks to cultivate the human person in full. And this, above all, is why it remains—quietly, firmly, insistently—subversive.

The ultimate aim of classical education has always been human flourishing, the full flowering of the human soul in accordance with its highest nature. This concluding reflection serves as an invitation to recover the ancient conviction that education is a fundamentally moral, philosophical, and cultural endeavor. It is a reminder that such a vision, properly understood, stands in contrast to many of the dominant narratives of our time.

Classical philosophers understood wisdom not merely as accumulated knowledge, but as the right ordering of knowledge toward the highest ends. Wisdom is not encyclopedic; it is teleological. It orders facts in relation to truth, means in relation to ends, and the temporal in relation to the eternal. It is integrative, giving coherence to the fragmented and scattered data of experience. Wisdom is the capacity not simply to know, but to judge rightly, to discern what is true, good, and beautiful—and to live accordingly. It allows one to distinguish not only between right and wrong, but also between the important and the trivial, the higher and the lower, the enduring and the ephemeral. Where cleverness may strategize and intelligence may compute, wisdom contemplates and directs. It is not merely concerned with utility, but with the ordering of the soul.

Wisdom is the capacity not simply to know, but to judge rightly, to discern what is true, good, and beautiful—and to live accordingly.

This high view of wisdom is embedded in the philosophical tradition of the West. In his *Nicomachean Ethics*, Aristotle divides the intellectual virtues into five: techne (art or craft), episteme (scientific knowledge), *phronesis* (practical wisdom), nous (intuitive reason), and *sophia* (theoretical wisdom). Of these, *sophia*—a combination of nous and episteme—is the most exalted. It concerns the knowledge of first causes and ultimate truths. It delights not in what is merely useful but in what is, and loves it for its own sake. Thus, for Aristotle, the life of contemplation is the highest life, governed by the virtue of wisdom.

This tradition was deepened by the Christian intellectual inheritance. Thomas Aquinas, drawing from Aristotle, refined the idea of wisdom within a Christian metaphysical framework. For Aquinas, wisdom is both a natural and a supernatural virtue. On the natural level, it is the habit of judging rightly about divine and human things through their highest causes. On the supernatural level, it is a gift of the Holy Spirit, enabling the soul to see all things in the light of divine truth. In both cases, wisdom grants a kind of sapiential vision that allows the knower not only to comprehend but to live in harmony with the order of reality. Wisdom, for both Aristotle and Aquinas, perfects the intellect and elevates the whole person, for right understanding cannot be separated from right living.

This commitment to wisdom as the goal of education has persisted, even if faintly, into the modern world. Mortimer Adler, the twentieth-century philosopher and educational reformer, sought to revive this understanding. He argued that the chief aim of education is not the accumulation of knowledge, but the cultivation of wisdom. Through his work with the Great

Books of the Western World, Adler emphasized the philosophical habit of mind—a habit that encourages students to ask fundamental questions, to test assumptions, and to consider truths in light of enduring realities. An educated person, he insisted, is not one who knows many facts, but one who can think well about what matters most.

This vision of education is quietly revolutionary because it defies the prevailing paradigms of modern schooling. Socrates understood this well. His method of questioning was not meant to dismantle truth, but to recover it. His inquiries sought to awaken the soul, to lead it from illusion to reality, from unexamined assumptions to genuine understanding. The unexamined life, he famously declared, is not worth living—not because it is inefficient or impractical, but because it is unwise, disconnected from its proper ends. His example continues to remind us that true education begins in wonder and proceeds through humility toward a life governed by truth.

To teach students to ask "why"—to invite them to contemplate first principles, to seek out the transcendentals, to prefer being over mere doing—is to push against the tide of our present culture. In a society driven by technocratic efficiency, ideological rigidity, and the idol of measurable outcomes, the classical educator proposes something radically different. He suggests that education is not about producing workers for an economy, but forming persons for a life well lived. In this light, the pursuit of wisdom is nothing short of countercultural. It challenges the instrumentalization of learning and reorients the educational endeavor toward truth, goodness, and beauty.

This is not to say that practical skills and marketable competencies are unimportant. But when these become the telos of education, something essential is lost. Students become mere inputs in an economic machine, and education is reduced to job training.

This is why wisdom remains the highest aspiration of classical education. It is the virtue that places all other knowledge in proper order. Without wisdom, we may become clever, efficient, and superficially successful—but shallow, confused, and morally adrift. With wisdom, we gain the power to live well: to align our intellect with reality and our will with the good. That is no small thing. In fact, it is the very definition of human flourishing.

This is not to say that practical skills and marketable competencies are unimportant. But when these become the telos of education, something essential is lost. Students become mere inputs in an economic machine, and education is reduced to job training. What is neglected is the formation of character—the shaping of a person's mind, will, and affections. Classical education reclaims this broader vision. It insists that to educate is not merely to inform, but to form—to guide the soul toward its highest fulfillment.

That is why the liberal arts—grammar, logic, rhetoric, arithmetic, geometry, music, and astronomy—have endured as the heart of classical learning. These disciplines train students not just in what to think, but in how to think. And they do so with a shared aim: to lead the learner toward wisdom and virtue. To embrace this path today is to swim against the current. It is to argue that who a student becomes matters more than what they can produce. It is to contend that education is not about manufacturing utility, but nurturing a life of meaning.

To call this pursuit subversive is not to romanticize rebellion. The classical educator does not seek controversy, nor does he delight in being contrary. The subversive nature of classical education lies rather in its fidelity—in its refusal to abandon the permanent things for the fashionable, its quiet devotion to what is true even when the world forgets. To teach Homer and Plato, Augustine and Dante, is to root students in a tradition that transcends the fleeting and offers them a standard by which to judge the present. It is to give them the cultural inheritance necessary to see clearly, choose wisely, and live nobly.

This commitment, paradoxically, is liberating. Though classical education is often seen as traditional or conservative, it frees students from the tyranny of the moment. It introduces them to enduring ideas, challenges their assumptions, and teaches them to look beyond slogans and trends toward the deeper truths of human nature and divine order. A helpful metaphor here is the gardener. The classical educator does not impose a rigid mold on the student. He cultivates the conditions for growth. He respects the nature of the child and the seasons of learning. It is a work of reverence, patience, and trust in the mystery of human development. In this way, it is a quiet resistance to the industrial model of schooling.

If the goal of education is human flourishing, then we must be clear about what flourishing entails. The classical tradition understands it as eudaemonia—a state of living in accordance with reason and virtue, of fulfilling one's nature as a rational and moral being. Such a life cannot be measured by test scores or résumé lines. It is seen in the person who loves what is worth loving, who reasons clearly and speaks persuasively, who acts with justice and compassion, who delights in truth, and who pursues the good even when it is difficult.

The fruits of such an education ripen slowly, revealing themselves not in instant triumph but over the course of a lifetime. A former student may return years hence, not to recount career achievements, but to offer thanks for having been taught how to think deeply, how to live well, how to read the currents of meaning that shape existence. True assessment lies not in a high school transcript or a title, but in a life seasoned with wisdom. In this way, the end of education is not a conclusion, but a beginning—a commencement. Classical education does not simply hand students a bundle of credentials at the threshold of adulthood. It sets them forth into the adventure of life, equipping them with habits of discernment, the steadiness of character, and the quiet joy that springs from knowing they belong to something larger than themselves. And in the end, perhaps one of the most precious gifts classical education offers is the restoration of joy and wonder to learning. In a system so often driven by anxiety—about grades, college admissions, and careers—the classical model offers a quiet but radical assurance: you are more than what you achieve. Learning is not just preparation for life; it is life. It is participation in the *logos*, the intelligible order of the cosmos. To read great books, to solve mathematical problems, to gaze at the stars or ponder the harmony of music—these are acts of reverence. They awaken the soul to meaning.

Learning is not just preparation for life; it is life. It is participation in the logos, the intelligible order of the cosmos.

This spirit of wonder is no naive fancy; it is the mark of maturity. It springs from the recognition that we are part of a cosmos far greater than ourselves, and that our calling is not to dominate it, but to understand it, to take delight in its order and mystery. Classical education cultivates what C. S. Lewis called a "rightly ordered soul," a soul humble before truth, receptive to beauty, and obedient to the good. Such formation cannot be mass-produced. It demands teachers who themselves love wisdom, schools that live as communities of learning, and parents who prize character above credentials.

And so, as this book draws to a close, we return to the beginning: classical education is a cultural project. It is a work of recovery and renewal, not of nostalgia but of restoration. It summons us to remember what it means to be human, and to teach in accordance with that truth. In this endeavor, we prepare not merely students, but citizens, saints, and sages—a labor worthy of the highest human effort.

Recommended Further Reading

1. *A Summa of the Summa* by Peter Kreeft. An accessible introduction to Aquinas's exploration of how natural and supernatural wisdom perfect human understanding and guide right living.
2. *The Nicomachean Ethics* by Aristotle. The foundational text on intellectual and moral virtues, establishing wisdom as the highest human excellence.
3. *The Great Ideas: A Lexicon of Western Thought* by Mortimer Adler. Demonstrates how wisdom integrates and orders all human knowledge toward ultimate ends.
4. *The Apology* by Plato. Socrates's defense of the philosophical life as the only life worth living, grounded in the pursuit of wisdom.
5. *The Consolation of Philosophy* by Boethius. Shows how philosophical wisdom provides guidance and meaning in the face of life's uncertainties.
6. *After Virtue* by Alasdair MacIntyre. Argues for recovering the classical understanding of virtue and human flourishing against modern fragmentation.
7. *The Everlasting Man* by G. K. Chesterton. Demonstrates how classical and Christian wisdom provide enduring perspective on human nature and destiny.

Acknowledgments

To the Great Teachers

First and foremost, I must thank those masters who taught me before I was born. To Homer, who showed me that education begins with wonder; to Plato, who demonstrated that the best questions have no easy answers; to Augustine, who proved that the mind must be trained before it can be trusted; to Aquinas, who revealed that reason and faith are allies, not enemies; to Dante, who mapped the geography of the soul; to Shakespeare, who taught me that language is not mere communication but incarnation itself.

To Chesterton, who showed me that the most profound truths often wear the mask of paradox; to Lewis, who proved that the ancient path is the most revolutionary one; to Dorothy Sayers, who insisted that children are human beings, not raw material for social engineering; to Jacques Maritain, who reminded me that education is an art, not a science. They remain the most demanding professors I have ever encountered, the most patient guides I have ever followed, the most faithful companions I have ever known. They ask no recognition, seek no tenure, demand no sabbaticals. They work for free, and their wages are the transformation of every mind they touch.

To the Living Voices

To my colleagues who daily choose the difficult path of teaching actual human beings rather than managing digital interfaces. To the Latin teachers who persist in conjugating verbs while the world conjugates pixels. To the mathematics instructors who still believe that mental discipline matters more than calculator fluency. To the literature professors who assign whole books instead of excerpts, who choose difficulty over accessibility, who trust their students with texts that require annotation rather than skimming.

To the administrators brave enough to choose substance over metrics, depth over data, formation over information. To the parents who have resisted the siren song of educational efficiency and chosen instead the ancient way of patient cultivation.

To Those Who Refuse to Be Obsolete

To every teacher who still writes on chalkboards, who assigns memorization, who insists on complete sentences, who believes that some things cannot be googled because they must be known. To the librarians who fight for physical books, who understand that wisdom cannot be downloaded, who create sanctuaries of silence in our cacophonous age.

To the students who choose Latin over computer coding, who prefer Shakespeare to social media, who ask why rather than what, who hunger for truth rather than information. You prove daily that the ancient hunger for wisdom burns as brightly in the twenty-first century as it did in the fifth century before Christ.

To the Patient Materials

To the paper that receives our thoughts without judgment, to the ink that makes our ideas visible, to the books that wait faithfully on shelves for readers who may never come. To the clay that teaches through resistance, to the wood that instructs through its grain, to the soil that educates through seasons. You are our first and most reliable teachers, patient masters who never grow weary of our questions, never tire of our failures, never doubt our capacity to learn.

And Finally

To those who came before us, who preserved the great inheritance through dark ages and bright ones, through times of persecution and periods of plenty. To those who will come after us, who will inherit what we leave behind. May we prove worthy stewards of what we have received, faithful guardians of what we must transmit.

The tradition does not belong to us; we belong to the tradition. Our names will fade, but the conversation continues. This is not our achievement but our assignment, not our possession but our privilege. We are links in a golden chain that stretches from Athens to eternity, temporary custodians of permanent things.

Deo gratias.

Index

Note: footnote information is indicated by n and note number following the page number.